PSYCHOLOGY A
SPIRITUAL TRADITIONS

PSYCHOLOGY AND THE SPIRITUAL TRADITIONS

EDITED AND
INTRODUCED
BY
R.J. STEWART

ELEMENT BOOKS

© R J Stewart 1990

First published in Great Britain in 1990 by
Element Books Limited
Longmead, Shaftesbury, Dorset

Designed by Roger Lightfoot
Typeset by Selectmove Ltd, London
Printed and bound in Great Britain
Cover design by Max Fairbrother
Cover painting by Monica Sjöö
(*Manu: African mother of us all*)

British Library Cataloguing in Publication Data
Psychology and the spiritual traditions.
1. Religious beliefs. Psychological aspects
I. Stewart, R. J. (Robert J.) *1949–*
200.19

ISBN 1–85230–180–5

CONTENTS

LIST OF CONTRIBUTORS

R. J. STEWART is a Scot who lives in Bath, England. He is author of twenty four books, including works on mythology, magic, music and consciousness, drama, and fiction. He is also a musician and composer, and designer of the unique eighty stringed concert psaltery; he has composed and recorded for stage, feature films, television, radio, and has made five LPs plus a series of cassettes of music and guided visualisations. His books have been translated into German, Spanish, Portuguese, Italian, Dutch, and Japanese. His music is known worldwide.

NGAKPA CHÖGYAM is an English-born lama of the most ancient traditions of Tibet. He has studied and practised under the guidance of several Tibetan Tantric Masters and completed a number of long retreats. In 1983 he became an Initiated Ngakpa (which means Awareness – Spell person) and returned to teach meditation and courses on the Tibetan Mystic Path. He is a healer, professional counsellor, and works increasingly with psychologists and those in the caring professions.

JOHN MATTHEWS is an expert on Arthurian literature and traditions, and has made a lifetime study of their relationship to human development and consciousness. He is author of a number of books an Arthurian and Celtic subjects, and has also co-written with his wife Caitlin a widely acclaimed two volume study of Western esoteric and spiritual traditions, entitled *The Western Way* published by Arkana.

DR GARETH KNIGHT is a Christian Kabbalist, working within the Western magical traditions. He has a wide experience of psychology and its relationship to the spiritual traditions, and is recognised worldwide as an authority on White Magic. He has published many books on subjects such as the Tree of Life, ritual magic, and the Rosicrucians.

WILLIAM G. GRAY is a senior figure in Western magical arts. His books have been influential in bridging the transition between the confused occultism of the nineteenth century and new and clear practise of magic with firm foundations in both ancient tradition and modern reassessment of human consciousness.

ADAM MCLEAN is an expert on alchemy. He is recognised worldwide as a writer and lecturer on the Hermetic tradition, and has published the unique Hermetic Journal. He has also published and edited a series of rare sourceworks, including many seminal texts that have influenced the development of Western traditions and techniques of understanding consciousness.

MONICA SJÖÖ is an artist and author. Her work explores the forces of the Great Goddess, and she has been active in the feminist movement for more than twenty years.

PROFESSOR DANIEL NOEL is an American educator specialising in the psychology of religion, and correlations between art, literature, and religion. He is Professor of Liberal Studies in Religion and Culture at Vermont College of Norwich University, Montpelier. His published works include *Approaching Earth: a Search for the Mythic Significance of the Space Age* (Warwick, NY: Amity House, 1986), and *Paths to the Power of Myth (Joseph Campbell and the Study of Religion)* (Crossroad/Continuum, New York, 1990).

IAN REES is a social worker and psychologist who has been involved in counselling offenders on behalf of the Probation Service.

LIST OF ILLUSTRATIONS

ACKNOWLEDGEMENTS

Daniel C. Noel's essay previously appeared in *Anima*, 16/1 (Fall 1989) and is reprinted here by kind permission of Anima publications.

Part of Monica Sjöö's essay first appeared in *Woman of Power* journal, USA in 1990.

William G. Gray's chapter is reproduced by permission of Professor Charles Tart, from *Transpersonal Psychologies*, Harper & Row, USA, 1975.

INTRODUCTION

R.J. Stewart

This book is broadly based upon material from the Fourth Annual Merlin Conference, held in London in 1989. The theme of the Conference was the relationship between spiritual traditions and psychology – the book develops this further. This is a vast and complex area to explore, and no one would claim to encapsulate its many potential realisations and possible statements in one anthology. My role as editor, therefore, has been to find a collection of unusual and, wherever possible, diverse contributors.

I was not interested, for example, in selecting world religions and running them through standard psychological interpretations – this type of thing has been done many times before. By the term *spiritual traditions* we are not limited solely to orthodox and political religions that have dominated human culture, but include other sources which those religions sought to suppress. These are found in folklore, mythology, magical arts, and the collective inheritance of religions, classical Mysteries and initiatory schools from the ancient world.

All of these, from the humble work of the shaman or folk seer to the grandly exalted structure of Church or Temple-based religions, are spiritual traditions. They seek to transform, one way or another, the human spirit, through a collective handing down and application of traditional arts, disciplines, beliefs and general lore, both written and unwritten. Some degenerate inwardly, and so come to rely on force and dogma, others retain their vitality, but are preserved in secret and, often, in a complex and entangled form.

The key to the seemingly arbitrary selection of chapters for this book is perhaps found within the composition of the Merlin Conference itself, a non-profit making annual event run by volunteers, yet one to which writers, scientists, psychologists, musicians, composers, actors, directors, artists and many other diverse experts and amateurs are willing to come. We live in a time when the arts and sciences are beginning, in some ways, to come together. Most significant in this context of fusion is the interaction between materialist psychology and the old spiritual and magical traditions, which are, of course, psychological traditions in their own right.

A decade or so past, this type of statement, that the old magical and spiritual traditions were truly psychological, would have been strenuously challenged, or more likely ridiculed. The perennial traditions were seen either as the sub-strata of orthodox religion, or as a confused mess of legend, myth, folklore and collective practices, eventually degenerating into the less savoury aspects of so-called occultism – the black mud, as Sigmund Freud described it. This was, at any rate, how Western esoteric traditions were frequently regarded by psychologists. Eastern traditions fared slightly better, but when taken out of cultural context and transported to the West tended to become the property of curious revivals and mutations, such as the Theosophical Society.

Today the vast and heavily commercialised field of New Age literature, teachings, practices and products is mainly derived from the impetus generated by Theosophy in the last century. Indeed, the dawning of a New Age was loudly hailed by Theosophists, even to the extent of acquiring and training their own spiritual Saviour or Messiah, in the form of the young Krishnamurti, his identity established by astrological and psychic and other occult methods. Perhaps he was a true spiritual master, for as soon as he was able he threw off all the garish trappings and New Ageism that had been forced upon him, denying it all utterly. The Theosophical Society never recovered from this event, but many other people followed to commercialise upon the New Age and the potential of Masters, leaders, teachers, and the like. Today it amounts to a multi-million dollar loose conglomerate of businesses.

Even as the Theosophicals were developing their own intellectual fusion of Hindu, Buddhist, and occult lore and language, C.G. Jung, one of the great founding figures of modern psychology, was giving mythology a liberal coating of respectability, removing it from the realm of the obscure academic or poet, into that of the therapist. Jung even wrote a psychological commentary upon *The Secret of the Golden Flower*, an oriental mystical text with a strong practical emphasis. But he never sought to approach directly the magical and spiritual arts and disciplines which are the practical and interactive aspects of myth. A short essay on Jung and Merlin is contributed to this book by Professor Daniel Noel (page 1).

Nowadays many psychologists, many therapists, are taking a head-on experiential approach to the old traditions – they are willing to try them out, to experience the techniques embodied therein for themselves, and even to apply them in practice. The sub-theme of the 1989 Merlin Conference was spiritual or totem animals, and in our chapter from Ian Rees (page 76), we find how the ancient technique of using spiritual or totem animals has been applied in modern therapeutic and counselling work with young offenders. This leaning of psychological therapists towards the spiritual traditions is perhaps due to the growing emphasis upon the *practical* aspects of these traditions and the firm move away from airy spirituality and vague knowingness.

Practical development has been the hallmark of the revival of Western spiritual disciplines, and indeed of certain branches of Eastern tradition, particularly that of Tibetan Buddhism, which comes afresh to the West with a new generation and a new emphasis. Some of this refreshing and inspiring contact is found in the interview with Ngakpa Chogyam, in Chapter 3.

Before any of this quite recent change, however, there was a long period, from approximately the turn of the century into the 1970s, when occultism and magic on the one hand, and orthodox Christianity on the other, tried to justify themselves psychologically. Because psychology had acquired the glamour and authority that often attaches itself to new 'explanatory' sciences in a materialist culture, and because it threatened to undermine the already confused and waning power of the Church and to explain the mysteries of the obscurest occult teachings, everyone tried to jump upon a vaguely psychological bandwagon. That particular school of apologetics does not appear here at all. It was merely a phase, and is virtually over. As a phase of development, however, it did some important work for the betterment of the spiritual and magical traditions: some of this is touched upon in our chapter by Dr Gareth Knight (page 10) who analyses the relationship between psychological and magical arts in the life and work of the influential magician and writer, Dion Fortune.

Another stream of old lore which has been revived in this century by both psychologists and esoteric students alike is alchemy, and our chapter from Adam McLean (page 118) gives a detailed series of insights into the appearance of animals in alchemical symbolism. This leads us back to the other greatly revived, indeed over-commercialised, primal psychological or magical art, that of working with spiritual or totem animals. Although there is a popular revival of this technique very loosely based upon native American traditions, it has always been a central feature of the Western tradition. In my own chapter (page 60) I have briefly described some of my own experiences and work with spiritual animals and birds during the last twenty years. To bring the subject out of mere analysis or discussion and into possible practical experience, I have included a typical visualisation which enables us to contact our spiritual animal or bird.

The spiritual animals often work through dreams, and there is a vast body or lore involving sleep, dreaming and visions, which long predates the modern theories of dreams for psychotherapy. John Matthews (page 100) discusses some of these older dream therapy and vision techniques in the context of Celtic and classical Greek cultures. In direct contrast to this essay into the techniques of the past, Monica Sjöö calls to account certain techniques of the present which claim to fuse psychology and spiritual traditions (page 41). There is a distinct undercurrent of scepticism and challenge towards New Age philosophy and techniques, not only in this collection, but among many contemporary thinkers, writers, therapists, artists and workers within the inner or spiritual traditions.

We gave finally an overview of the Western tradition from W.G. Gray, one of a small number of influential writers and magicians who have brought the Western traditions out of the obscurity of the nineteenth century into the present day through a constant process of simplification and elucidation.

Thematic Links and Order of Chapters

The chapters are not arranged in the order in which I have generally mentioned them in the Introduction above, but have a thematic order, as show in Figure 1 (page xvi). The first chapter from Professor Daniel Noel gives a possible psychological overview of the entire subject, while the last from W.G. Gray gives a magical overview from the standpoint of a senior practitioner of the Western magical arts. There are many links between the various chapters, which were written quite independently of one another, and I have tried to bring out some of these links in my introductions to each chapter.

The main thematic connections between chapters and their running order are as follows:

1. Professor Dan Noel and 2. Dr Gareth Knight, each using biographical material of important individuals, C.G. Jung and Dion Fortune, in the fields of psychology and magic in the early twentieth century. Each of these chapters discusses the interaction

between psychology and spiritual magical arts as evident in real lives and the work produced by those lives.

3. Ngakpa Chögyam compares, in an interview, the potential of modern psychology with a spiritual tradition, that of Tantric Buddhism. He also discusses the claims or illusions of the New Age movement. This leads to 4. Monica Sjöö, who challenges many New Age attitudes, therapies and concepts. She reveals inherent flaws and dangers within the New Age movement, showing that it is by no means new, but a reworking of an old, outmoded and potentially weakening stream of philosophy and symbolism, claiming to merge psychology and spiritual traditions. In 5. I draw some comparisons between modern psychology and counselling, New Age techniques and theories, and the ancestral Western tradition of working with spiritual animals.

This leads to 6. Ian G. Rees describing his work with the old animal visions and mythic structures in counselling and therapy.

In 7. John Matthews also discusses animal and bird lore, but in the major context of dream work, temple sleep, and incubation in the Celtic and Greek cultures. This leads us to 8. where Adam MacLean gives a detailed exposition of animal symbolism in alchemy, and how the alchemical physical transformations were harmonised with inner psychological and spiritual transformation of the alchemists themselves. We conclude with 9., a highly individual and detailed overview of the Western magical tradition, from the influential writer W.G. Gray.

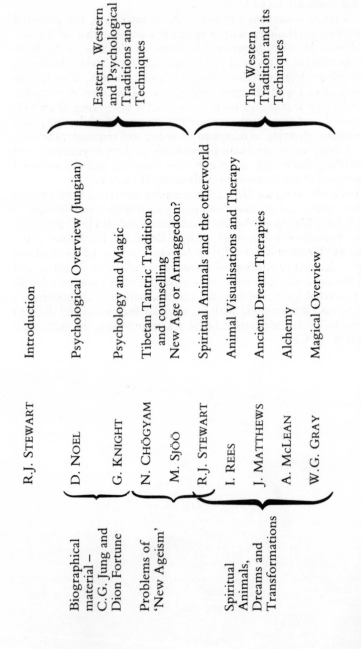

Fig 1. An overview of the areas covered in Psychology and the Spiritual Traditions.

ARCHETYPICAL MERLIN AND THE NEW SHAMANISM

by Professor Daniel C. Noel

INTRODUCTION

R.J. Stewart

In this essay, Professor Daniel Noel touches upon and links together a number of themes concerning psychology and spiritual matters that are individually developed by other writers in later chapters. Most important is his discussion of the potential existence of a 'new shamanism', and the possibility that Jung's psychological techniques represent one path by which such a new shamanism might be realised in Western culture. This discussion leads to the strong implication, of course, that C. G. Jung was somehow tapping into the old Western shamanism, as represented by the figure of Merlin, but restating it through his own life and work for the twentieth century. This is no mere intellectual theory, as Daniel Noel makes clear, for there is biographical evidence that supports it.

The image of Merlin, and our following of his distant cry in the forest, has influenced both the arts and psychology: various interpretations are put upon this haunting sound and our inner quest in pursuit of its maker. C.G. Jung, as Dan Noel suggests and offers evidence for, sought the inner Merlin in the forest of the collective unconscious, where he is buried deep but permeates extensively. Jung must also, of course, have sought Merlin in his own soul. This type of psychological realisation has bridged between the ancient traditions of Merlin and modern reassessment of such traditions.

We might take the overall image of Daniel Noel's essay a little further, for just as Merlin buried himself in the inner world of the Western psyche, laying strange trails and clues for our pursuit, so do the old traditions teach that he linked and merged himself with the physical land (something significantly different to a psychological interpretation). Our new awareness of our wholeness and inseparable link to the environment, now that have brought it to the brink of destruction, is part of that Merlin-awareness that comes alive for us today, when we need it the most.

If we turn to the enigmatic *Prophecies of Merlin*,[1] we find them concluding with sequences that seem to lead into the twentieth or twenty-first centuries, with what are (to us) clear images of modern technology, nuclear disaster, pollution and incurable disease. Though we might argue historically or intellectually against the validity of such Prophecies (set out from oral tradition in the twelfth century), they strike a haunting note for us today – as if the past and the future are harmonically linked together. Discussion as to their origins and accuracy is, in fact, irrelevant.

According to Celtic tradition Merlin merged with the land after his prophetic life: and now, at a time of a deep need for such inner skills and arts as Merlin represents, now when he seems to be coming alive in the imagination again as never before, is exactly the time when the sequence of his Prophecies ends. This is perhaps, to borrow boldly a Jungian term, an example of synchronicity.

★   ★   ★

1. Anglos and Shamanic Transformation

My Norman ancestors probably crossed the Channel to England before they crossed the Atlantic to Virginia and later migrated to Georgia and Mississippi (where I was born). Likewise my own life has included several brief journeys back across to England since I moved from Pennsylvania to *New* England in 1973. It was not until I spent a sabbatical in Santa Fe in 1987, however, that I actually noticed that I was and am an 'Anglo'.

In the American Southwest, of course, anyone of non-Hispanic European ancestry is referred to as an Anglo – even Irish-Americans who would resist being lumped in with the English! But beyond mere labels I was made to rethink my own cultural identity there by the powerful presence of living Hispanic and Native American traditions which are, at best, very much less obvious in Vermont. Food, architecture, accents, festivals – all around me was 'contrapuntal' evidence that would not let me ignore my Anglo heritage. Above all there was the intensely attractive but alien spirituality of santuario and kiva: observing public rituals gave me a glimpse of realities apparently not available in *my* native culture.

I suspect that this blend of attraction, alienation and dissatisfied self-revelation is one that shapes the experience of many of the Anglos who have come to the new shamanism in the two decades since Carlos Castaneda's first book. For 'the new shamanism,' or 'neo-shamanism', is what we should call the recent upsurge of interest, largely on the part of educated Euro–Americans, in that archaic style of spirituality. Shamanism, as defined by scholars such as Mircea Eliade, involves an ecstatic trance-journey from which the shaman returns, transformed, with healing images or techniques for his or her tribe. Whether attempts by Anglo seekers to alter their consciousness by similar means – prolonged drumming, for instance, or solitary vision quests – qualify as authentic shamanism of the traditional sort is debatable. But the widespread impulse to make such neo-shamanic attempts is itself worth pondering, and may contain its own kind of validity.

We are drawn to the shamanic spirituality of other cultures, indigenous cultures in particular, because we seem to be fed little ecstasy or healing power from our Anglo roots. Cut off from our own primal lifeways by distance and disaffection, the example of Native American, Asian, Australian or African shamanism is tempting medicine, and we flock to workshops and tours – or at least to the local bookstore for the latest fascinating account of someone else's apprenticeship.

I have not, I confess, tried the various avenues to shamanic transformation offered by fellow Anglos drawing on still-living wisdom from other cultures, and I do not rule them out. For me, however, freshly aware of those cultural roots I had too long taken for granted, the transformative journey – if it were to *become* transformative – had to begin with a trip from New Mexico to Old England.

2. Merlin as Anglo Shaman

In June of 1987 I made my sixth visit to England in fourteen years. On previous trips I had been moved, even enchanted, by the sacred spaces in the English West Country, and had been teaching summer seminars there on topics related to the legendary landscape of Somerset, Dorset, Devon and Cornwall. So I was aware of Merlin as one of the characters of Arthurian literature who still haunted that countryside. At Tintagel on the Cornish coast, at South Cadbury and Glastonbury in Somerset, and at Carmarthen in South Wales there are sites that seem to accord with references to Merlin in the primary textual sources: Geoffrey of Monmouth's *History of the Kings of Britain* (1136) and *Life of Merlin* (ca. 1150), Robert de

Boron's *Merlin* (ca. 1200), and Thomas Malory's *Morte D'Arthur* (1485).

What I did *not* fully know until 1987 was that long before Merlin was Arthur's advisor and court magician in the late-medieval texts he was seer, bard, Druid, Wild Man, and, at base, shaman. He could therefore be an ancestral model for any Anglo's efforts at shamanic transformation, even today.

I learned this initially from Count Nikolai Tolstoy – an heir, I take it, of the great Russian novelist. His 1985 book, *The Quest for Merlin*, which I encountered in England two years later, turned out to be only one of several manifestations of a recent Merlin resurgence. It has remained the most important one to me, however, because of how strongly it makes the case for Merlin's shamanism.

Above all Count Nikolai taught me to take Merlin seriously as a shaman. In Disneyfied versions of Arthurian legend he had seemed a slightly buffoonish old wizard, charming but nowhere near psychologically captivating or archetypal. Tolstoy's quest, on the other hand, had revealed a composite figure who could be an authentic guide on the neo-shamanic journey. As the Irish Suibhne, the Scottish Lailoken, and the Welsh Myrddin, Merlin's identity had deep Celtic layers beneath the medieval texts of Geoffrey and surrounding the work of his successors all the way down to Tolkien, T.H. White, and others in our own time. Tolstoy even points to the possibility that in pre-Celtic times Merlin descended from a divine figure of prophetic inspiration worshipped in southwestern Wales (where the bluestones for Stonehenge were quarried) but identified with all of Britain – which one ancient manuscript calls 'Myrddin's Precinct'.

And with these oldest mythico-historical layers now showing through and combining with more modern ones we have an archetypal Anglo shaman who is resurfacing right about now.

3. Jungian Manifestations

As the term *archetypal* implies, there is a strong Jungian element in all this, and it is this connection which further helped me to see Merlin as a model for shamanic transformation today. I do not have thousands of dreams to draw on, as Jung did in determining that certain recurrent images were suggestive of the few major psychological predispositions, unrepresentable in themselves, which he called 'archetypes'. However, Merlin's persistent presence in the lore and literature of the western imagination – to the point where this one barely-verifiable figure now automatically embodies the role and powers of every magician – allows us to see him as a guiding image, at an archetypal depth, in our cultural and personal psychology. There is, in addition, evidence that the inner circle of associates around Carl Jung felt Merlin manifesting himself on this level.

Even before my own view of Merlin was deepened in 1987 I knew that Emma Jung and Marie-Louise von Franz had written about Merlin. I also knew that another of Carl Jung's associates, Heinrich Zimmer – best remembered for his works on the myths and symbols of India – had done so as well. And beyond casual reading about these connections, I had been preoccupied for some time with Jung's travels in England and had learnt a few details which pointed to Merlin's presence.

On a 1979 visit I was able to interview Mrs Anne Baynes at Reed House, her home in Surrey. Anne Baynes was the widow of H.G. Baynes, a founder of Jungian psychiatry in England and one of Jung's treasured assistants. Forty years earlier Mrs Baynes and her husband had accompanied Carl and Emma Jung on a journey out to Glastonbury, in Somerset, because of Emma's research on the psychology of the Arthurian Grail quest, with its many associations to the folklore of that town. Until her death in 1955 Emma Jung worked on a book about this material which von Franz, herself a distinguished Jungian analyst, later completed.

As I sat in the garden of Reed House at sunset, Anne Baynes described a dinner party there on the evening before the two couples were to make their 1939 pilgrimage. A third couple had joined the Jungs and Bayneses: Heinrich and Christiane Zimmer. Since that was the year when Heinrich Zimmer's essay, 'Merlin', appeared in a Swiss journal which the Jungs would have known well, and given the imminent Glastonbury sojourn, it is very likely that Merlin was a subject of dinner conversation.

In any case a quick glance at Emma Jung and Marie-Louise von Franz's *The Grail Legend* indicates that Zimmer's perspective is honoured with several references in that volume's final five chapters: all on Merlin. Likewise von Franz refers to the Zimmer essay in her own biography, *C.G. Jung: His Myth in Our Time*, which closes with a chapter called 'Le Cri de Merlin'.

Once I had read Nikolai Tolstoy's *Quest for Merlin* in 1987 I began to reconsider these Jungian manifestations. It became clear to me that not only was Jung himself fascinated by Merlin – while deferring to Emma as regarded pursuing detailed research – but he actively identified his psychology, if not his own personality, with Merlin's powers.

4. Comprehending Merlin's Cry

The von Franz biography underscores the Jung-Merlin connections by retelling the tale of the latter's disappearance, imprisoned in a spell by Viviane or Niniane (Nimue), to whom he had relinquished his magic. Merlin's cry can still be heard in the forest, it is said, and this is something that certainly captivated Jung.

As we know, during the process of constructing his retreat tower at Bollingen on Lake Zurich, Jung chiselled images and sayings on a large granite cube mistakenly brought by the builders. He later recalled that he had had the idea to inscribe the phrase 'Le Cri de Merlin' on the back face of his Bollingen stone because

> what the stone expressed reminded me of Merlin's life in the forest, after he had vanished from the world. Men still hear his cries, so the legend runs, but they cannot understand or interpret them . . . His story is not yet finished, and he still walks abroad. It might be said that the secret of Merlin was carried on by alchemy, primarily in the figure of Mercurius. Then Merlin was taken up again in my psychology of the unconscious and – remains uncomprehended to this day!

Uncomprehended, that is, by those who remain insensitive to the imaginal language of the unconscious psyche. In his own life and work, of course, Jung *listened* to images, both the inner imagery of dreams and the outer images of the *anima mundi*, the soul in the world's things. While he never carved 'Le Cri de Merlin' on his stone, he did chisel the face of Mercurius as Trickster – surely an aspect of Merlin's shamanism, as Tolstoy emphasises – on a nearby wall when it seemed to be laughing out at him in the shapes of masonry, sunlight, and shadow.

Jung, as an old man dictating his autobiography in the six years left to him after Emma's death, knew that both her researches and Zimmer's 1939 essay had stressed Merlin's disappearance. That disappearance, seen with Jungian sensitivities in mind, is a major key to the mode of Merlin's *re*-appearance today, a central clue to how he becomes accessible again to Anglos' experience – and to everyone else's, given the modern sharing of transformative resources which until now has drawn mainly on *non*-Anglo shamanic treasures.

5. How Merlin Returns

Heinrich Zimmer tells us that 'the lord of the enchanted forest is made spellbound, wittingly and willingly, in his own domain, and by an enchanting fairy child who is the incarnation of the magic depths of the forest itself . . . The unconscious, through Merlin, has manifested itself to the world in revealing symbols, and sinks again into its own primeval stillness.'

In other words, Merlin has voluntarily renounced his worldly powers – Niniane's tricking of him is in this view a *cooperative* venture – and resides ever after in a fairy-forest rendition of the collective unconscious. It is, therefore, not surprising that Jung's explorations into the symbolic imagery of the unconscious felt like a rediscovery of Merlin, available once more to those who can employ Jungian tools of comprehension.

But Zimmer's Jungian sensitivity to Merlin's disappearance goes even further than the insight that it may have been a deliberate withdrawal. He closes his essay by saying that 'Merlin and Niniane seem, in the end, to have exchanged sexes. He is content to be vanquished and to rest peacefully, while she, with the knowledge he has given her, is free to come and go.'

Merlin returns, to judge from this large clue, in our attentiveness to the cries of the unconscious, the murmurs of the imaginal or soul realm which we Anglos lost as we went about the business of 'modernising' the world through science, technology, colonialism and commerce. And he returns not necessarily or exclusively in male manifestations. Not only does Zimmer's 1939 insight suggest Merlin became his own anima-figure, the contrasexual soul-manifestation within masculine personality development (according to a later essay by Emma Jung which refers to Merlin's disappearance). Even to imply this much would importantly indicate that his wisdom is accessible through all of the soul-women with whom he is associated: his wife Guendoloena, his sister Gwenddydd, and Morgan le Fay/The Lady of the Lake, as well as Viviane/Niniane.

Yet such anima images would remain within the domain of masculine psychology, whereas Zimmer's reading can just as well be extrapolated to say that in being 'the incarnation of the magic depths of the forest itself' – the Anglo or Celtic unconscious into which Merlin subsides – Niniane, as an independent female personification, fully and freely incorporates Merlin's potentialities. This seems not so much an endorsement of a bland androgyny as a plea for all of us, men and women alike (and in interaction), to heed Merlin's cry, to practice a re-animating, transformative attention to all expressions of soul.

For whatever imaginal voice soul may choose, Merlin intimates – whether dreams or visualisations, stories or music, magic shows or movies, or simply the evocations of friends, lovers, mentors – is where this renewed shamanic option offers itself to our suffering, for our deepening, in our life-journey of transformation.

6. Merlin's Guidance: Shamanic Transformation as Soul-Making

I would also suggest that an absolutely essential teaching of whatever sort of shamanism is that we have to experience *more* imaginally than we have become accustomed to doing, value the activity of the imagination *much more* centrally than our modern world view has allowed. It certainly need not embarrass us Anglos that Merlin is not literally here to lead workshops – neither is Castaneda's don Juan, for all we can find out, and his suspiciously *literary* teachings are certainly the sacred text of the new shamanism.

More positively, and probably more to the point, Merlin's invisibility to physical vision *de*-literalises our experience just as don Juan sought to do when he tried to teach Carlos to 'see.' Non-ordinary perception, or what the Jungian psychologist James Hillman calls 'seeing-through,' is one lesson we can all learn from Merlin's return: in particular from the imaginal *mode* of that return. The subtle experience of seeing-through can remedy the cultural loss of soul to which Anglo efforts over the centuries of modernity have contributed so greatly.

'Image *is* psyche,' said Jung, and since the word *psyche* means soul his statement affirms that the equivalence of soul and imagination is at the crux of Jungian thought. Consequently it is very much in the Jungian tradition for someone like Hillman to speak of 'soul-making' instead of psychoanalysis and to emphasise, as part of his perspective, the poetic basis of mind.

Soul-making – the term originally comes to us from the English poet John Keats – is the type of shamanic transformation we Anglos and others will undergo as we listen to the symbolic imagery in the 'initiatory traumas' of ordinary life, the sacred wounds of our suffering world, comprehending the Merlin's cry in every symptom, every perceived denial of the unconscious psyche in self or society as well as any imaginal voice which reasserts soul in whatever medium.

Surely we have much to learn from native shamanic wisdom holders towards the recovery of soul, if they will honour us with their teachings. But a kind of spiritual colonialism is very much worth worrying about – in order to avoid committing it – and soul-making can genuinely come from the subtly experiential Anglo shamanism which Merlin brings. Indeed, maybe the imaginal deepening which

Merlin represents can even make us more fit to receive the proferred healing powers of primal peoples from other traditions.

Everywhere today in the dominant culture, in any case, the soul and its imagination are denied: by reductive materialism on one side, but also by an image-denying spiritualism on the other, and by ego-manipulations from the well-intentioned as often as from the 'philistines'. I am far from advocating that every neo-shamanist sign up for a formal course of Jungian therapy, or fly to Britain to seek out Merlin's haunts. Clearly there are less obvious (and less costly) means to soul-making: everyday life offers them constantly if we can see through the screen of a soulless society. But the *investment in imagining* that such specific activities represent can be an immensely valuable first step in retrieving soul and re-animating the world.

Another, to take a personal favourite, might be attending to the 'mere make-believe' of talented storytellers such as Mary Stewart or Marion Zimmer Bradley or Jane Yolen. They dream the myth of Merlin onwards into the present, into publication and therefore public waking reality. They take the surviving fragments of his factual history not primarily as objects of scientific analysis, or even as supposedly firm traditional footing for clear-cut spiritual formulas, but as occasions for our re-enchantment: inconclusive signposts on a metaphoric journey of soul-making in the midst of a dis-enchanted world fixated upon unambiguous certainty and control.

And along all such subtly transformative paths, we would do well to imagine, Merlin is again a guiding model, an evocative voice. Archetypal Merlin returns, and his – or her – cry can be our shaman's drum.

Notes

1. R.J. Stewart, *The Prophetic Vision of Merlin*, Penguin Arkana, Harmondsworth, 1986
R.J. Stewart, *The Mystic Life of Merlin*, Penguin Arkana, Harmondsworth, 1986. Both books contain translations and commentaries upon the original Merlin (12th C.) texts of Geoffrey of Monmouth.

THE IMPACT OF PSYCHOLOGY UPON ESOTERIC SOCIETIES

by Dr Gareth Knight

INTRODUCTION

R.J. Stewart

Dr Gareth Knight draws upon the life story and work of the influential magician and writer Dion Fortune to show us how psychology and magical tradition interacted in the early years of this century. He focuses specifically upon the effect developing psychology had upon magical orders and their members, mainly through the example of Dion Fortune's Society of the Inner Light.

It would not be extravagant to say that Dion Fortune was a pivotal figure in mediating new levels of magical art and new methods of elucidation for the twentieth century. Much of the work that she started has been continued, in individual ways, by W. G Gray, Gareth Knight, and other modern researchers and developers of the Western tradition. But it must also be admitted that without the organising and materialising impetus of modern psychology, we might not have the clear developments in exposition and publication of spiritual traditions that are now emerging and, of course, pulling away from the interim effect of psychological reductionism and superficial explanation. This is a matter of cultural or social history as much as any deep philosophical or metaphysical discussion. Dion Fortune wrote a text called *Sane Occultism* among her many books, probably the first attempt of many that were to follow, from other writers, to demystify and simplify the irrational responses to magic that were rife in her time, among would-be magicians just as much as among the suspicious authorities, vested interests, and the general public. The aim for the next century might be for us all to say 'occultism? what occultism? There is only the imagination, magic, and spiritual realisation.' The less occult the better.

★   ★   ★

There is an ill-defined and indeed shifting boundary between the practical concerns of the occultist and the psychotherapist. This is perhaps not so surprising.

Even our awareness of the physical world through the outward senses of perception raises deep philosophical questions to which we still do not know the answers, despite our skills with neurological mechanisms. The questions (let alone the answers) are even more problematical when we try to account for 'inner' experiences or motivations, of whatever kind.

Sigmund Freud anticipated some of the problems, and possibly tried to evade them, when he warned C.G.Jung about the dangers of clinical psychology sinking into the 'black mud' of occultism. Psychologists of various persuasions will have their own views about all this but it may help to give a view from the swamp, so to speak, and see how things looked to the occultists, and particularly to those with a psychological bent.

Prominent among these was Dion Fortune, whose occult development more or less coincided with the rise to popular awareness of modern psychology and its analytic techniques. Born in 1890, she was a woman in her early twenties when psychoanalysis became something of a craze. This followed upon the publication of Freud's *Interpretation of Dreams* in 1900, shortly followed by *The Psychopathology of Everyday Life* and *Wit in Relation to the Unconscious*, which brought what had been a clinical subject to popular awareness.

Such an impact did these ideas make that Dion Fortune, or Miss Violet Mary Firth as she then was, could find her services very much in demand as a 'lay analyst' in London, although a medically unqualified 23 year old. She worked out of a medico-psychological clinic in Brunswick Square that appears to have been under the jurisidiction of the London (Royal Free Hospital) School of Medicine for Women, and attended relevant external courses at the University of London.

In the course of time the British Medical Association felt that things should be brought under closer control and the practice of psychoanalysis was reserved to medically qualified practitioners, which in effect put an early end to Miss Firth's promising career, although it seems likely that she would in any case have soon drifted from the paths of orthodoxy.

This was in part due to her having begun to have some odd psychological experiences that were difficult to account for in terms of accepted medical and psychological theory. These commenced at a club for students of Theosophy, which she had joined because of its convenient location to her clinic and its superior catering facilities. One day she attended one of its meditation classes in a mood that she describes as 'one of mischief rather than enquiry' only to find herself experiencing thought transference, which brought her to the conclusion that if telepathy was a fact of life then it ought to have a bearing on psychotherapy; perhaps as an alternative to the lengthy, painful and cumbersome process of psychoanalysis.

At the outbreak of the war she went off to take up war work, first on the land and then in a food science research laboratory. During this time she had ample opportunity to venture inwards and the visionary experiences so induced led her towards a greater study of occult theory which in turn brought a deepening and widening of experience, of apparent memories of past lives, contacts with beneficent entities, and all the worst that Freud had warned against.

After the war, in seeking to bring the two worlds together, she met up with Dr Theodore Moriarty, whom she may have originally met at the Brunswick Square clinic. Moriarty was not a doctor of medicine but he was evidently a man of some charisma as well as occult and psychological knowledge. He became in fact the model for a series of short stories that she wrote for the *Royal* magazine that were later published in volume form as *The Secrets of Dr Taverner*. The stories purport to be written up from the casebook of a mysterious doctor who ran a private nursing home that specialised in cases beyond the reach and understanding of current medical psychology. The patients included vampires, werewolves, elemental changelings, victims of black magic and the like.

Dion Fortune claimed that she had written the stories 'down' to make them acceptable to the general public, rather than hyping them up. However, this must be taken with something of a grain of salt. She was certainly capable of telling a good story by an amalgamation of some of the more odd-ball cases that she had come across at the London clinic together with occult interpretation or speculation provided by Moriarty's teaching. Moriarty never had a nursing home of the type described but he was the leader of group of students who met together from time to time on a residential basis.

Her involvement with Moriarty did not prevent her from casting her net wide and in 1919 she also became initiated into a lodge of the Hermetic Order of the Golden Dawn, later to form her own group, which was initially intended as a kind of 'outer court' to the Golden Dawn but which soon took on independent status and became a powerful fraternity in its own right. Through all of this she retained her interest in psychology and wrote some early books on the subject, either as Violet Firth or as Dion Fortune. The very titles indicate their era: *Machinery of the Mind*, *The Problem of Purity*, *The Psychology of the Servant Problem*. The last of her titles in this genre uncompromisingly incorporated her occult interests. This was *The Esoteric Philosophy of Love and Marriage* and although it is regarded with some levity in the climate of modern times it was taken very seriously in its day by her superiors in the Golden Dawn on the grounds that it betrayed 'esoteric secrets'.

The occultists of the later nineteenth century were obsessed with secrecy, an attitude which persisted well into the twentieth century, and it was not entirely without good reason. For instance, Dr Wynn Westcott, a London coroner, was threatened with loss of his professional post because he was a member of the Golden Dawn. A large part of this attitude was however part of the general tenor of sexual repression of the period and the realisation by those who had any practical acquaintance with magical psycho-dynamics that they depended upon what some psychologists call the libido, or which in oriental yoga is termed the *kundalini* or 'serpent power'. In more general terms it is the life force that wells up into human creativity and that can be expressed in a variety of ways.

However, as Freud discovered in his early clinical work, there is a phenomenon known as 'transference' whereby the patient may transfer sexual or other emotions upon the analyst. Insofar that some types of occult practice are broadly similar to those of psychoanalysis (free fantasy for example), it follows that 'transference' can also occur in occult circles. Indeed I have heard it taken for granted by those on the wilder shores of occultism. And it has also been expressed to me by an experienced analyst that 'transference' is inevitable in any analysis. This of course does not imply that occultists or psychoanalysts lead lives of sexual promiscuity.

All this was enough to cause a certain call for discretion amongst responsible occultists, although Dion Fortune tried to put a wider awareness of it to positive good use. This was a time of campaigning for sexual liberation; of information by Dr Marie Stopes on the one hand and D.H.Lawrence on the other. And when we speak of sexual liberation we have to try to imagine ourselves back to rigid and inhibited attitudes and assumptions that would be quite unthinkable nowadays. Whether the lower classes should be instructed in the existence, let alone the methods of contraception. Or whether residential domestic servant girls should be allowed to have 'followers'.

This Dion Fortune strove to do in the guise of fiction and so the writings of her mature years can be divided into two complementary sectors. On the one hand non-fiction works explaining the general philosophy and theory of occultism, (e.g. *The Esoteric Orders and their Work, The Training and Work of an Initiate, The Mystical Qabalah*, etc.); and on the other hand the novels, which have a story line elucidating principles of psychic polarity between hero and heroine, (e.g. *The Goat Foot God, The Winged Bull, The Sea Priestess, Moon Magic.*)

The heroes of her books therefore tend to be somewhat repressed men, ill used by society, whose creativity is released with the help of a woman. This is achieved by directing their mutual desires through a subtlety of psychic interplay to open up inner depths that bring a fulfilment that may or may not then be expressed physically by the act of love. There is something of the popular romantic novel in all of this, although her works would certainly never have been quite suitable for the publishing list of Mills and Boon. Her intentions were also to reawaken the knowledge and technique of the ancient mystery religions as a method of individual and social healing in modern times.

In an article in her society's magazine she wrote, 'My novels have a purpose, which is the purpose of initiation . . . they are closely akin to the initiation dramas of the ancient Mysteries, in that they take the reader by way of dramatic representations to a realisation of the nature of the soul.'

It was her original intention to write a whole series of such novels, possibly ten in number, (corresponding to the ten spheres of the Tree of Life of the Qabalah). As she said, 'The Mystical Qabalah gives the theory but the novels give the practice.' Furthermore, 'Point by point I am taking the great problems of human life, analysing them in characters' experiences, and finding the ultimate happy ending in a definite practical psycho-magical solution – showing exactly how it was done so that anybody with a similar problem can go and do likewise.'

It was perhaps, in practice, not quite so simple as that, but in the general run of her intentions we seem to be coming close to elements of C.G.Jung's analytical psychology. His favoured sources were to be found in mythology, legend and ancient mystery traditions, including even alchemy, which were also the pabulum for Dion Fortune's aims.

C.G.Jung's works, when they became available in English, certainly had a considerable impact upon her. Jungian psychology seemed an excellent way of 'explaining' occultism to the outside world. And it was certainly something of a fillip to respectability to have an eminent psychologist talking in similar terms to the occultists.

Bernard Bromage, an occult commentator of respected integrity, interviewed Dion Fortune at about this time and found her full of psychological terminology. This led him to write that she 'had attained the greater part of her knowledge of magical techniques solely by study of psychological principles . . . She had attended many courses at . . . the University of London, in such related subjects as psychology, psychoanalysis, mental therapy and the like, and she tended to use the terminology employed in these circles in what seemed to me a rather over-facile and slightly too-credulous manner. She was full of "ab-reactions", "compulsive neuroses", "psychosomatic conditions" and the like.'

Part of this emphasis may have been put on for Bromage's benefit, and when the article was published, many years later, (in *Light* magazine in 1960), some of those who had known Dion Fortune intimately found his pen portrait unreal to the point of hilarity. The point being that psychological terms can play a useful part in presenting some of the dynamics of the magical philosophy in a way that is likely to be more readily understood, and Dion Fortune no doubt made the most of this, as I and no doubt many others have done when faced with media interviewers.

Convenient though it may be as a type of shorthand, it is nonetheless misleading, although perhaps just how misleading is perhaps not readily apparent. William G.Gray performed an important service when in his occult books, from *Magical Ritual Methods* onwards, he drew attention to the fourfold structure of practical occult symbolism in its own right, without recourse to Jungian psychological interpretations. The fourfold system had been there for all to see of course, from time immemorial, in Celtic legend, the Tarot, the Amerindian medicine wheel, the Tibetan Book of the Dead and so on. Indeed there is a certain circularity in the process in that the term 'mandala' coined by Jung for a symbol of psychological integration, means in fact 'magic circle'. However, whether Jung means quite the same thing by the term as the occultists is somewhat open to question.

At root the occult and the psychological premises differ very considerably, and we have to ask ourselves very carefully how far the 'collective unconscious' equates with the 'astral plane', and whether the 'Self' is the same as the 'Divine Spark', or how far the 'Anima' resembles the 'Holy Guardian Angel', and whether the 'Masters of the Wisdom' are manifestations of the 'Animus' of the female medium.

However, there was sufficient evident similarity for Dion Fortune to encourage the members of her society in the study of Jungian psychology, and until at least the late 1950s a book on the subject, by Jacobi, was part of the curriculum for all intending members. It was indeed the aim for some time to try to have at least one member trained in Jungian analysis in order to provide a service for members in the resolution of any psychological problems, which can become acute in the forcing house of a working occult group. However, there was a tendency for those who took up such training to leave the ranks and not return. There was clearly some kind of undefined chasm, between allegiance to Jungian psychology and allegiance to the occult society, that was not easily bridged. In later years, the reverse was known to happen, of at least one Jungian psychologist coming to the occult fold, and then ceasing to practise. In the end the society turned to other forms of therapy for the benefit of its members.

Israel Regardie, a contemporary of Dion Fortune, whose occult writings gained a wide following, was also much influenced by the Jungian psychology, and his early books lean heavily on psychological interpretations of magical dynamics. He had something of an irascible streak and was roundly contemptuous of the tradition of contact with superior spiritual intelligences. He castigated all who sought 'that commonly found fantasy . . . of being in touch with Masters', which, he averred, 'is so evidently neurotic, or even blatantly delusional, that most of those claiming it would have done better to have included some kind of psychotherapy in their magical training.'

Dion Fortune, who certainly did believe in that 'commonly found fantasy', and practised it, nonetheless also felt that 'some kind of psychotherapy would be an advantage in magical training' and went some way towards trying to implement it, as we have described. Regardie did modify his views somewhat in later years, although of course much of the alleged communications put about by various 'channels' merits the full force of his polemic. What he called the 'inepti' outnumber the 'adepti' very considerably.

Regardie himself went on to other forms of psychology and became a practitioner of the techniques of Wilhelm Reich. Dion Fortune's society also switched away from an emphasis on the Jungian psychology to look at alternative forms of psychotherapeutics. There was considerable interest in Ron L. Hubbard's 'dianetics' when it first came out, in the 1950s, later to develop into 'scientology'. This movement has had something of a bad press in one way and another but in its early days senior members of the Society of the Inner Light took a lot of trouble to study it. Once again, as with the Jungian interface, some did not return. However, for some time elementary psychotherapeutic techniques from this system were provided for members, either in group sessions or for individuals. I experienced some of this myself and have to say I found it nothing but beneficial.

However, it was a phase that passed and the society developed a less psychological and more mystical orientation, while at the same time producing some perceptive instruction on 'spiritual pathologies', in which psychological insights were intimately bound up with occult and mystical dynamics. It is to be hoped that some day these papers will be made available to a wider public.

As an example of this new approach, greater emphasis was placed upon the ability and indeed the will of the spirit to express itself efficiently and intelligently in the world. It was recognised that many seekers after the higher wisdom do so partly on false pretences, not as elevated souls seeking to give selfless service to humanity, but as reluctant and inadequate citizens of the cosmos in full retreat from the problems and responsibilities of material expression.

Typical symptoms of such a spiritual pathology would include:
1. difficulty in finishing a job or a cycle of activity completely; giving an impression of other-worldliness, or spiritual 'top heaviness';
2. a reincarnationary record demonstrating sequences of lives spent withdrawn in religious or occult orders occasionally interspersed with a life of extreme violence – in short, lack of balance in life expression;
3. a mind dominating the feelings, thus having no real warmth of 'heart', even when outwardly apparently kind and considerate;
4. difficulties in relating to the opposite sex because of a compulsion to be independent, aloof, self-sufficient;
5. a tendency to be unmarried, or else married to a similar type with little interest in children or domestic and family life;
6. very often in the right, but intolerant of imperfections in others or themselves;
7. at heart lonely and unfulfilled, seeking 'higher' consciousness to compensate for the hollowness of expression and experience at the lower levels.

In such an approach as this, the Society of the Inner Light would appear to have developed a mode of psychological analysis particularly related to their own field of endeavour, and also incorporating their own assumptions as to the importance of the spiritual element in human psychology, and to the phenomenon of reincarnation. And when we come to look at the esoteric field generally, there has been a tendency to pursue lines of psychological analysis in similar fashion. Thus it would seem that, for the committed and experienced occultist, the Jungian and Freudian orthodoxies leave something to be desired. This is most readily apparent in the question of 'masters' on the one hand, and re-incarnation theory on the other.

There remains however a considerable margin of overlap, both in theory and practice, and even in intention in that much 'New Age' interest in occult dynamics is geared to psychotherapeutic aims; that is, to the resolution of personal problems and the integration of the personality as ends in themselves. We may even see psychologists using esoteric techniques and 'maps of the soul' as a means of therapy. For instance, the Psychosynthesis of Dr Roberto Assegioli bears much similarity to the esoteric psychology and cosmic groundplan of Alice A. Bailey, who in turn derives her inspiration from H. P. Blavatsky, the founding Theosophist. Indeed it is a moot point as to who used 'free association' or 'free fantasy' first, the psychologists or the occultists. The latter tend to call it 'path working' or 'scrying in the spirit vision', although there is a latter day halfway house in the term 'initiated symbol projection'.

Various other esoteric themes have permeated the psycho-therapeutic sphere. There is, for instance, the Enneagram, favoured by Gurdjieff and Ouspensky and their followers. This is a device like a nine-pointed star that serves as the ground plan for an esoteric cosmology and general yardstick of inner and outer experience, in much the same way that the Qabalistic Tree of Life or the Twelve-fold Circle of the Zodiac is utilised by other occultists. One may nowadays find Roman Catholic pastors using it as the basis for psycho-therapeutic workshops and also linking it to more objective mystical and religious principles such as the personality of Jesus Christ or to the personal prayer life. Of course the enneagram does have an esoteric and religious origin in that it comes down to us from or through the medieval Sufis, and possibly from Pythagorean number mysticism before that.

We therefore find that as well as there being several schools of clinical psychology there are also various schools of esoteric psychology. And when we come to practical experience we find that the theoretical assumptions of the practitioners seem to influence the results and to dominate their interpretation. It has been observed before that the different schools of psychology seem to develop self-validating experience: Freudian patients come up with Freudian symbolism, Jungian patients oblige with Jungian, and so on. The same might be said about the various schools of occultism.

This does not necessarily mean that all involved, on either side, are dishonest or deluded. Materialist critics with their own reductionist preconceptions also affect, or inhibit, the results they try to observe, even if they like to think that they are the only ones who are 'truly objective'. (In fact, in this field, it is probable that this question-begging term is quite meaningless.) There is nothing quite so pathetic as the sight of an anthropologist, for example, fluttering like a moth against a lighted window, struggling to get in to the lighted world of spiritual experience, the restraining glass being their own academic assumptions. Jungian psychologists, to the occultist, seem to occupy an intermediate position; the window is open, but they will not come all the way in!

A lot of the problem of intercommunication stems from a lack of well-defined terms and also from the related problem of an unsound philosophical basis upon which to measure the subjective and the objective and their interrelationship. It is possible that the greatest contribution to solving these problems has been with us for more than 150 years but has not been recognised yet. This is the epistemological ontology of Samuel Taylor Coleridge.

Unfortunately he never quite got round to expounding this concisely and systematically, but it has been reconstituted to some degree by Owen Barfield, in his monumental work, *What Coleridge Thought*. Barfield was a close lifelong friend of C.S.Lewis and J.R.R.Tolkien, and one of that famous discussion group the 'Inklings'. As a protagonist of the thought of Rudolf Steiner, he was for long highly regarded in anthroposophical circles, and latterly he has been increasingly encouraged and respected in American academe.

I have endeavoured to show something of the modern relevance of Coleridge's thought and its subtle and far-reaching ramifications in *Magic and the Western Mind* (previously published as *A History of White Magic*), and in more detail in *The Magical World of the Inklings*, although Owen Barfield's work, whilst not perhaps being too easy to read, is certainly more profound. Ultimately, of course, one has to go to Coleridge himself, a prodigy whose youthful reading included Plato, Plotinus, Giordano Bruno and Marsilio Ficino, for the most part in the original, and who later travelled in Germany and learnt the language to study the roots of the romantic tradition, which includes the contributions of the Rosicrucian–based mystic Jacob Boehme on the one hand and the poet/philosopher/scientist Johann Wolfgang von Goethe on the other.

Most of these trends point to the fact that, in the last analysis, human psychology cannot be understood without recourse to the spark of divinity in man. And if, in our modern prejudice, we prefer to leave out the personal term God, then we may, for want of something better, perhaps utilise the concept of Pure Reason that served Plotinus. This is the 'lux interna' that infuses the imagination with inspiration, and the concrete understanding with intuitive insights. In Coleridge's imagery it is the Promethean fire that was stolen from heaven and which we have not yet learnt how to handle – what Existentialists have called the challenge to accept our freedom. This also implies a dreadful responsibility, but one which we may, like cosmic adolescents, learn how to grow into without too much hooliganism.

It is this concept of the evolution of consciousness that Barfield illustrates in the light of Coleridge's thought. We have a parallel from the psychological side represented in such works as Erich Neumann's *History and Origins of Consciousness* and *The Great Mother*. Here we have the lineaments of the growth of human spiritual awareness and responsibility from the group consciousness and 'participation mystique' of animal man, through the individual ego development represented by the myths and legends of the hero, to our present dilemma of what to do with our quasi-divine powers in the fields of ecology, genetics, nuclear power, and so on.

Psychology has done much in this respect to point the way, but still has a tendency to confine the extent of the cosmos to the contents of the human skull. If we need the help of spirits from the vasty deep, they may well speak to us through our intuitive and imaginative antennae, but they are likely to be rather more than archetypes of the unconscious. This is a thought that is so profound in its implications that we might well feel a great deal safer within a psychological subjective bunker should such spirits turn out to be not 'goodies' but 'baddies'. And, indeed, demonology and the constitution of the angelic hierarchies have somewhat fallen out of fashion during the current epoch. This does not necessarily imply that they, any more than God, have been annihilated by our ostrich-like posture.

As a balanced way of coming to terms with the problems involved, perhaps a synthesis between the occult and psychological positions might be found, whether or not it is good practice to build permanent houses upon bridges. One example of such an approach may be found in *The Inner Guide Meditation* of Edwin Steinbrecher. This is a system that combines psychological dynamics with the astrological birth chart, the mediational consequences of which are conversations with helpful beings as represented by standardised Tarot images.

The symbolic mechanism is based upon the Golden Dawn system of attributions between astrological planet, constellation or element on the one hand and Tarot Trump image on the other. There are arguments that this system is largely arbitrary but in the light of experience this is no great objection to virtually any system of occult symbolism. If correspondences are believed in, and worked out in a reasonably balanced and consistent way, then the chances are that they will work. William Blake provides an example of this, with his endless identification of Biblical locations with parts of London or

'Albion' in general, along with tribes and patriarchs of the ancient Hebrews and representative figures within his personal life (such as the soldier who accused him of treason). They may be arbitrary but they are not inconsequential. Whoever is prepared to work with them sympathetically will find that they work. And it follows that if one prefers to modify them, or to substitute one's own system entirely, than that too is likely to work.

For Steinbrecher's students, starting off in visualisation of Plato's cave, and being guided by an animal (a personal totem), one may be led to a communion with the representation of the Sun in glory of the Tarot Trumps. From this healing and integrating contact one may be passed on to others, and the whole thing may eventually be worked out in terms of the configuration of the astrological birth chart, with relevance to personal life history and relationships. This, it may be judged, is both psychology and occultism.

We have noted that a fundamental divide between the occult and the psychological approaches is two-fold: 1. an objective recognition of superior spiritual beings, and 2. process of reincarnation of the soul. As an illustration of the type of psychology into which these occult assumptions may lead us, we can examine 'an anatomy of the subtle bodies' promulgated by Dion Fortune in 1940, well after she had become familiar with Jungian interpretations. These ideas were published in her private news letter as part of a series entitled *Words of the Masters*, indicating that they are attributed to a higher external source than the personal theories of the writer. Here a diagram may prove helpful to clarify the essential concept from the detail. (See Fig. 2 on page 22).

We have a threefold spiritual entity, commonly called the Higher Self, or Individuality, that is cosmically self determined, and so fundamentally harmonious, and which expresses a particular spiritual 'ray', 'harmonic', or 'archetype'. This unit is responsible for building a series of incarnations within the lower worlds of ideas, feelings, sensations. In this sense it has a sort of architectural role in relation to the lower bodies, which ideally are the temple of the spirit. These lower bodies are represented by the projected Personality or Lower Self, which is shown in anthropoidal shape in the diagram, as opposed to the star-like configuration of the Individuality or Higher Self.

The problem now lies in the means of communication between these two expressions of a single human being: the Higher with its background of harmonious cosmic eternity, and the Lower, developed in the familiar way within the world, subject to heredity, genetics and environmental conditioning. All reductionist approaches treat only of this latter system of consciousness.

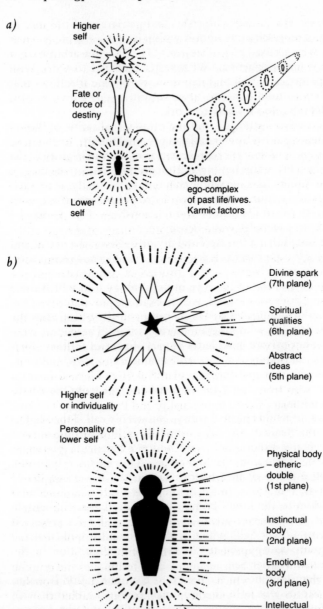

a)

Higher self

Fate or force of destiny

Lower self

Ghost or ego-complex of past life/lives. Karmic factors

b)

Divine spark (7th plane)

Spiritual qualities (6th plane)

Abstract ideas (5th plane)

Higher self or individuality

Personality or lower self

Physical body – etheric double (1st plane)

Instinctual body (2nd plane)

Emotional body (3rd plane)

Intellectual body (4th plane)

Fig 2   Bodies of Consciousness

Much of the background to all of this is to be found in Theosophical and other related writings, including 'communicated' material that Dion Fortune herself recorded as far back as 1922, later published as *The Cosmic Doctrine* but also having an influence on other of her occult and psychological works. In this 1940 teaching, there is put forward an additional two-fold connection, one called the Fate and the other the Ghost.

The Fate is described as the abstract essence of the past, acting as a causative agent upon the current Personality. It is therefore experienced as a 'force of destiny' or our own especial mode of expression which leads us to inner fulfilment and outward expression of our own unique potentiality, which will be an amalgam of basic spiritual type together with the abstracted experience of previous lives on earth or of more direct cosmic experience in the higher worlds. The Ghost, on the other hand, is an image of the ego of the last incarnation, and it contains within it, rather like a nest of Chinese boxes, or a succession of mirror reflections, previous ego images.

Its attributes, then, are to provide a composite picture of memories of previous form experience. Although itself never more than one incarnation old, it contain memory images of the previous ghost and so on down the time track. But whereas the Higher Self contains the integrated and harmonised realisations of past form experience, the Ghost is a repository of *unassimilated* experience, and is thus similar in nature to the subconscious of the current Personality, and in its remoter memory images to the Jungian collective unconscious.

It will be seen from the diagram that both Fate and Ghost have different relationships with Individuality and Personality. The Fate is, in a sense, a channel itself, between the two sets of vehicles. The Ghost, on the other hand, is more of an extraneous appendage. It can have a determining influence upon the Personality, perhaps overriding that of the Fate, whilst it also has a tenuous link with the Individuality, without which it would become a completely dissociated shell. It is by no means an evil entity when in touch with the spiritual life of the Individuality, (which is in a sense ultimately responsible for it), but it tends towards the past, and to unresolved problems of the past, as opposed to the Fate, which looks toward fruitful growth, new experience, and to the future.

This has an important bearing upon occult techniques and training methods, the aim of which should be to open up Personality consciousness to the Individuality, via the Fate, rather than to the drag from the past represented by the Ghost. One may see herein the reason why mainstream esoteric teaching from the responsible schools heads students away from undue interest in past incarnations. Wherever such is not delusory speculation, or pandering to a hypnotist's will, it is liable only to set up a drag from unresolved problems of the past, particularly if the 'memories' are cloaked in glamour and self admiration. This is in fact but another form of spiritual pathology.

It might be thought that stirring about in the past in this way was a means of relieving or releasing or abreacting past repressions. This is a point of view, and in line with Freudian aims and techniques. The more positive pursuit of the strengthening of the influence of the Fate is however an integrative approach that in the psychological field characterises the approach of Jung.

Enhanced contact with the Individuality ought to be an act of positive achievement and healing, and this is borne out in other schools of esoteric thought. We have been looking at the human psyche in spiritual extension in terms of Dion Fortune's teaching. Much the same pattern may be found in the esoteric psychology of Alice A. Bailey, which in turn derives from H.P.Blavatsky and traditional oriental sources. For instance, Dion Fortune's concepts of the Individuality or Higher Self, in Alice Bailey's works are called the Soul. And Dion Fortune's identification of the Fate as a channel between Higher and Lower Selves has close correspondence with Alice Bailey's *astaskarana* or 'rainbow bridge'. Furthermore the memory images of the Ghost are another way of looking at the Theosophical conception of Seed Atoms. It will be gathered that esoteric psychology is no simplistic panacea, but rather adds dimensions on to the more rudimentary conceptions of conventional psychology.

It may therefore be of interest if we take an actual case history, and we have one more or less in the public domain, in the life and work of Dion Fortune herself. We may find, for example, some exemplification of the Ghost in the comments she made on her later novels, *The Sea Priestess* and *Moon Magic*, for the protagonist of these two novels has many attributes that suggest she might be well be a manifestation of Dion Fortune's own Ghost. In her preface to *Moon Magic* for instance, she writes, 'when I imagined the character of Vivien Le Fay Morgan, or Lilith Le Fay, as she variously called herself, I brought into being a personality . . . she is very far from being a puppet in my hands, but takes charge of the situation.' And, 'After the conclusion of *The Sea Priestess* she would not lie quiet in her grave, but her ghost persisted in walking. It walked to such good purpose that it forced upon me the writing of this book.'

After several abortive attempts at writing a sequel to the first novel, she finally set the narrative in the first person, allowing the heroine to, so to speak, write it herself, whereupon, she reports, the book more or less wrote itself. As to the final result she records, 'I have not a very high opinion of it as literature but it is certainly a psychological curio. It contains, moreover, an amount of very odd lore, much of which I did not know anything about until I read it in these pages.'

'What have I created in Lilith Le Fay?' she asks, 'Who and what is Lilith, and why did she live on after the book about her was finished (i.e. *The Sea Priestess*), and insist on appearing again? (i.e. in *Moon Magic*). Have I furnished myself with a dark familiar?'

It is of course not uncommon for authors to find characters taking on life of their own in any story, and similar phenomenon can happen to actors. In many cases it is felt that his gives a sense of vitality to their work. It is, of course, in either case, an example of the 'magical' use of the imagination, or in popular psychological parlance, 'working off the subconscious'.

However, we enter a further dimension when such characters become compulsive or obsessive in their effect, or take on a more objective reality. And in the case of Dion Fortune and her fictional heroine it seems that we are moving into this area when she writes, 'Lilith lives after a curious manner of her own; she lives for others as well as for me; and it may well be that to some of those who read these pages she will come as a shadowy figure half-seen in the twilight of the mind.'

It should be said that such a visitation is not likely to be tremendously helpful, as an examination of the character of this figure may show. We could, for example, take our previous checklist of symptoms of spiritual pathology and see what evidence there is for 'otherworldliness', 'spiritual top-heaviness', 'lack of warmth', 'mind-dominated feelings', 'aloofness and self sufficiency, particularly in relation to the opposite sex', 'lack of interest in children or domestic ties', 'intolerance of imperfection', and an 'inner hollowness'. It should be clear, that on the evidence of the novels, Miss Lilith Le Fay does not score very well as a rounded human being.

She undoubtedly is a lady of some charisma and power, and she is certainly well intentioned, but nonetheless all her relations with the men she selects are power seeking and manipulative. She is therefore not an evil person but a profoundly out-dated one, and her vitality stems not from what she is but from what she knows. Her own justification for her actions would be that the current age is in need of some of the ancient wisdom which she has to teach, but it is arguable that she also could have benefited if she had lived a more complete and whole life in the world as she found it.

Conventional psychologists might interpret the action of *Moon Magic* in terms of Dion Fortune's unsuccessful marriage. In 1927, she married Dr Penry Evans, in character somewhat similar to the Dr Rupert Malcolm of the novel, but the relationship had foundered by 1939. Alan Richardson, in his biography of Dion Fortune, *Priestess*, deals with the situation from this point of view in some detail, but with the proviso that 'we should beware of dismissing her ideas on sexuality as "nothing more than" a matter of compensation. She had these ideas all her *lives.*'

The italics are mine but the plural is Mr Richardson's, and it is significant to our thesis that the heroine of *Moon Magic* is at least in part an expression of Dion Fortune's Ghost, with its reflected memories of previous incarnations. However, rather than dwell upon this manifestation of unequilibrated experience from the past, let us look to the other side of the coin and try to discern the influence of Dion Fortune's Fate. This will give evidence of itself as all the good things that were achieved by Dion Fortune in her life and which have lived after her, and to this end we have an impressive catalogue. In general terms it may be summed up by the early expressed intention to try to revivify the powers of the ancient mystery religions in the modern age, and in this she to a large part succeeded, not only in the contribution to the general consciousness of her Society of the Inner Light as an organisation in its own right, but in the influence it has spread and work that has been done by various individuals who have been trained in its methods and who have then gone on to set up their own centres of teaching and spiritual activity. This is a natural type of seeding in work of this nature, where individuals are encouraged to discern and to carve out their own pattern of destiny within the world. Thus much that can be traced back to the influence of Dion Fortune points to her own Higher Self and to her own Fate. Much of this comes through in the early textbooks and essays, with their consummate commonsense and dedicated good faith, and also again in some of the Weekly War Letters, where her courage and good humour in the light of considerable adversity and indeed physical danger, reflect a Personality well expressing the Fate and the Individuality.

She was at something of a disadvantage in being lumbered with assumptions about being the withdrawn head of an enclosed order. And in this she was as much a victim of the expectations of her disciples as of her own predilections. It is her husband, Dr Penry Evans, who perhaps finds his way as an initiate in the world with rather more success. As Alan Richardson says, 'Merl had several masks: he was the Sun Priest, he was a physician; he lived his life through many outlets, none of them really overlapping.' He had been one of the first to volunteer at the outbreak of war in 1914, and after active service in the Artists Rifles and the Machine Gun Corps, left with the rank of 2nd Lieutenant. He studied medicine and qualified as a doctor in 1924, when he took on a 'house job' at Charing Cross Hospital, followed by positions in public health in East Ham. He met and married Dion Fortune with whom he developed his esoteric side, but rather than become an enclosed adept he went on to run his own factory engaged in research into health foods based on soya bean products. When civil war broke out in Spain he worked on the republican side to try to alleviate problems of malnutrition in children. After having to fly for his life from General Franco, abandoning all his medical equipment in Barcelona, he became Assistant Tuberculosis Officer for Southwark before eventually becoming Medical Officer for Health for Beaconsfield, where he designed his own house, (called 'Pan'), and settled down with the second Mrs Penry Evans. In his latter years he was described as 'a man that was happy with life, very droll and kind, quite passionate about music and possessed of a very definite charisma – a kind and kingly presence.'

So we find in Dr Penry Evans, an example of an esoterically minded idealist who was at the same time able to a large degree to express his ideals in the world. And as we have mentioned above, there was in the War Letters of Dion Fortune, (which to date have regrettably never been published), particular evidence of a commonsensical, humorous and compassionate woman of the world, concerned with political and social issues, and by no means the encloistered *femme fatale* of the image of the novels.

As she writes elsewhere, the Higher Self may tend to come through to greater contact in times of physical danger, and in this respect the letters to her students, during the dark days of 1940 during the London blitz, may give a closer idea of the Individuality of Dion Fortune as expressed through a dedicated Personality.

For instance, after being bombed out of her headquarters in October 1940 she can write:

> In our last letter we asked our members and friends to invoke for the protection of 3 Queensborough Terrace and in this letter we have the ironical task of informing them that we have been bombed out of it, though without casualties; so it may be maintained that the invocation was at least a partial success, though your Leader and her Librarian look like a couple of sweeps owing to a difference of opinion with the roof, which fell in on them, but tactfully refrained from hitting them.
>
> It has often been alleged that Dion Fortune is a Black Occultist, and we regretfully admit that the allegation can no longer be denied; however it is hoped that soap and water will restore her to the Right Hand Path and

her students will once more be able to hold up their heads before a world always too ready to think the worst.

Thus we trust we have made a sufficiently clear demonstration of the two concepts of the Fate and the Ghost, at any rate as they impinge upon and influence the expression of the Personality within the world. The more valuable exercise of course, will be for each one of us to attempt to make the distinction within our own lives.

There is, however, a further element from which we should not shrink in any discussion of the difference between the occult and the psychological points of view. This is the degree of objectivity of thought-forms.

As Dion Fortune remarked in her preface to *Moon Magic*, others beside herself had become conscious of the figure of Lilith Le Fay. She also says, in her article on the subject, that 'the Ghost is not a living entity but a thought-form, and the methods of dispelling thought-forms are applicable to it.' A problem may be that many occult aspirants who do not know any better might well go out of their way to invoke the thought-form, assuming it to be a power or knowledge bestowing experience. So it might be for those who have the ability to handle it but one cannot universally recommend the practice of trying to catch a tiger by the tail, or perhaps not a tiger but something more like the crowned serpent in Charles Williams' novel, *The Place of the Lion*, that dominated poor Dora Wilmot, and induced this weak and hitherto ineffectual woman to write a number of malevolent anonymous letters and then to try to coil sinuously round the gentleman who caught her at it.

A problem is that a thought form such as that of the heroine of *The Sea Priestess* and *Moon Magic*, having been built up by a powerful imaginative consciousness such as Dion Fortune undoubtedly had, will tend to be very powerful and persistent. And coming out of her own bank of 'Ghost' memories it will have the validity of being based upon ancient realities, and will tend to appeal to others who have a similar bank of memories. In other words it will stimulate and reinforce their own Ghost.

This is unlikely to do them very much good. Not only does it deflect attention away from the healthy influence of the Fate, it brings yet more unbalance to bear upon the unbalance that made the thought-form seem attractive in the first place. Thus do we get a certain class of houri on the occult fringe obsessed with fantasies of 'polarity' and yet never really making a start in the real business of human and social relationships. Such are also unlikely to want to accept the boring prospect of sustained training in meditation and contemplation aimed at the true contact with the spiritual dynamics of the Fate and the Higher Self. The more highly coloured exercises of the active imagination will have much more appeal, particularly if they feed the deviation.

The acid test as to whether all is well or not will be found in the circumstances of daily life – are they balanced or chaotic, relationships sustained or promiscuous, is mental confusion evident through failure to be punctual, or emotional confusion evident through inability to be tidy? In Qabalistic terms, the ethic of Malkuth, of daily outer life, is Order, and a persistant failure in this indicates that all is not well on the higher levels, no matter what the pretensions may be.

Also, the more the thought-form is brooded upon, the more powerful does it become, which is a point of general public hygiene upon the astral plane, not just a personal psychological problem. This is an area that psychology seems unwilling to address, at least in these terms, although it may well be covered in terms of group psychology and analysis and manipulation of the public psyche through the mass media, be it in terms of advertising, or political propaganda, or more subtle ways of manipulating the 'spirit of the times'.

Indeed it might well be asked how far the 'image making' of modern times is not a magical operation in the pure sense, of manipulating the consciousness of others through symbols and sonics. Dr Goebels was the first modern exponent of it on a massive scale but it is nowadays almost a commonplace. Indeed we might further ask ourselves, in the way that we use the media of mass communication, how far it is possible to invoke a *national* Fate or Ghost.

In terms of Britain, the Fate, as channel to the Higher Self, or Folk Angel, might be regarded as Logres, the realm of King Arthur and his Round Table Knights, as C.S.Lewis has suggested. Whilst the Ghost might to be found expressed in the football hooligans who invade the continent of Europe chanting xenophobic slogans. It would be an interesting point of debate to determine into which category the fighting of the Falklands war would fall.

Needless to say every country has its own Fate or Destiny to fulfil, and its Ghost to lay. And ultimately we have to think in terms of the human race as a whole. A problem at the same time occult and psychological.

A DISCUSSION
WITH NGAKPA CHÖGYAM

INTRODUCTION

R. J. Stewart

At the Fourth Merlin Conference in 1989, at which Ngakpa Chögyam was a guest speaker on Tantra and Shamanism, a debate took place. The formal proposal was that 'modern psychology is a shard stolen from the vessel of spiritual traditions'. As is always the case with such deliberately grandiose debate proposals, this was first qualified, and even intentionally aggravated (though not to the point of unpleasantness) to generate discussion. Afterwards, a discussion arose on this theme. In true Tantric Buddhist manner, Ngakpa Chögyam disposes of the entire root of any such debate as being absurd. But because he is also experienced in Western methods of counselling and therapy, he proposes the integration of such methods within a spiritual tradition – in this chapter, Tantra.

This proposal is, perhaps, the only balanced resolution that might be reached. No true spiritual tradition is rigid or dogmatic, but protean and ever developing, its roots far back in the illusion of time and culture, its branches reaching into the unknown. It is the potential integration of our infant modern psychology into any one of the true spiritual traditions that is an important possibility, and not simply the choice of the tradition itself, be it Eastern or Western. But the converse, for a materialist study of the human psyche to seek to negate or absorb the spiritual traditions and replace their function in human life, has always been a possibility in the West.

The rest of this discussion I will leave to the humour and clarity of Chögyam, but there is one point which he raises that is worth further attention at this introductory stage. He seems to be telling us that the real ragbag and confusion of psychology-spirituality is found in the New Age movement. Some of the worst aspects of New Ageism are amply described by Monica Sjöö, in Chapter 4. But the inherent vacuousness of much of the New Age impetus and methodology is neatly pinpointed by Chögyam, speaking as he does from a long active tradition of spiritual transformation and enlightenment. This vacuous quality of New Ageism may not be in itself imbalancing – but there is great potential for it to be applied unscrupulously, like any fashion, for straight profit. During that debate in 1989, this aspect of a self-proclaimed link between spiritual traditions and psychology, a claim often made by New Age teachers, courses, publishers, therapists or schools, did not capture any attention. My guess is that the real debate probably lies in that direction now, unless as Ngakpa Chögyam reminds us at the outset, we can realise our Beginningless Enlightenment.

★   ★   ★

Q. Ngakpa – from your perspective as a Lama of the Nyingma Lineage, and as a professional counsellor; what is your reaction to modern psychology as 'a shard stolen from the vessel of spiritual tradition'?

N.C. It sounds a little bit like the theme for a science fantasy movie (laughter). Well, what indeed. I need to explain that from my perspective, from the perspective of Tibetan Tantra, we are all Beginninglessly Enlightened. Everything I say is going to be based on this. When I say that we are all Beginninglessly Enlightened, I mean that we all have the *answers* within us. Within our own being, we have all we need to unravel our own condition. Any power or knowledge to which we can aspire, is already there – has always been there. So, what of modern psychology? As a loosely defined Rogerian counsellor, I would say something quite similar – I would say that people are all fundamentally good, and that they have within them all the resources necessary for arriving at creative solutions to their own problems. Am I saying that Carl Rogers stole this from the Nyingma Lineage? I don't think so; maybe he stole the idea from some other spiritual tradition? Maybe it's been 'stolen' all the way down the line, the Tantric rape and pillage of reality (laughter).

Q. Well, let's not say stolen, let's say. . . .

N.C. Lifted, purloined, ripped off, plagiarised, unconsciously borrowed, morphogenetically transferred (laughter). I don't think it matters how it is phrased. It still implies that the primal facts of human reality cannot be repeatedly discovered afresh without reference to what went before. I'd have to oppose such an idea fairly vigorously; I think (laughter).

Q.   (laughter) Why?

N.C. Why? Because it's very limiting (laughter). It reduces human capacity for inspiration and innovation to the width of a blood-drip tie!

Q.   But you represent an ancient spiritual tradition.

N.C. Yes; but only as a young child of the Lineage. I value the Nyingma Lineage beyond all else, but that doesn't mean I'm chauvinist about it. I value the Nyingma Tantras for their ferocious ability to butcher the demons of the neurosis. These Teachings enable us to enter into the Space of our *primal Awareness*. But it is just this very *primal Awareness* that gives rise to *all* systems of transformation. Modern psychology in many ways is the 'Dharma' for the extra layer of 'samsara' we have at this present time.

Q.   That's a very interesting view. I'd like you to say more about that but first (for those who are unfamiliar with the terms you have used) could you explain what you meant by the words Dharma and samsara?

N.C. With pleasure. Dharma actually means: what is; that which is there; reality; the natural existence of everything. But Dharma also means: the methods whereby the nature of reality is discovered. These methods are naturally based on the many different and complicated ways in which we've divorced ourselves from the nature of our own real Being. Samsara means: going round in circles, and describes the condition of having misunderstood the nature of reality. Basically, samsara is the pain we experience when we hide from our own enlightenment.

Q.   So in what way do you see modern psychology as being the Dharma for our extra layer of samsara?

N.C. The Teachings of Buddhism, in all its levels and Schools is addressed – or was addressed – to a certain kind of person. That kind of person was the product of the extended family system. The extended family is actually the most psychologically healthy basis for human development. The child has numerous role models – especially when there are a fair gaggle of brothers and sisters. Beyond the parents and grandparents, there are uncles and aunts and their children . . . there's a word for them, isn't there . . . ?

Q.   Cousins.

N.C. Ah yes, cousins. So, I'm not saying that in ancient times we had 'better' role models – it's just that (in our formative years) we would have had more of them. It's the multiplicity of role models that enables the child to recognise that *being human* is not restricted to the narrow pattern of behaviour witnessed in the parents. In addition, we would have had a greater number of siblings – brother and sisters. All this makes for a more balanced; less emotionally vulnerable; less convoluted; less self-destructive; more grounded; less co-dependent; less maladapted person. But now most of that relative 'simplicity' is lacking. I mean; Buddhism used to address an audience who had a relatively uncomplicated motivation for wishing to engage in the spiritual path. Now; people enter into the practice of Buddhism (and probably most other spiritual paths) for all manner of fantastically intricate purposes. What confuses matters more, is that some Lamas take a while to realise that the motivation of their students can be their main obstacle. Students will often express great fervour, and expect to be taken seriously. But often it's the case that they simply wish to act out childhood dramas under the guise of dealing with 'spiritual' dilemmas. This is often why people in 'spiritual' communities connected with Eastern Teachers can be so unpleasant and conspicuously lacking in social skills. So, to return to your question, I feel that it's very important that people look at their own personal pain in a 'non-esoteric' manner before they shroud their own neurosis in the cloak of arcane mysteries. The intrinsic Mystery of Being is mysterious enough without filtering our involvement with its methods of Realisation through the web of belligerent potty training (laughter).

Q.   (laughter) So, you would say that people need to undergo therapy before they consider their spiritual life?

N.C. Well, I would say that there is no 'one answer' for everyone. People need to have some kind of honesty or integrity about how they actually are. Teachers also need to be more involved at the personal level – especially Teachers from other cultures who may not be sufficiently aware of the issues that afflict some of their students. I wouldn't say that people should complete a thorough course of analysis before tackling the spiritual dimension, but I do think that it could go hand in hand with their spiritual work. I think that could be invaluable; *if* they could find a therapist or analyst who could work creatively in that way without undermining their spiritual priorities. This is obviously a very difficult area. Ideally, any Teacher who addresses *any* particular audience should evolve methods of adapting the method and approach to suit the particular culture and mental set of that audience. When Padmasambhava (the Tantric Buddha) took the Teachings and Practices of Tantra to Tibet, he absorbed the ways of the indigenous Bon tradition. It was in this way that Buddhism could become a suitable Spiritual vehicle for the Tibetan people. If Buddhism is to become a suitable vehicle for western people, it is going to have to integrate *into itself* the appropriate methodologies of Modern Psychology.

Q.   But is the same true of the pre-Christian spiritual paths of the West?

N.C.   Yes, unfortunately the same factors apply. Even though such paths are, in a sense, 'nearer to home' – they're still addressing an audience with the complexities of having been raised in the psychological bonsai pot of the nuclear family (laughter). We have to know *why* we want to enter a spiritual path. We have to be able to distinguish between wanting to change, and wanting to play out the tightly locked-in patterns we learnt in childhood.

Q.   Could you elaborate a little? I'm not quiet sure what you mean by 'tightly locked-in patterns'?

N.C.   Well, in the extended family system, we learn that there are a wide variety of options in terms of what it means to be human. We also learn that male-female relationships do not necessarily have to be played out according to the model performed by our mother and father, strangely enough (laughter), and I'm sure this may upset some people: children *can* be psychologically healthier with two sets of parents (having evolved out of the break-up of a marriage). At least they then have *two* models for what marriages can be like. If the divorce is acrimonious, that's obviously very disturbing – but with a relatively mature and compassionately handled separation, children can even learn that change *is* fundamentally acceptable.

Q.   But don't children often manipulate such divorced parents, setting one against the other?

N.C.   Yes. But that doesn't *have* to happen. It's not built into the process of separation – it's not an inevitable outcome. It depends entirely on *how* the parents separate, and on who they were as partners whilst bringing up the children or child. Obviously children brought up without sufficient attention evolve manipulative ways of gaining attention and love from the separate parents. If the parents have been warm, loving and adequate to the role of parenting then such manipulative behaviour need not arise – if the parents have had a relatively good relationship and can approach their break-up in a caring and maturely considered manner.

Q. Wouldn't such well-balanced people stay together anyway?

N.C. Quite possibly, but that makes it sound as if separation isn't a healthy choice or that it cannot be a healthy choice. The concept of a life-long relationship itself *can* be very unhealthy, and distort people in their relationships with each other. You see, everything that comes into being – passes out of being. Everything that arises out of Emptiness – dissolves back into Emptiness. Pattern emerges out of chaos and merges back into chaos. From the Tantric perspective, the fact that form is impermanent doesn't make it wicked, naughty or delusionary. You cannot say, within this view, that because a relationship comes to an end that it was not a good relationship. You may as well say that because a meal came to an end, that it was not a good meal – or that if a period of time comes to an end, that it must have been unsatisfactory. We should attempt to enter into the spirit of endings in the same way as we enter into their beginnings. We should clink our wine glass as cordially in the toilet as we do at the dinner table (laughter). But let's not dwell too long on marriage, divorce and developmental psychology.

Q. (laughter) No, we're getting away from the subject a little.

N.C. Yes; the basic issue for me, is that any spiritual practitioner needs to unravel certain aspects of his or her personality before they walk too far down any spiritual path. That, from my point of view, and based on the experience of what I've seen among Western people, is absolutely crucial.

Q. How did you go through this unravelling; or did you have to go through it at all?

N.C. I did have to go through it, very certainly! And very painful it was to be sure. But I didn't have recourse to therapists – I went through it in long solitary retreats in the Himalayas, where I experienced my neurosis explosively and in a way that made it impossible to hide from what came up.

Q. How did that happen?

N.C. (laughter) Well, in retreat it's not possible to take evasive action. You can't hide from yourself if all there is, is what you are in the moment. It can actually be quite terrible! (laughter) It *was* quite terrible, and at one point I'm surprised that I didn't get dehydrated from crying! Any period over six months in solitary retreat exposes everything there is to expose if you maintain your meditation practice.

Q. Why then wouldn't you advise retreat as the best way to

unravel this extra layer of samsara?

N.C.   Why? (laughter) Because it's a bit of a kill or cure method.
The possibilities of going over the edge, of ending up in
the locked ward of a psychiatric hospital are fairly high.
Solitary retreat is very valuable at a certain stage of spiritual
experience, but not really for people at the outset of their
spiritual journey.

Q.   So why did you choose to go into retreat; was it because you
were in some way ready?

N.C.   No, I was certainly *not* ready! (laughter) I can't think of
anyone more unready than I was. You have heard of Ethelred
the Unready? Well, I was Chögyam the Unready.

Q.   So why did you go into retreat? What made you choose to
do that if you felt you were unready?

N.C.   Well, I didn't choose, and I didn't know I was unready!
(laughter) I merely followed my Lama's instruction and
advice, and discovered later that I was unready.

Q.   And having discovered yourself to be unready, couldn't you
have come out of retreat or was that not permitted?

N.C.   Oh sure; I could have left the retreat at any point – that was
the hell of it, especially in the beginning. I had to learn why I
was there, what I really wanted from what I was doing. It was
in that situation that I realised that I had been relating to my
Lama as a substitute father figure. He was the kind, encouraging father I felt I never had. He was the father who actually
instructed me never to cut my hair again – the hippie's dream!
(laughter). Everything up until the suggestion of retreat had
been pleasant; joyful; fascinating; mysterious; intriguing;
wondrous; absorbing; stimulating – and then: the retreat.
This was the complete opposite: humiliation piled on top of
humiliation; death after death; boredom on top of boredom;
fear; anxiety; panic; painful memories; dreadful internal
turmoil; conflicting emotions; cognitive dissonance; massive
self-doubt; insecurity; isolation; depression; overwhelming
sadness and bewilderment. A fabulous soup of existential
angst, and it tasted ghastly! (laughter)

Q.   Why did you stay in retreat if it was so painful?

N.C.   Because I felt as if I could not live with myself if I came
out. Because I wanted my 'father's' approval. Because I
was an ego-maniac, albeit a fairly amiable one; because in
some sense there seemed to be no reasonable alternative.
But actually, because I was seduced by existence and non-
existence, and because I'd made the commitment to remain.
And it was this commitment, based on the power I felt to

exist in the Lineage of Padmasambhava, that kept me in there. There was something real about my connection to the Lineage and my devotion to my Teacher that existed as well as my neurosis and my extra layer of samsara.

Q.   So your Teacher obviously thought you were ready.

N.C. (laughter) Well, I should imagine that he was confident that I wouldn't go crazy – but as to being ready . . . You see, he'd not met more than a few western people, and they were doubtless quite hardy robust types – whereas I was something of a teddy bear (laughter). You see, three-month retreats are nothing for a Tibetan – and he was treating me more or less like a Tibetan. I had a very traditional training as a Ngakpa, I learnt a great deal about the complexities of Tantric rites from him. It was only later when I met H.H. Chhimed Rigdzin Rinpoche, who became my principle master, that I learnt about the profound psychology of Tantra and Dzogchen.

Q.   Now, we've talked about the problems of failing to deal with the extra layer of samsara – but what about those who get stuck with psychology when what they actually need *is* a spiritual path.

N.C. That's the other end of the scale. Certainly, I think it's crucial that there is some end in sight with counselling or psychotherapy – these processes are valuable, but only deal with one aspect of our being. That's not to underplay modern psychology – after all, as I said before, if this one aspect of our being isn't unravelled then the others are likely to be just a fairy tale. But therapy can become its own fairy tale – we can become addicted to it, and spend our lives investigating the goblins of our childhood. Through therapy, we could even make these goblins super real. These ugly aspects of unsatisfactoriness could invade our present experience and create very bizarre sub-plots on what our lives *are*. Our memories of childhood and the traumas we experienced are important – but not *that* important. The totality of *what we are* is *there* – in the moment. It's not the infinite detail of our childhood, but the spectrum of pain as it manifests here and now that is really crucial. It can be valuable to allow the past to throw light on the present, but the process can become addictive. We can become addicted to the on–going trauma of past pains and end up living metaphorically. We can become prisoners of past events. On the other hand, we could approach the Transpersonal workshop market as if it were the equal of the ancient spiritual traditions. I'm not saying that it's impossible to grow through encounter groups and other psychological process work – I've seen considerable benefit from such work; but it can become rather lop-sided. The spiritual traditions are highly balanced and have evolved over a great period of time in which the 'Being' of being a human being has been penetrated to the core. The same cannot be said for psychology; (laughter) no one has yet attained enlightenment through psychology – or even through having their aura Rolfed! The New Age spirituality market is probably the most useless of all alternatives – it has neither the bare integrity and honest caring of modern psychology, or the dynamic insight and all-inclusive effectiveness of the ancient spiritual traditions.

Q.   You're not too fond of the New Age?

N.C. (laughter) No – at best it's harmless. I'd say it's almost a complete waste of time.

Q.   (laughter) Why not complete?

N.C. Well, many things can be a springboard to more authentic methods and spiritual systems. There are all sorts of stories in the Nyingma tradition of great robbers becoming Great Yogis!

Q.   And the purveyors of the New Age could be like these great robbers?

N.C. If only they could (laughter). I think that all they rob is people's time and their own intrinsic resources. I would say that if anything, the New Age is an assemblage of randomly pilfered shards from the vessels of both ancient traditions and modern psychology. A truly useless mixture – when it's all stuck together, the result is something like a cross between tea-strainer and tea-pot . . . I'm sorry if that sounds unkind (laughter). I suppose it's impossible to please everyone!

Q.   Would you agree, to whatever extent, that individuals or groups use psychological counselling as an alternative to religion or as an alternative to addressing spiritual insights?

N.C. Yes. (laughter) Would you like me to qualify that?

Q.   If you would.

N.C. I think you're right . . . But I think that this is just the other side of the coin. 'Heads' or 'tails' – it's a valid system used in a manner that makes distorted use of its validity. You can't go to the ancient traditions to work out childhood neurosis, and you can't go to therapy for profound spiritual insights. But the two don't have to be divided.

Q.   You think there can be a synthesis of modern psychology with ancient traditions?

N.C. No, not synthesis – but integration. From the perspective of Tantra, synthesis is not even a consideration, but the integration of modern psychological methodology (with its insights into our particular twentieth century neurosis) into the Tantric View of reality would be extraordinarily valuable. I am, at the moment, working towards such integration with a number of working psychologists. I think that for me personally, it is the most valuable work at this present time. Unless this integration can flourish, I fear that the ancient spiritual traditions may merely remain enclaves for the weird and socially maladapted. Not that I'm saying that there is no place for weirdness – Britain has a rich tradition of eccentrics; but the spiritual path shouldn't be dominated by those who need an alternative life-style. There was nothing 'alternative' about Tantra in Tibet. In Tibet it was very conventional and respectable to be a spiritual practitioner. Even Crazy-Wisdom Masters – the Wisdom-Eccentrics of Tantra – were quite within the bounds of acceptability. I think this is a serious point to grasp – if you're attracted to a spiritual path because you want to drop out in some way, you've maybe got the wrong idea. I'm not saying *either*, that it's wrong to drop out – *or* that conventional society is healthy. But, what I *am* saying is that we shouldn't lump the ancient traditions along with the other 'alternatives' that have evolved and relate to them as all being under the same umbrella. I'm making a distinction here between the value of 'alternative life-styles' and the neurotic approach of needing to be 'alternative'. There is a difference, and I think that's it's important to be aware of where we're coming from in that. I mean (laughter) if I want to get milk out of a petrol pump – I won't have much joy. If I want to indulge my need to be different through becoming the practitioner of an Eastern spiritual path, I won't get what I want either. There is what we want, and what we need, and what's available to fulfil those requirements. If both psychologists *and* spiritual teachers were more in touch with this particular area of confusion, then they could be of far greater service to either their clients or disciples.

Q.   And this is something you're trying to do, isn't it?

N.C. Yes.

Q.   Does that mean that you would refer people to a psychologist if you felt it inappropriate for them to enter a spiritual training with you?

N.C.   Well; I've not done that yet . . . I've not taken on many Apprentices; and those I have taken on, I've got to know very well. Being a counsellor, being familiar with therapeutic methodology, enables me to . . . actually, it enables me to work with the person. I don't really see divisions any more. In Tantra, it's the relationship with the Lama that is important; and that relationship is traditionally *unlimited* in its form. The Tantric relationship is based on the Tantric View, and all activity that springs from that View *is* Tantric by virtue of that. With this understanding, therapeutic methodology becomes Tantra because it is *informed* or *resonant* with Tantric View. But having said that, I would certainly like to see some kind of training made available within the ancient spiritual disciplines for psychologists (interested as practitioners within those disciplines) to learn how to integrate their skills within the context of the particular spiritual view. My word that was a long sentence! (laughter) Probably my last – thank you; I hope this will be useful in some way.

NEW AGE OR ARMAGEDDON?
Questioning the New Age Movement

by Monica Sjöö

INTRODUCTION
R.J. Stewart

I first met Monica Sjöö in the late 1960s in Bristol, when we were virtually neighbours in Clifton, which was an artists', writers' and musicians' zone, an airy cliff-top suburb of fading gentility and seedy Georgian houses filled with Flower People and drop-outs. At that time she was committed to radical, political feminism, and producing paintings which were, in those distant hazy days, deeply shocking to men and, I am sure, to many women. I was an aspiring musician, seeking the spurious goals of fame and fortune, but also committed irrevocably to creating and communicating. In the twenty or more years that passed, turning into 1990, we had no contact whatsoever, yet in many ways, through quite different paths, we seem to have shared certain experiences deriving from the ancient traditions of the Great Goddess.

For Monica this has been a progression through the feminist activism of the sixties and seventies, towards a deep realisation of the Goddess who is beyond, yet is still inherently relevant to, modern politics. Indeed, the recent awareness of 'Green' issues that has permeated into general consciousness may be traced in many ways to the revival of awareness of the Goddess among a smaller number of people, particularly among women. Monica describes some of her own insights and experiences in the chapter that follows, and they may of course be experienced directly through her paintings.

For myself, as I have described in some of my books, the Goddess experiences were in the form of painful and terrible visionary experiences, arising from my own work within an ancient, practical Western tradition of psychic transformation. When I say visionary, I do not mean the type of psychic-television found in so many modern exercises and tapes, but a type of experience that works right through into the physical body: the visual aspects of it are the merest surface presentation within the imagination. I suspect that this tradition, that of the Underworld Initiation (as I have termed it) is the Western parallel or equivalent of *Tantra*, particularly as found in that branch of Buddhism which absorbed chthonic Tibetan magical arts, just as Western Celtic Christianity absorbed the chthonic arts of Britain and western Europe.

These chthonic arts, even when found within a world religion, are not beloved of orthodox priesthoods and political cults, for they may lead, under certain circumstances, to a sequence of powerfully liberating transformations. My own understanding has always been that these traditions existed as collective lore upon a very simple level, preserved by tales and songs, in every land. But they may be activated, so to speak, through the perennial magical and meditational techniques, into vehicles of enormous power. Little wonder that such traditions were ruthlessly suppressed, yet, paradoxically, remained utterly exposed and open to access. Only the convoluted intellects of the Victorian occultists and psychologists simply could not see these open secrets.

Historical origins are, however, unimportant. The deep traditions, particularly those concerning the Goddess and her Dark and Light manifestations in all life, are timeless. It is upon this ground, within this timeless Underworld, that ephemeral life-conditions, politics, education, beliefs, and all the outer forms, are dissolved . . . and perhaps re-created.

In my own case, the psychic transformation was also closely linked to the environment, not in any general sense, but in the very specific way of living for more than a decade upon a powerful sacred site. While this may sound superficially glamorous, living upon a power site and ancient temple is not an experience I would lightly recommend to anyone. Having spent some years, more recently, in quite different surroundings, I have been in the fortunate, or at least interesting, position of being able to make a comparison between life on a geomantic site and life away from one. This is an entire branch of esoteric or magical psychology which could well be developed for the next century. No attention is paid to geomantic forces at all in modern western psychology, though there has been a recent active revival of Chinese Geomancy in California, with regard to siting of houses and their shapes and so forth, and the relationship of this to psychic and physical health.

I feel a particular affinity for much that Monica has to say in this chapter – she states, in no uncertain terms, many matters which I have touched upon in my own writing, but she takes them much further and assesses them directly as modern cultural phenomena. For some years I have repeatedly voiced my uneasiness over New Ageism, mainly because it seems to have no tradition whatsoever behind it. New Age philosophy and practices, claiming to be a fusion of the best of spiritual traditions and psychology, are rooted no earlier than the late nineteenth century, probably originating with the Theosophical Society. That this rootlessness may be a matter of pride, even a central dogma of the New Age 'we take the best of all beliefs and methods and make them into something New', is not sufficient in itself.

Christianity also made great headway in its early years by claiming newness, originality, and being the vehicle of – guess what – the coming New Age. It sought to throw away the old paganism (which in its decadent Roman Empire form was certainly worthy of disposal), to herald a new dawn of a new world – and within a mere fifteen hundred years (or less, as it was by no means widely established for the first five or more centuries in the West) has brought us to the brink of world destruction. Of course New Ageism would never become a dogma or a political religion enforced by rule of arms – it has learnt that most subtle of lessons, developed by political Christianity, to be *inside* the ruling system and not to oppose it.

My own experiences with New Age matters are not as personally profound as Monica's have been, but that does not make my uneasiness any less valid. Whenever I have criticised New Age music, for example, people have stood aghast, as if I might be uttering obscenities or exposing myself during an audience with the Pope. Yet most of it is, and always will be, synthesised pop-product, the blandest of the bland, mixed with artificial bird song and other pseudo-natural effects. When in the mid-seventies I and a number of other people working in the Western tradition were approached by various parties to establish 'New Age' centres in Britain, I reacted adversely, and was deemed to be an unspiritual chauvinist for not rallying to the cause of Light, and, of course, to the vision of money. Some of the centres and trusts, started through that particular impetus, are now beginning to fail, to find the inevitable darkness that must come after the first day of light. Will they survive the night?

When my book *The Underworld Initiation* began, in a small way, to acquire a kind of cult status, I received letters from people, particularly in America, and particularly from therapists. A number of them wanted me to 'authorise' or 'licence' them to use the techniques (very loosely and sometimes incoherently described) in the book. When I refused to have any part in such activities I was again branded as mean-spirited, selfish, unnaturally enclosed, and uncooperative. As far as I am concerned people use the ancestral traditions at their own risk . . . no licence from me will help such use or abuse, though like all writers I am jealous of my copyright and of unscrupulous people falsely making money from my work. Now, more than twelve years after writing *The Underworld Initiation*, I am working on two further books developing the techniques, exploring many of the open ways and reweaving certain loose strands in that first effort; these will be published by Element Books in 1991 and 1992.

On the other hand, I also received letters and had conversations with a large number of people who said that they simply saw no point whatsoever in going down into the earth in visualisation, in encountering a Dark Goddess, or in working with any such negative (as they saw it) forces – surely, they argued, we need to ascend, to find the light, to be positive. The answer is found in meditation, in attuning to the perennial tradition that the stars are within the earth . . . and that the Goddess weaves light out of the darkness. We ignore these deep ancient truths at our utmost peril, a peril that is upon us, here and now, and may not be avoided.

*   *   *

We are fast approaching the Millenium. The question now facing us all is whether the Earth-Mother, Spirit, Planetary psycho-physical being – will be able to renew and transform Herself. Or whether She is by now so irredeemably abused, polluted and choked in Her very blood/water arteries – from rainforest devastation, acid rain, ozone-layer destruction and the direct poisoning of the oceans and underground waters – that it is just too late.

If She dies so do we; if She transforms and survives so do we.

These different prospects awake different responses in different contemporary movements. The New Age movement speaks much of 'Earth Healing', but being patriarchal and male-initiated it sees Spirit as transcendant and male by definition and as NOT inherent in Nature or the Earth.

Therefore to me the New Age is part of the problem and not its solution.

Any movement that sees the 'material world' – whatever that is supposed to be since even physicists now speak of matter as dancing particles or waves of pure energy and light vibrating at different rates – as 'fetters of the Spirit' is directly descended from Christian and other monotheistic Godfather religions that deny Spirit, Mind, intelligence and autonomous creative powers to the Great Earth Mother.

Patriarchal cultures are anti-evolutionary, as they attempt to cut us off from the Mother-source of life itself. Our experience has been, during several millenia of necrophilic patriarchal cultures (or non-cultures), that any religion that speaks of Spirit and creative Mind as male and transcendant, and not immanent or indwelling (a word derived from that for mother-matter), both welcomes and actively encourages the rape and exploitation of the Earth and the Death of Nature. This is then perceived of as a 'Liberation' of father-created Spirit from female Matter.

Some New Age writings seem indeed to welcome the Death of the Earth – and the White Light, that is always invoked by them, is the Divine Radiance of the Father of Cosmos, the Light of Christ-Consciousness, of supreme power, purity and perfection – in typical New-Age speak. As opposed to impure, weak and imperfect mortal and dark, negative and passive female realities, according to the same way of thinking.

I want to explore the differences between beliefs and assumptions of New Age followers, or White Lighters as they are called in California, and that of genuine Green, radical and Earth-based Pagans, both women and men, who experience Earth as a great

Divine, life-creating and conscious/intelligent planetary Spirit-being; she who is a Mother contained within the womb of the greater Cosmic Mother-Spirit of eternal Space.

The Universe is not manufactured nor is it made, it does not come from a 'Big Bang' either, but it is part of a birth process; it is born.

Physical birth from a mother is a microcosmic reflection of a macrocosmic event. As they say: as above, so below. Our blissful existence within the Dark Womb of the Mother, both physical and cosmic . . . born into the Light from its darkness and returned again, through a dark birthchannel or tunnel, into the radiant White Light of Her Otherworld realms after 'death'. Darkness and light co-existing as do past, present and future in other space times than our own.

Vicki Noble has suggested, in her new and Californian-based women and Shamanism journal called 'Snake Power', that we are in fact now experiencing a kind of collective Near Death experience and that 'the blinding Light of it is showing us how to transform our lives'. By this she means, I am sure, that in just about every Near Death experience known, where the person has encountered the great White Astral Light, she or he has returned from the experience a changed person, far more loving and caring of everything that is and lives.

I myself had this same experience, but indirectly, at my young son's death in 1985 when, in an altered state brought on by extreme shock and grief, I felt myself flying on great white wings with him into a radiant White Light and a loving Spirit presence (no gender involved). I received from my son the telepathic communication that 'the only thing that matters is love'.

It was this experience that set me on the search that led me to write my book (*New Age or Armageddon?*, Women's Press, forthcoming). I want to point out the dangers of the New Age movement that so seductively seems to speak of the very same things – of love, light and Earth healing – while in fact it is reactionary in most senses, it is anti-feminist and racist, it does not believe in the benevolent Mother Spirit of Cosmos and the Earth and it originates amongst the children of priviledged white people in the rich western world.

There is just no recognition in the New Age movement that women were the creators of ancient cultures and that the original mother of humanity and Ancestor Goddess was African and therefore Black; Hers was the luminous Darkness that creates life. There is no recognition that women's sexuality is evolutionary as we experience Shamanistic death and rebirth every month when we bleed, that women are the guardians of the Twilight zones between life and death as we risk our lives giving birth bringing Spirits from the Otherworld womb into this Earthplane.

We were always the Shamans, oracles, sibyls, shape-shifters, wise women of the Craft, healers, psychics and mediums . . . the communicators with the great Unknown. We are so because the rythms of our body-minds are in tune with that of the Earth's, the tides of the saltwater oceans incorporated in our very beings as we rythmically menstruate with the Moon, the Radiant Queen of Heaven, in Her changes. The Moon . . . home of Spirits and the maternal giver of Mind, knowing intelligence, wisdom, visions, psychic powers and lucid dreams. She who is both Dark and Light – anathema to New Agers who fear the Dark-Maiden, Mother and Crone.

I have always believed that only if women rise worldwide will there be a future. It is after all women who know the cost of life as we bring if forth and nurture it from our own bodies, facing our own deaths as we do so. I also know now (I wish I didn't) that the psychic umbilical cord that connects mother and child extends into the Spirit realms before birth AND after death.

We have a conversation going with the Earth all the time – She is after all our Mother and there is a silver astral umbilical cord that joins us to Her – whether we are aware of this or not. Our response to the Violated Mother is that our own immune systems will cease to function and we will develop all kinds of lethal and mysterious illnesses and that some men's sexual violence towards women increases as our Mother, the Earth, is cruelly plundered and raped.

She speaks through our bodies and what we do to Her we do to ourselves.

Within Earth – Her internal fires, ores, minerals, crystals and waters – there are mysterious life-creating powers that we do not understand. And why should we?

Paul Devereux, who is involved in the British Earth Mysteries movement and is the editor of the Ley Hunter journal, writes in *Earth Lights Revelation*[1] that it is possible that Earth communicates with us through White Lights that emanate from deep within Her subterranean caverns and womb. In past ages these lights – often in the form of floating globes/spheres/balls/or columns of varying sizes and sometimes glowing in different fiery hues from orange to blue – were interpreted as being Spirits, Fairies (the Shining Ones), the Dead as Ghosts, White Lady figures, fire-spitting Dragons – and most resently UFOs. These Earth Lights, as Devereux calls them, seem to respond to and to imprint human thought and are trance-inducing. He thinks that they are an intelligent energy form unknown to science but known to the Ancients who created their sacred places, such as the Megalithic stone circles, precisely where these Lights were to be found because these are 'window' areas into the Spirit realms. They are Places of Power where Shamans, women and men in all ages, undertook Out of Body journeys to Otherworld realms in altered states of mind.

It is thought that possibly the Lights are produced by crystals in ores that are being rubbed and crushed against each other underground in areas where there are geological faults and fault lines, places prone to earthquakes.

In other words . . . intelligence, light, creation and evolutionary energies emanate from deep within the fiery womb of Earth Herself. I find it interesting in this context that Bride/Brigid, the ancient Goddess of both the dark Neolithic peoples and of the later Celts on these islands, was both Serpent as well as Sacred flame and the miraculous waters of sacred wells. She was a Northern Kore or Corn Maiden and to Her belonged all of animal and plant life. She possessed the Shamanic powers of ecstatic poetic utterance and inspiration. She controlled the applied fire of smithcraft and she was imaged as the luminous White Lady, while in Her Hag aspect she was Black and Blue as Kali the Indian goddess. She was subterranean Darkness, the fiery magma, the sacred waters and radiant Light.

It is also interesting that the Californian West coast, where so much of the New Age movement has originated and where also so many radical and spiritual movements have been born, is situated along a great geological fault line and is very prone, as we saw recently, to major earthquakes.

It has been suggested that we are truly Children of the Stone – the bones of the Earth – and that human intelligence and mind developed in interaction with stone and flint from earliest Palaeolithic times. Perhaps crystals are indeed a form of intelligence whereby our Earth Mother is trying to teach us and to heal us, if we would but sense and hear this instead of attempting to overlay all with our own (New Age or otherwise) ego based motives. I thoroughly dislike the way crystals are being ripped off from the Earth and sold at high prices in expensive New Age shops. Could this be a travesty of Earth's real attempt at communicating with us?

We have now reached a time, nearing the Millenium, when the 'Ring of Fire' – the active volcanos of the Pacific basin – is awakening within the Earth . . . having possibly been negatively activated by underground nuclear tests in the Pacific and under the Nevada desert in the USA. However this might be the means whereby the Earth is attempting to cleanse and heal Herself as I understand that volcanic eruptions replenish the Ozone-layer and also the soil. The ancient Polynesians believed that the souls of the Dead are kept by the Goddess Pele deep in Her volcanoes. They are sent up on to the Earth in volcanic eruptions along with the lava and are reincarnated. Native Americans believe that human beings first came from inside the Earth through a labyrinthine birth entrance or exit from the subterranean womb.

There is within the Earth an enormous and dormant coiled Serpent/Dragon of electromagnetic powers. It is Kundalini the Rainbow Serpent, the fiery She-Serpent, that also dwells within the etheric Chakra system of our subtle bodies. She is now awakening within the Earth and She is rising within us. She is raising Her vibration and shifts our consciousness to a new and faster level of transformative energies. Brigid – the Sacred internal fires, Serpent and Mother of Wells and springs – is returning; Hawaiian Pele – Goddess of the volcanoes – is coming alive; White Buffalo woman of the Native American peoples returns in the West, bringing Vision Quests and Out of Body trance states – and the African Goddess Oya is the wild winds, tornadoes and uncontrollable forces of Nature.

As Vicki Noble writes 'We must now channel fierce energies or be destroyed'.

Surely this is what the 'Harmonic Convergence' (16 and 17 August in 1987) was about, or should have been about . . . the fiery energies of the Subterranean Mother in conjunction with the powerful energies of the major Lunar Standstill, that happened that summer, and in interaction with other planetary beings.

Instead of this . . . New-Age male gurus advocated the return of assorted and transcendant male Sun/Son entities and refused to recognise them as Divine messengers of the Divine Mother transforming Herself. But . . . now has come the time when all of us – who in past ages were burnt as 'witches' because we loved and cherished The Moon Goddess and magically communicated with our Mother Earth – to fight anew on life's behalf.

This, in summary, is what I believe about Mother Earth and what we have been doing to Her. How did I come to see things this way? In recent years, I have been in the unlikely situation, for a feminist of many years, of getting to some degree involved in, and gaining a rather uncomfortable insight into, some of the thinking and practices of the so-called 'New Age' movement. The reason for my involvement was the sudden and tragic death of my fifteen-year-old son, Leif, in August 1985, and then, the drawn-out illness and death from virulent cancer suffered by my oldest son, Sean.

I spent thirty anguished hours by Leif's brain-dead body, in the hospital in Bayonne in the Basque country on a beautiful late August day in 1985, and as I said earlier, experienced flying with him on great white wings into a great loving light-presence. A few hours before the life-support machine that had kept his heart beating had turned off, a message came telepathically flooding into me from my son telling me that 'the only thing that matters is love. Absolutely the only thing that matters is love.' Leif also visited me soon after his death in a lucid dream and told me that he would often come back to me in dreams.

At that time, I had not as yet come across the now-so-numerous accounts of near-death and 'out of the body' experiences, and even though in theory I believed in the 'living dead' in the Goddess Underworld, this actual experience totally stunned me. I simply didn't know how to handle this or how to apply it in my own life.

After Leif's death and my psychic journeys with him to the Otherworld realms, there were many things I desperately needed to find out and to understand about the Afterlife, about near-death experiences and lucid dreams. And my other son, Sean, was in great need of healing on all levels. So I read a great deal on parapsychology, became involved in Spiritualism, and joined meditation and healing circles with him. We received a great deal of support and kindness and healing from both women and men.

Sean then made the mistake of seeking out some New Age therapists who he imagined would help him. He became involved with Rebirthing. This California-based movement, founded by Leonard Orr in the 1970s, is, as far as I am concerned, one of the most dangerous, mercenary, irresponsible, and reactionary of the patriarchal therapies of the New Age movement.[2]

My son received very little support from them, and was virtually blamed for his own illness. Rebirthers claim that you create your own reality, and if you are poor, ill, abused, and oppressed, you are a loser, and suffer from 'victim consciousness'. I watched my son go downhill and become more and more ill, through the weekly, expensive sessions with the Rebirthers, until he relapsed, never to recover again.

In the meantime, I became more and more uneasy about the patriarchal and politically reactionary views so prevalent in the New Age movement. It is important to remember that in no way had I come into all this with a negative or critical mind. On the contrary, I had been at my weakest, barely wanting to live, experiencing a descent into the Underworld where I was stripped to the bones, as was the the Goddess Inanna, and grasping at anything that would help me and my son. I was even willing to read innumerable New Age and spiritualist books which consistently used patriarchal terminology such as 'mankind'. This gave me the eerie feeling that the women's movement, which I have been an active part of since the beginning of the second wave of feminism in 1969, just had never been; that feminists had simply not been heard and that our struggle had just come and gone without a trace. I had to pinch myself many times.

After my honeymoon with the New Age, having met many kind and loving women and men, things started to grate on me, once I started to resurface after the first paralysis of total grief. This was, I suppose inevitable, coming as I do from a Pagan and a left-wing Anarcha-Feminist perspective, and having had much experience, first in the anti-Vietnam-war movement (in the sixties in Sweden), then in the Women's and Lesbian movements in the seventies, and more recently in the Peace and Radical Pagan/Goddess movements.

New Agers attempt to do social transformation and Earth Spirit healing without being grounded in a cosmology that reveres and defends the Goddess Earth. And so they flit from Zen Buddhism, to Gestalt, to Rebirthing, to Native American Shamanism – whatever is the latest trend or craze – and pillage the East and the Native peoples for spiritual support and iconography in the same way that the conquering British collected material and artistic wealth from Africa and Asia two centuries ago. They then translate into pop-European language such ideas as the Rebirthers' 'Eternal Physical Immortality' – the retardation of the natural process of ageing – in the interest of affluent Wersterners who have heard tales of swamis hundreds of years old living in the foothills of the Himalayas. New Agers have adopted a pseudo-Hindu way of seeing life on Earth as 'the pigsty of Life', as an illusion and/or a punishment, even though in Western Christianity we already have entirely home-grown Nature-hating, life-hating teachings. By proposing the possibility of gaining heightened spiritual powers, these New Agers consider themselves part of a new spiritual elite.

There is in the New Age movement simply no political questioning – no awareness of race, sex, class, and imperialism – and it seems not to have heard what women have been saying now for many years. Toni Morrison, the African American writer, said recently, in a talk she gave in Bristol, that to say that one is 'apolitical' is a very political statement because it implies that either one thinks that everything is just fine the way it is or one doesn't care.

I do not, however, think that the New Age is 'apolitical'. I think that it is often highly reactionary and verges on fascist ideologies.

It became obvious to me that the so-called New Age movement had emerged just at a time when women were rising worldwide, rediscovering our own powers and spirituality, and honouring the reawakening Goddess within us.[3] It is yet another attempt by (heterosexual and white) men to co-opt women's energies, to divert us from the struggle to free ourselves. New Age men take it upon themselves to define for both women and men what are 'feminine' and 'masculine' energies, so-called yin and yang, and attempt to convince women that all we need is a male guru or 'master', whether he is a New Age therapist, a Hindu guru, a Native American shaman, a Tibetan lama or a Zen master. When I found that in New Age gatherings it is just as intimidating for a feminist to stand up and confront the patriarchal attitudes and language and imagery used by these much-adored gurus of all shades as it had been in the left-wing movements of the 1960s, I felt increasingly angry and had a strong sense of having seen this all before.

New Age ideologies are on the whole developed by white, privileged, heterosexual males who are perfectly comfortable speaking of 'spirituality' divorced from economic and political realities. As a feminist who has been involved in the Lesbian movement and many other aspects of the women's movement, and as an artist and writer concerned with the re-emergence of the Goddess and our women's spirituality, sooner or later I was bound to react strongly against the blatantly male gods and Fathers-and-sons emphasis of the New Age and its degrading of the Goddess to some kind of Jungian 'archetype', or to just a figment of the human imagination, or to a passive Earth Mother who awaits sexual embrace and fertilisation from a masterful Sky Father, who is defined as the true parent and creator of life.

The New Age offers women 'happiness' – like that of 'happy' women, barefoot and pregnant, cooking the brown rice in ashram kitchens – and romantic/spiritual love. Women become present-day 'Brides of Christ' and substitute god or guru for husband. They are offered mystical joy, blissed out with the perfect Master, while fulfilling traditional roles as housewife and mother. Women who are struggling to develop an identity are now taught the benefits of 'non-ego'.[4] And homosexuality is presented as a blockage of the lower chakra which limits the natural expression of the truth inside a man or woman, which is to be 'complementary' to each other.

Renaissance artists, sponsored by the Catholic Church, the merchants, and the aristocracy, painted idealised Madonnas. Meanwhile, actual women were tortured, raped and burnt at the stake in the town squares in front of the church for attempting to protect the Mother and Her nature, for having women's traditional knowledge of herbal healing, astrology and midwifery, and for practising the magical/psychic arts.

Today millions of women and their children in the Third World live abject lives and suffer miserable deaths from hunger, while white Western New Agers are producing idealised 'beautiful' images of anorexic young women. The concept of female subjugation and persecution has been sanctified by the patriarchy, and is justified by its male religions. The Catholic church with its all-male priesthood and woman-hating celibate monks went as far as persecuting and murdering millions of women during three hundred years of the witchhunts, or 'Burning Times', in Europe. In this they were supported by that era's 'great' male thinkers and intellectuals.

Today the Virgin Mary gives birth to a deformed 'jelly-fish baby'[5] in the Pacific. She is a sexually mutilated girl-child in an African Moslem country. She died from a back-street abortion in a South American Catholic country or was burnt alive by her parents-in-law and 'husband' in a dowry murder in India. The awaited Messiah is a Black woman in detention in a South African prison. She was just shot by Contras in Nicaragua, or died from alcohol poisoning on a Native American reservation. Or she died at birth in Ethiopia where there was no stable at all.

A disturbing trend in the alternative holistic health movement is its middle-class bias, which emphasises the individual in isolation from community and political realities. Many believe there is a 'cancer-prone personality', a person with a history of basic rejection and negative life patterns. Cancer patients, so the theory goes, have often had unhappy, emotionally deprived childhoods that led to negative, suicidal and despairing attitudes that encourage malignant growths. Grief, bereavement, and psychological conflicts are very common triggers of cancer. According to this theory, it is almost as if some have chosen to feel the inherent sadness in the Universe and have legitimised this sadness by becoming terminally ill.[6]

I would say that growing up in patriarchal societies in oppressive patriarchal families is a good recipe for becoming maimed emotionally for life. Certainly this is true for both women and men. It would seem, then, that we are living in a fundamentally cancer-producing culture.

There do not seem to be many question asked, though, within the New Age movement, about why so many people grow up unwanted and unloved; about poverty and real deprivation; about class, sex and race; about how we can possibly stay healthy and happy while the Earth is raped and polluted all around us. My son Sean did have an unhappy childhood and had experienced loneliness and rejection. But Bristol is also surrounded by several nuclear power stations, and the cancer that Sean suffered from is becoming very common among farmers who come into contact with chemical pesticides.

Many New Agers believe that we all create the Universe with our minds. 'You create your own reality' is the catch-phrase of New-Age-speak. If you should question this you are told that you

Fig 3 My Sons in the Spirit World *by Monica Sjöö*

are 'negative' and you should 'take responsibility for yourself'. If someone feels hurt at being treated without care or consideration, s/he is told that s/he is adopting a 'victim stance' or that s/he is 'having expectations' or is 'choosing to be hurt'.

By concentrating solely on the individual mind-body-spirit, the blame and guilt is thrown straight back on the person, who is made to think that s/he should be able to heal her/himself by mind alone. Rebirthers even say that if one becomes ill or dies, this is a 'sin against God'.[7] This is the kind of guilt-tripping that was not at all helpful for my son, Sean, ill with cancer. It implies that one chooses to die from cancer, even though we live a polluted and cancer-producing world where it is a miracle that anyone is still healthy at all. There is also an implied denial of the Mother's natural cycles of birth, death, and rebirth.

If someone suffers abuse and oppression it is only because that person has a 'victim consciousness'; it is never acknowledged that we all live in patriarchal, homophobic, racist societies. It does not take into account the collectively created 'karma' accumulated by the generations before us and that we now have to live with. With incredible cynicism, New Age white Americans, who live in the world's most powerful and exploitative imperialist and war-mongering nation, say that people dying in the Third World from hunger and disease choose to do so with full conscious awareness, before life. They believe that a Black child in detention in South Africa created the reality of apartheid, and that women living in patriarchal societies choose to be raped and physically abused, because these are lessons they needed to learn in this life. Or because they deserved it due to past karmic actions.

This kind of thinking takes the responsibility for violence, suffering and disease away from the obscene and death-dealing structures of imperialism, multinational corporations, and nuclear war industries. This thinking justifies the neo-right-wing policies of Thatcher and Reagan/Bush free trade, mass starvation in the Third World, and yuppiedom in the West. Inequality, wrongdoing, hurt and pain are erased, and so is society's responsibility for them. This becomes a recipe for selfishness, lack of compassion and political awareness, inaction, congratulatory smugness, self-righteousness, and often, cruelty.

New Age therapists commonly talk of money as just an energy that one might or might not attract to oneself. When talking of so-called 'prosperity-consciousness', New Agers, particularly Rebirthers,[8] teach that the poor are poor simply because they are not capable of attracting or receiving money. They believe in individualism and the rightness of money and class. They seem to think that being wealthy, white and healthy in this life is the result of deserved and earned good karma.

New Agers also adopt ancient Hindu and Buddhist ideas of karma, developed originally by the privileged, upperclass Brahmins in India to justify the caste system, by which they enslaved the dark-skinned Goddess-worshipping Dravidian people. This is a good example of how jargon can be applied to oppressed groups to achieve social control and manipulation.[9]

And the New Age practises the ultimate form of spiritual imperialism within the USA itself. New Age shamanism is left out of the context of tribal life and the struggle for survival and sacred communication with the Earth and Cosmos, and is used by wealthy privileged white people.

White Americans ripped off the Native lands and left the indigenous peoples dying from diseases and hunger on the reservations, while the children of the privileged white oppressors enrich themselves on Native shamanic spiritual teachings without actually returning anything to those peoples.

That perhaps the universal spirit is affronted by precisely such worldwide misery, and by those in the West who perpetuate it, and that the Western world is building for itself a truly terrible collective karma by these actions, does not seem to occur to the New Agers.

To understand the New Age movement, it is important to understand white North Americans' attitudes to money and power, and to do this we need to look at its Puritan Christian heritage. The Puritans came from the Old World to the New World to do the Lord's bidding, to build a place from where the Light could shine, where Christ could usher in the Kingdom of the Millennium, and to expand trade and business opportunities. The massacre of the Native peoples and profits from the slave trades were justified in the name of the Lord's Will and 'Manifest Destiny'. American protestantism damned the 'Indians', reduced the Blacks to 'soulless animals', and made a virtue of expanding capitalism, racism and 'democracy'. Might was right.

White intellectuals moulded a 'God' to reassure Americans that what they were doing – no matter how bloody, as they occupied Indian, Innuit, Mexican and Hawaiian lands – was right, pious, and necessary. The Puritans had of course learnt much already from the persecution of the European Pagans during the centuries of witchhunts.

The Christian religion was traded to the 'Natives' because 'The influence of the Gospel will have the tendency to make them more submissive.' It was said by both Native Americans and Africans that: 'The missionaries came and they had the Bible and we had the land. And then they said 'Let us pray.' And when we opened our eyes, we had the Bible and they had the land.' All the indigenous peoples – with their belief in a mystical relationship between Earth, Sun and collective land, and who saw no separation between daily life and religion – were seen as obstacles to 'progress' and expansionism.[10]

White North Americans entirely ignored the ancient sacred pathways and centres of the Native lands. Cut off from their own psychic roots, they created a society that is violent, mad and one-dimensional, an alienated culture that has run amok in the world and believes that anything natural or organic can just simply be blasted aside. They created a culture that believes that anything artificial or synthetic is superior, because it is 'man-made' and not created and nurtured by Mother Nature.

With the Puritan work ethic went the belief that wealth and success were blessed by God the Father. 'Prosperity is next to godliness' is today believed by Christian fundamentalists and New Agers alike.

Today we find the New Age movement in solidarity with U.S. politics and economy – which utterly depends on its weapons industry and needs wars and hunger in the Third World – and honouring the belief that the United States is the 'land of the free' and of democracy and has a special role in the coming planetisation of mankind. In the meantime the United States – the anticipated initiator of the New Age global neo-Atlantean civilisation – has given the world nuclear weapons and energy, the H-bomb, nuclear waste, and new radiation-induced cancers.

White Americans, involved in the now so fashionable New Age shamanism, will turn around and say . . . Our Native American Shamans speak of the Great Spirit as male and a Sky father, at the same time as they show uttermost love, respect and reverence for the powers of the Earth Mother. The answer to this one is – as the Native American poet, feminist and writer Paula Gunn Allen has shown[11] – that confronted with the planned genocide of their people and political/religious pressure from white male Christians, many Native American men, and that only in the last hundred years or so, have come to elevate localised male spirits and guardians into a monotheistic Sky Great Spirit being.

Paula Gunn Allen says that Thought or Spider Woman – who spins all of Creation from Her luminous fibres of pure energy and cuts them at death, as did the three Norns of Scandanavia – was the Great Spirit. Thought Woman dreamt us into being from Her great Mind and Corn Mother gave us substance and nourished us. We are joined to Spider Woman through the silver cord that is attached to 'the hole on the top of the head' and it is up to all of us to keep that hole open, to be able to 'see' with our Third Eye, because this is the way she communicates with us. If we deny Her and all the Spirits in Nature, in the name of scientific 'rationality' – a 'rationality' that is now killing us all – it is our own loss.

Some New Age thinking that I find particularly worrying is connected to very reactionary and pro-fascist religious views – via the Theosophists and the medium Alice Bailey writing in the 1930s – of secret and elite 'Masters' who through hidden/occult means somehow control world events and human minds . . . and who are attempting to bring about an Aryan 'superrace' on this Earth. Such technological/scientific developments as nuclear power, space exploration and even 'the Bomb' were welcomed by the 'master' speaking through Alice Bailey, who herself was obsessed with imagery of Light and Fire. She has, through the Findhorn community – or 'Light centre' – in Scotland, become a prophet of the movement. Many New Age adherents speak of the 'Brotherhood of Man' and the 'White Brotherhood of Light.' Underlying such New Age concepts is a tradition of male spiritualist imperialism that expresses itself in terms such as 'Lord, God on High' and 'King Jesus the Saviour'.

The Other or Heavenly realms are envisioned as replicas of the man-made (the proper word here) hierarchical/patriarchal structures on Earth. There a gland – the third eye, or Ajña, attributed with spiritual visionary powers, our cosmic receptor – transmits biological messages of its light perception to the pituitary gland, which stimulates growth hormones. We are in fact a kind of human plant.[16]

All of life was born in the womblike environment of the planetary ocean of Moon-tide-blood-waters. The Lunar-tidal rhythms were transferred into the female body. Our menstrual cycle of sexuality is an evolutionary force strongly connected with the Moon's cycles.

We are meant to live cosmically and biologically by the natural light of the Moon in Her phases. With eternal daylight we would all go crazy and nothing would grow. It is in the dark womb that life is born, in the dark soil that the seed germinates. It is in the dark night that we dream lucid dreams when the Ancestors and Spirits speak with us and take us to their realms. The Ancients always believed that not only fertility but also all powers of the Mind – wisdom, visions, inspirations and psychic powers – were given by the Lunar Mother.

Patriarchal societies are truly anti-evolutionary, as they suppress these spiritual-sexual-psychic powers in us all. People involved in

God the Father and Sun/Son religious thinking – as is most of the New Age movement – collude in the illusion that spirituality has nothing to do with life on this Earth as it unfolds, because to them 'Spirit' is disembodied, pure, uncontaminated by matter, never born of the Mother, and always male. They can the distance themselves quite comfortably from actual economic and political realities.

I have found that many New Age adherents are unable to empathise with illness, old age and dying. Rebirthers in particular seem to want to escape into an eternal Light-existence divorced from the Dark Earth and Womb. They desire 'Physical Immortality' instead of being magically and ecstatically recycled by the Immortal Cosmic Moon Mother. Rebirthers appear to envy women's actual birthing powers and deny the Great Mother, who is the source of all Creation and Transformation.

Beneath all the New Age talk about Healing the Earth is the arrogant assumption that the human (male) mind is the self-aware consciousness of the Earth and that without it She is passive, unaware, and dormant.[17] There is no recognition that it is because She is alive and conscious that we are alive and conscious; we are of Her essence and intelligence.

Women do not generally feel comfortable with abstract discussions about the death of Nature. We feel her pain and grief in our bellies and wombs. Women were the shaman guardians of the sacred places of the Earth in ancient times. We dream Her being.

The religion of the Ancient Mother is radical and revolutionary, as it calls for the freeing of all the oppressed – we are all Her children – and the freeing of Earth and all Her creatures from their present bondage to patriarchal unrealities. Patriarchy is set upon turning the Earth into the Wasteland or into a nuclear furnace. Considering its obsession with 'Light' seemingly at any cost, one might be forgiven for thinking that the patriarchy would welcome even a radiated Earth.

It is absolutely essential, if we want to survive, that we tune into Earth's real being and that we collectively meditate on and visualise the Mother Goddess and call on Her benevolent powers.

But we also must realise that as the Death-dealing Hag or the raging Kali, she might just explode and erupt in utter rage, in unimaginable catastrophes, to sweep us off the surface of Her body, as so many unwelcome and exploitative parasites that have out lived our time.

This chapter is based upon material in Monica Sjöö's forthcoming book *New Age or Armageddon?* to be published by the Women's Press in 1991. Some parts of the chapter have appeared in the USA in the journal *Woman of Power.*

Notes and References

1. P. Devereux, *Earth Lights Revelation*, Blandford, 1989.
2. L. Orr and S. Ray, *Rebirthing in the New Age*, Celestial Arts, 1977; and J. Leonard and P. Taut, *Rebirthing: The Science of Enjoying All of Your Life*, Trinity, 1983.
3. M. Sjöö and B. Mor, *The Great Cosmic Mother*, Harper and Row, 1987; M. Gimbutas, *The Language of the Goddess*, Harper and Row, 1989; and M. Stone, *When God Was A Woman*, Dial Press, 1976.
4. S. Boucher, *Turning the Wheel: American Women Creating the New Buddhism*, Harper and Row, 1988.
5. Many women in the Marshall Islands have given birth to what they call 'jelly-fish babies,' whose extreme deformities result from nuclear bomb tests conducted by the United States from 1946–1958 on the Marshall Islands. See Women Working for a Nuclear Free and Independent Pacific, *Pacific Women Speak* (pamphlet), Green Line Publishers, 1987.
6. O.C. Simonton, M.D, *Getting Well Again*, Bantam, 1980.
7. Orr, *op. cit* (Note 1).
8. P. Laut, *Money Is My Friend*, Trinity Publishers, 1978.
9. Gimbutas and Stone, Sjöö–Mor (Note 3).
10. Ward Churchill, ed., *Marxism and Native Americans*, South End Press, 1983.
11. P.G. Allen, *The Sacred Hoop – Recovering the Feminine in American Indian Tradition*, Beacon Press, 1986.
12. Among those who expound these ideas are the Theosophists, led by Helen Blavatsky, who wrote *The Secret Doctrine* in 1888, and Alice Bailey, who wrote many books in the 1930s and '40s.
13. B. Rogers, *Men Only: An Investigation into Men's Organizations*, Pandora Books, 1988.
14. Blavatsky and Bailey, *op. cit.*
15. Sjöö and Mor, *op. cit.*
16. L. Lacy *Lunaception.*
17. P. Russell, *The Awakening Earth: The Global Brain*, Houghton Mifflin, 1982.

SPIRITUAL ANIMALS, GUARDIANS, GUIDES AND OTHER PLACES

by R.J. Stewart

INTRODUCTION

The Fourth Merlin Conference had as its sub-theme the subject of totem or spiritual animals. This appears in Chapter 8 from Adam McLean in the context of animals in Alchemy, and Chapter 6 from Ian Rees in the context of using animal visualisation for therapeutic work within the Probation Service, mainly with young offenders. During the Conference a practical workshop was undertaken for two groups, one guided by Ian Rees, and one by myself. As I have written extensively on spiritual or totem animals and some of the related techniques in my earlier books, this seems an apt place to summarise some of my own experiences and understandings of this important and neglected branch of the Western spiritual traditions, found repeatedly and inevitably from paganism to alchemy, even through to the animals that traditionally attend Christian Saints.

I am not fully aware of how much, if any, emphasis is given to any aspect of this animal-working tradition in modern psychology, though obviously it has become very commercialised and fashionable in the current revival of shamanism and primal techniques of altering consciousness. It seems regrettable that we are so ignorant of our own potent heritage in this respect, that we must needs seek heavily amended or emasculated forms offered through New Age promotions, often far removed from their true cultural context.

*   *   *

When I came into contact with the powerful British traditions and techniques associated with spiritual animals, in the late 1960s and early 1970s, it was simply as part of the Western magical spiritual tradition that I was seeking to understand; I had no concept that variants of this branch might grow to such sudden, and perhaps unfortunate, popularity as they have today. There is still much to be done in restating the tradition of spiritual animals and its empowering techniques for modern use, and indeed, to develop it further for the future.[1]

Later in this chapter, I have included a version of the visualisation that I led at the Merlin Conference in 1989, one which I have developed with groups of people in both the UK and USA, often with surprising results, even to myself as someone who is supposed to be used to such material. I say a version, because like many items rooted in tradition, even with a modern individual's style or content, it is not a rigid script, but built of certain active key images and themes, leaving considerable leeway for adjustment according to intuition and the nature of the group involved in the working.

I will return to and briefly list some typical and some surprising results shortly. But before doing so, and before we experience the visualisation itself,[2] I would like to describe some of the important differences between the old collective traditions of spiritual or totem animals, and a modern psychological approach to using such traditions in guided visualisation. The distinction is very important indeed, for there is a disconcerting tendency among modern meditators, visualisers, psychologists and therapists to assume that it is perfectly acceptable and beneficial to use parts of the old traditions, separated from their main stream of teaching and collective lore, for therapeutic visualisations. I would suggest that in some circumstances, despite the wide-ranging benefits that are possible from such a simple psychological adaptation of traditional imagery, there are potential dangers, even disasters, inherent in methods and exercises which avoid the core of the tradition.

So what is this core that is ignored or avoided? One major feature of the core tradition in the west, with parallels worldwide, is that the animals are always real animals – living creatures in the holistic world of the Goddess in which we live, or ought to live. The core is also that this Goddess-world contains other specific and substantial and real worlds and places, 'dimensions' as we might call them: this is quite absent from psychological concepts and methods, in which other places are always imaginal or restricted solely to the process of visualisation.

It must be stressed, even to the point of repetitiousness, that nothing like this modern psychological materialist approach ever entered the minds of our ancestors: the animals were always real animals, seen in the land, and the other places or worlds were always real solid places. When I say our ancestors I am not merely referring to some remote or idealised time in the past, but to any of our relatives anywhere who grew up in a relatively collective community with traditional folklore, including ballads, songs, tales; and the mass of material relating to other worlds such as the Fairy realm, or animal and bird lore. Such lore can be traced back through the centuries, from the twentieth century in many communities, to at least as early as the traditions of Bronze Age Ireland (circa 1–2,000 BC and archaeologically for many thousands of years prior to that period). These ancient Irish traditions are preserved in a late form by medieval monastic collections (drawn from oral tradition) such as the extensive epic poetry relating to Cuchulainn.[3] There are many classical Greek, Egyptian, and other cultural parallels that might be included if we were to make a historical or anthropological study of the theme and its appearance in magic, myth and religion.

In some primal traditions, the spiritual animal leads the human into the physical Otherworld. This understanding of a physical other dimension is found, for example, in Scottish and English fairy tradition, and was clearly described in the late seventeenth century by the Reverend Robert Kirk, though it must be said that animal traditions are absent from his treatise *The Secret Commonwealth*.[4] Kirk does not list or even imply spiritual animals or related techniques at all, and the hosts that he describes in the Fairy realm are human-like beings, true to the original nature of the fairy people of Celtic tradition (rather than the whimsical sprites of Victorian fantasy and sentiment). These fairy people, Kirk says, can relate to us, and become Co-Walkers or subtle allies and partners: he recounts a number of experiences of this sort from among his Gaelic parishioners, who had regular and almost casual contact with the fairy world and its people. In other words, it was a normal everyday occurrence, and neither portentous spiritualised channelling or therapeutic visualisation.

The magical or spiritual animal traditions, despite their absence from Kirk's *Secret Commonwealth*, abounded in Gaelic and English (and of course European) folklore, and are too numerous to list here. We find similar concepts published more recently in the books of Carlos Castaneda, who says that he is restating his experiences within a native American tradition. These include physical translation to other worlds (as in Gaelic tradition) and the use of spiritual animals (also as in Gaelic and other primal traditions worldwide).

We should add, at this point, that conscious group visualisation probably played no part in the old traditions except in formal ritual or temple circumstances. Some of these, in the context of dream and vision, are described by John Matthews in Chapter 7. In earlier cultures most of the visual sequences and narratives that we might identify as 'spiritual' or 'magical' were absorbed through listening to and learning songs, tales and epic poems. After this long and organic absorption of mythic images, which was part of everyday life, a small number of people might go out into isolation and seek a spiritual animal, having been given some instruction by another well versed in the deeper lore of tradition. The concepts of 'visualisation' and group working are quite modern, and we have to accept this major difference between our way, divorced from a collective culture, and the roots of the tradition itself. We must never pretend that we are truly restoring the mystic lore of our ancestors and experiencing it exactly as they did. I would even go so far as to say that it is the differences between the way modern people and their ancestors work with inner or initiatory arts that are more important than the similarities: we must search out these differences, for in them are the keys to our own further transformation.

My own early experiences with spiritual animals came directly as result of meditation, of altering consciousness while living in fairly isolated simple circumstances. They did not come from books, courses or personal teaching. Such aids were, for the Western tradition, almost non-existent at that time, other than the complex, heavily intellectual and often unworkable occult treatises of the nineteenth and early twentieth centuries. Well known examples are the works of Eliphas Levi, the Golden Dawn texts, books by Aleister Crowley, eventually leading to the more accessible work of Dion Fortune (for whom see Chapter 2) and related works. In retrospect I must acknowledge that some of these complex and often tedious works contain a great deal of information and symbolism concerning spiritual animals, though mainly in alchemical, Egyptian, and Eastern contexts: the material is there nevertheless, but not in an accessible form as a direct tradition in its own right.

My first experience of the effects of spiritual animal working were, or seemed to be, spontaneous. I now think that certain individuals are naturally attuned to certain creatures, some animals or birds are more or less permanently attuned, while others work for specific phases of a lifetime. If we are able to find these creatures, many of our individual energies are greatly enhanced, and in many cases, rebalanced harmoniously in areas that were previously weak or out-of-tune. There is an implied exchange, always, with such workings. The human benefits from the animal, and the animal also benefits from the human. This is not, in my opinion, identical with therapy, though the effect is undeniably therapeutic. In other words, the benefit is a side effect of the contact, which is sought solely for its own sake, and never with an ulterior motive of therapy in mind.

In ancient and primal societies there were and still are a number of complex rules or taboos or *geasa* upon people concerning animals – in Irish tradition these gradually degenerated into superstition, and we still have remnants of such folkloric animal superstition today – the lucky black cat, the number of magpies, and so forth. One of the most powerful restrictions was that one should never kill or eat one's own spiritual animal: this could be a personal animal or family totem, or a tribal or even national animal. So the restrictions were sometimes considerable.

As we live today in a society where animals are regarded as soulless flesh, an attitude which is the direct result of Christianity, we abuse them in very conceivable way. It would be difficult, if not impossible, for a modern man or woman to live according to the ancient animal taboos, but if you contact a spiritual creature, you will never seek to hurt or eat its physical counterpart. This is different to our modern concepts of animal rights or vegetarianism, which I think are separate ethical issues that we must all address. We need to remember that in early cultures where certain animals were taboo or sacred or blessed, other animals were quite happily hunted, killed, and eaten. We find a remnant of this worldview in traditions preserved by the native Americans, who frequently say that humanity should kill only what they need to eat, and that the cycle of other lives must be respected.

My own first experience of a spiritual creature, when I was twenty years old, was as follows:

While out walking very early one morning in the country, during a period of very simple (but by no means ascetic or excessively frugal) living combined with regular daily meditation, I had my first conscious spiritual animal contact and experience, one that has remained with me actively ever since, though it would be truthful to say that nothing has ever equalled that first spontaneous experience. While walking along an isolated track, I suddenly found that I was, to all intents and purposes, high in the air above myself. I moved at great speed, and saw my body walking along the road below: my eyesight was greatly enhanced and seemed to cover a field of vision that I had never previously experienced. I was most alert to all movements below, the grass in the wind, tree branches and leaves, and to many small creatures moving secretively to and fro all around the body walking the road below at dawn.

After a period of disorientation, in which I almost fell over, I realised that I was seeing through the eyes of a bird. Looking up, I looked down and saw myself looking up: the bird was a hawk, which slowed in its distance-flight and began to hover only a few metres from me, ready to strike into the field nearby. It was much later, years later in fact, that I learned that the hawk is one of the specific spiritual animals within the Celtic bardic tradition, and has many links back to ancient Egypt and the god Horus. It is possible that if I had had this intellectual information in mind as a precondition or preconception, the event would have been coloured by it, but at that time I had made very little study of Celtic or Egyptian tradition. Somehow I had awakened this link with a spiritual bird, and it had worked through a real physical bird. There is much more to this type of experience, but the merest outline of the personal account is enough for the present.

A second experience, of a different sort, for it occurred in a dream, involved that classic totem animal, the cat. While in that same isolated rural area where I had encountered my spiritual bird (the hawk), a tiny kitten, born wild on the moor, found its way to me. This grew into a large and rather savage temperamental cat which remained as my companion subsequently in very urban town-centre circumstances, for the next fifteen years. Like many people who live with cats, I could report apparent instances of telepathy, communication, and so forth. But I will instead recount a dream involving the cat as a spiritual animal.

In this dream, I found myself in a large house, a type of mansion or country hall, at night. As I descended a large carved staircase, I could see an open door, leading to a deep blue star-lit landscape beyond. This landscape was intriguing and drew me strongly, and as I set off towards the door, my cat darted past me and ran out into the night. Just as I was about to follow him, a voice seemed to speak into my ear, saying quietly 'He can go there and return, but if you go you shall not return, for you will die and never come back to the human world.' In my dream I took heed of this rather disturbing advice, and eventually awoke to find the cat sleeping upon my bed.

This dream experience may have a number of rational psychological explanations, certainly more than that of encountering the hawk, but it is firmly within the old traditions of totem or spiritual animals, who act as messengers and guides between the worlds, and are at one and same time real physical animals. The implication was that, as with the hawk, I could travel in that mysterious realm of the starry night through the consciousness of the cat, but not simply on my own, for it was beyond the threshold of human life for me at that time. In recent years I have been able to move within that world independently, but could not have developed this ability without the interim period of working with a spiritual animal.

A third experience involves the sacred animals on an ancient site, and is of a different category again. In the early 1970s I spent several years exploring, in meditation and visualisation, the power centre and ancient temple site upon which I lived. To do this I used the traditional methods of western magic, employing the known symbols from the temple remains on the site, and building these in my imagination. The result of this technique is, or should be, that one attunes eventually to the deeper levels of the sacred site, which exist beyond physical expression time or space, and yet are still attuned to a specific locus, the geomantic power centre. All this sounds very grand in retrospect, but at the time it was a simple matter of studying, building in visualisation, and awaiting results – often for long periods of time with nothing apparently happening.

To assist my explorations I began to construct a visionary journey leading deep into the heart of the sacred site (a version of which is published in *The Underworld Initiation* and is found on my recording *Journey to the Underworld*).[5]

It soon became clear that while I could travel alone to a certain depth or inner location, I could not proceed directly beyond this. I realised that I needed a spiritual animal to guide me further, and assumed, from the archaeological and legendary material relating to the site, that this would be the Pig. Yet whenever I worked with the image of pig or herd of pigs, the result was inconclusive. Eventually I realised that I had to wait for the spiritual animal to appear of its own accord, rather than try to visualise something, even if that something was apparently the correct animal.

During a harrowing and memorable session, I encountered a huge dim form in a mist, threatening and visible mainly as bearing wide curved horns. I felt fearful that I had aroused some monster with my imaginative work, but determined to still my panic and await what would come. The mists parted, and there was a small pure white cow, with wide horns, one of an ancient breed virtually extinct today. It was to be many years until I saw one of this rare breed of cattle in the flesh, in a wildlife park, though once sacred herds of them roamed special preserves in Britain. Seeing these animals for the first time in the flesh, in 1989, was like meeting an old friend, though intellectually or rationally the whole emotive response to a mere cow seemed absurd.

So I followed the cow into the mist, and she led me to the brink of the entrance to the Underworld, after which I had to proceed by descending alone. Some time after this experience, I discovered that while the Pig was one of the spiritual animals of the black hag goddess of Welsh tradition, Kerridwen, the Cow was the creature of Brigid, the goddess of secret fire, smithcraft, poets, inspiration, and healing. I also found that this Brigid type of goddess had certainly been worshipped by the ancient Celts at the very site that I was exploring, though we only know today of her Roman form as Minerva. So a further pursuit of archaeology and legend revealed that which inner visualisation and encounter had shown to be true.

By the beginning of the 1980s I started to work with the Merlin traditions[6] and found many links there to the totem or spiritual animal work and experiences which I had already undergone, and which I had published in some of my earlier books on symbolism and traditional techniques of altering consciousness. The Merlin tradition, more than any other western esoteric tradition, seems to embody a vast cycle of spiritual animals[7], and when I designed the Merlin Tarot[8] in 1984–5, I tried to include this cycle of animals and birds according to the ancient pattern of the Four Elements and Seasons, but also as specific key creatures appearing in each of the trumps and court cards. This simple direct use of spiritual animals as visual images is worth more than thousands of mere words.

So it was with fifteen years or more of this type of direct experience, supported by study and research in a more prosaic academic sense, that I began to work with spiritual animal visualisations with groups of other people. Not on a regular or commercial basis, but occasionally, as and when such events arose naturally, at meetings, workshops, or private gatherings.

Here is the place where we can turn briefly to some of the experiences of other people, coming afresh and often unwitting to the use of animals and birds in visualisation. A few examples will suffice:

The general method for unpractised groups seems to be to put the group into a situation where they may freely encounter an animal or bird: strictly speaking the creature chooses them and not vice versa. This in itself can be a deeply disturbing and stressful experience for some people, though blissful and wonderful for others. Many have reported that they resisted the animal that chose them, that it was sometimes a creature which they feared, but upon accepting it, their fear vanished (usually for good) and an empowering energy filled the place where the fear had been.

Those who related to a spiritual creature without this threshold problem often encountered difficulties later, welcoming their spiritual animal or bird, but finding that it led directly into places where they feared to go. This second level fear was not necessarily one of dread or loathing, but often accompanied by what was known in the old days as 'holy terror', for the spiritual animal would lead the human to an encounter with a god or goddess, or a potent power place, into which he or she hardly dared enter. This is where the Guide, the spiritual animal, leads the human to the Guardian, often in the form of a god or goddess within a specific spiritual or magical tradition. The animals of your own land or heritage tend to lead always to the gods and goddess of that same land. Thus working in Britain, one tends to find that British animals lead to encounters with ancient Celtic or Saxon deities, the Guide leading to powerful Guardians, or to sacred inner locations of great transformative power.

I first rationalised and formalised this guide-guardian sequence of the tradition from my own difficult experiences with it in the late 1970s, eventually to be published as *The Underworld Initiation*[5] in 1985. I am certain, however, that it was a method known and regularly practised in the ancient Mysteries of both the classical and Celtic worlds, and that it was also preserved in folk tradition as an oral teaching, based upon ballads, songs and tales.

I found that this method worked as effectively with groups of people in Manhattan as it did in rural weekend retreats in England. The Americans, however, tended to encounter animals not only from the American land, but from very early history, animals now extinct. In the Merlin visualisation (which is found on page 71) there is often a preference for horned and hoofed animals, which may lead to the great god Cernunnos, also known as Pan. The actual limitations or expansions of the animal and bird roll-call depend very much upon the feeling and presence of each individual group, so there are no specific exclusions. While conducting this visualisation on one occasion in New York, several people met with horned and hoofed spiritual animals from Africa – the hippopotamus, the giraffe. This rather threw me at first, as I was well versed in relating to the Western European creatures, but not to the African. But the realisation came rather rapidly that these animals were indeed correct for those individuals, for they were tapping into a collective heritage that included African ancestors or deep memories.

One last group of examples from experience springs to mind; those people who had already worked within modern presentations of native traditions, such as commercialised seminars on shamanism or classes on native American tradition. Very often these people would come into a group and declare that they were brothers of the Eagle, sisters of the Wolf, and so forth. But when they entered into the Otherworld Journey, they found that these creatures were absent, and that other quite spontaneous and unexpected animals or birds came to them with considerable power and impetus.

My guess is that this demonstrates that simply choosing an animal intellectually or through superficial attraction to traditions may not work. Sometimes the person does indeed choose the right spiritual animal instinctively, but sometimes it is only a matter of glamour or suggestion or wishful thinking. In the type of visualisation which follows this introduction, no suggestion or choice or list of potential animals or birds is given, so there can be no mere force of suggestion at work in the creature that chooses you. I will say, however, that I have not been able to follow up on those individuals who seemed to lose the totem beast of their choice and be chosen by something surprisingly different. A comparative study might be interesting, but surely the time would be better spent in working with spiritual animals?

THE VISUALISATION: MEETING YOUR SPIRITUAL ANIMAL.

1. *The first stage* is a period of silence, stilling and calming the awareness, with steady regular breathing. This period of approaching silence and stillness is important, and should not be bypassed. The aim is not to enter into any meditative state as in a modern meditational group, but very simply to be still and silent: this period of preparation should not be combined with special techniques from other traditions, as the effect can be contradictory or enervating. The silent period should not be too long, nor should it be allowed to float into any kind of free association, fantasy or reverie. A simple brief period of stillness is always effective. These general guidelines should be explained to the participants in advance. Before this brief explanation of the period of silence, the group should also have a short summary of the intention of the entire visualisation which is:

(a) To enter through visualisation into another world, which is very close to our own but not identical to it. This is the primal world, the image from which our own world has been separated.

(b) Within that world we will meet certain people, animals and birds. It is likely that a creature will come to us as a companion, and that this companionship will lead to a journey into a place of power.

(c) In that place of power we may meet with other beings, or experience visions and sensations.

(d) We will then return to the regular world by retracing our steps, though in some experiences we find that we return by a different route to the one by which we entered.

(e) Our spiritual animal or bird will remain with us as a guide for future meditations and visualisations. If possible we should seek out this creature physically, not in a sense of ownership or any typical human–animal situation, but merely to spend some time with or near to such a creature. This physical contact or communion is very important, and greatly enhances the power of the inner or imaginative work.

Having listed the intentions and simplest of guidelines, the visualisation is usually guided or loosely steered by an experienced visualiser and teller. In early stages of group or individual work the material can read from the printed page, using, for example, the visualisation given below. Tapes may also be used[2], and these are a very effective application of modern technology within an ancient tradition. Nothing, however, can equal the effect of the teller or leading visualiser knowing material by heart, and being able to tell the story simply and clearly. This method of working takes time and experience, and should not be rushed into. Eventually it leads to that essential intuitive flexibility in group work, where variations upon the main narrative and images are made even as the experience progresses.

2.   *The second stage* is entering the Otherworld through the power of the imagination.

3.   *The third stage* is encountering an initial contact in that world: this will vary. In the visualisation given below, we use the tradition of Merlin, appearing as a mysterious wild man of the woods, whose call draws us further into the wild, while we seek him, but never find him face to face. The Wild Wood figure may be male or female, of course, and there is no reason why the imagery should not be adapted to a wild woman of the wood. Traditionally, however, the wild figure is the prophet Merlin, inspired and maddened by the power of the Goddess of the Land, and this image and the very real contact that it generates brings great energy with it.

4.   *The fourth stage* is being chosen by a spiritual animal or bird. At this stage, the group encounters a large number of creatures, who appear spontaneously from within forest surroundings. Each person is chosen by one creature.

5.   *The fifth stage* is the journey to the place of power.

6.   *The sixth stage* is the experience within that place, which is not preconditioned, guided or controlled in any way. This includes a period of silent contemplation or communion with whatever arises in that place.

7. *The seventh stage* is the return journey through the Otherworld, usually, but not inevitably, by the same route as the inward journey, again in companionship with the spiritual creature.

8. *The eighth stage* is the individual and collective return to outer consciousness. This should not be rushed or forced, nor should it be drawn out and lingering. The transition must be made simply and firmly by everyone concerned, and if necessary the teller or leading visualiser should be sure that each person present is fully focused upon the outer world.

Discussion and sharing of experiences can be very helpful, but is not an essential requirement or an inherent aspect of the tradition.

Here is where the spiritual traditions differ in a major way from modern psychology: there is no emphasis upon long discussion, dissection or rationalisation of inner experiences. The older psychological methods, rooted in the magical and spiritual arts, tended to give the individual very little in the way of formalised sharing or discussion: there was, and is, always a marked preference to let the student experience direct transformation, without gradual stages and slow progressions or easy long drawn-out sessions. This aspect of the older traditions is discussed in a Tibetan context in Chapter 3 by Ngakpa Chögyam, who also discusses the relationship between modern counselling and the cathartic effects of spiritual disciplines.

The entire issue of interpretation and discussion can be a serious burden and block, particularly if, as is often the case, some members of the group are used to such methods, and tend to demand them. Individuals may need some preliminary grounding in the fundamental differences between the older techniques and the modern, though we need to be cautious not to build up an a unnecessary mass of comparisons and restrictions. The key is always in the experience itself, rather than any analysis of it.

THE VISUALISATION

1. (A period of stillness and silence with eyes closed and relaxed breathing precedes this visualised narrative.)

2. 'Let us build in our imagination a landscape: it arises before us, and we pass into it. It is a great primal forest, with towering trees and many deep shadows and pools of light. The light is green and gold, and we hear the wind shaking the high leaves and branches. We stand upon the forest edge, and at our feet is

a tiny trail, leading off among the trees and through the thick undergrowth. As we stand at the threshold of the forest-edge, we hear among the sounds of moving trees and calling birds, a faint distant laughter. Darting between the trees we catch fleeting glimpses of a figure in a ragged robe, with long flying hair. For a moment he seems about to turn and look back at us, then laughing again, he runs way into the forest. We know that we must follow him, follow his cry in the wild wood.

As we cross into the forest and down the trail, we sense the presence of the great trees, their vitality feels warm, and they seem to be aware of us as we pass among them. The trail is narrow, a deep slot made by passing animals among the thick carpet of fallen leaves, branches, and tiny forest plants and flowers.

Again we hear the wild laughter, coming from a tree close by, then the sound of footsteps scurrying off. Again we hasten to follow, running deep into the forest. Even as we move, we can hear many birds calling and flying, seeming to move with us, and hear many animals moving through the undergrowth. Yet we see nothing of them, as if they remain hidden from us.

A third time we hear the wild laughter, and suddenly we emerge into a forest clearing. In the centre of this clearing is a tiny spring following from red rocks licked smooth by creatures seeking salt. Sitting upon the rocks is the wild man, staring at us, laughing. As we enter the glade, he takes a small wooden flute from his robe, and begins to pay a high, haunting melody. As he plays, a wind rises, and a shower of rain falls into the clearing. As the rain ceases we hear a great beating of wings and rushing of creatures, and in an instant the glade is filled with birds and beast of all kinds. They stand around the edge of the clearing, looking upon us with no fear, calm and ready.

To each of us a creature comes, and chooses us as a companion, and even as this choice is made, the wild man leaps over the rocks, and onto the back of a huge stag. They race off at great speed into the forest, we follow them, with the animal host, each of us travelling with our companion. As we rush headlong through the trees, the company of animals gradually draws away, until there is only our own group, each with their new companion animal or bird, and the wild man riding the great stag, leading us onwards.

Suddenly the trees end, and we emerge upon the shore of a great lake. Beyond the lake are high snow capped mountains, and in its centre is an island, with a dark building upon it. Our guiding creatures stop at the lake shore, and wait. The wild man upon the stag rushes straight for a stone causeway that leads over the water to the island, and within a moment they disappear from sight into gateway of that dark castle.

We pause and look upon this island place: it is of dark smooth stone, with a central round tower, and two smaller towers flanking an arched gateway. We can see no windows, and the surface of the stone seems polished like glass. Beyond the central tower we can just see two further towers on the opposite side, balancing those of the gateway facing us.

We know that we must enter this mysterious place of power. Our companion animals quietly withdraw into the forest, after pausing to drink from the clear waters of the lake. We walk slowly over the stone causeway to the great arched gate, which we find to be closed. There is no sign of the Wild Man of the woods and the great Stag, and all is still and silent. We hear the waves of the lake lapping gently, and the lonely cry of shore birds. In the distance the sun shines, reflecting brightly from the snowy mountains. We wait, and try to find within ourselves our true reason for being at this gate. (*A short pause is made here.*)

As we seek and try to find that true reason, a small section of the gateway opens, a narrow door within one half of the great double-gate, just wide enough for one person to pass through at a time. From inside we hear a faint echoing laughter, and one by one we pass into the chamber beyond. We find this to be a simple courtyard open to the sky, with three doors, one into each of the gate towers, and one into the great central tower. Even as we look the central gate opens slowly, and as it opens a gust of wind rises, and a shower of sharp rain scatters into our faces. Within that wind we hear the sound of many voices, and of people moving about us, as if the castle is filled with an invisible host. The wind and stinging rain cease, silence falls again, and we enter the central tower.

We come into a circular chamber, with a low, domed roof. It has a floor that slopes gently to the centre, leading down to a deep well. Around the walls of this well chamber are many carvings of figures, animals, birds, humans, and other beings. First we look upon these figures. (*A pause here.*)

Now we turn to the central well, and slowly, one by one make our way towards it, and lying flat upon the floor, look into its depths. This is the well of transformation, and within it is all power, all potential. Let us look into the well in silence. (*Here a longer pause for silent contemplation.*)

One by one we rise from the floor, and make our way around the well chamber towards the door: keeping in our minds and hearts whatever we have seen and felt rising up from the well. As we draw back, one of the carved figures on the wall comes to life: this figure approaches us one by one and gives to each of us a small gift. Look well upon the figure, remember who or what it is, and keep the gift safe.

We now leave the central tower, and as we do so we hear again the sound of that great host, this time with music and laughter, as if a huge celebration goes on invisibly all around us. (*Joyful music may be played here.*) In the courtyard our companion creatures wait for us, and we greet one another with pleasure, as old friends.

The great gateway out of the castle stands wide open, and ahead of us on the causeway we see the Wild Man riding a huge stag, but now in the company of two other creatures that we look upon and remember. Suddenly our entire company picks up speed and rushes headlong over the causeway to the shore and forest beyond: as we move we hear the sound of many horns blowing in the castle behind us; they echo back from the high distant mountains across the lake. Now we enter the shadow of the trees, and realise that the sun is beginning to set. Our companion creatures carry us rapidly to the forest edge, and we look out over a night landscape towards a distant land. We hear again the haunting laughter, and the sound of hooves lightly over the forest floor. Then one by one our companions depart, each looking fully upon us and giving a final communication.

It is time to return to that outer world, that distant land in which we spend our lives. Let us step over the threshold of the forest, and even as we do so it begins to fade. We pause in silence, and gradually find that we are sitting in a familiar room. Let us return fully to our outer awareness, and quietly waken to the customary world. When we seek to return to the Otherworld, we can draw upon our companions, and the contact and gifts given to us in the heart of the mysterious castle. Now it is time to return fully. In our future meditations and contacts with our spiritual animal or bird, we will know how to use the gift given to us in the mysterious castle.

The group takes notes, discusses if required, and disperses.

It is often useful, especially in the early stages of this type of work, to write out individual experiences immediately following the visualisation. A simple check list would be sufficient, though often more details come to mind when we start to write. The list would include, as a minimum:

1. What animal or bird chose you as a companion.
2. What happened when looking into the well.
3. What figure came alive from the wall of the chamber.
4. What gift was given by the figure.
5. What were the two new creatures attending the Wild Man and the Stag.

(I would be pleased to hear of any experience with this visualisation, and you may write to me at BCM 3721 London WC1N 3XX. If you wish a reply, please enclose a stamped addressed envelope or an addressed envelope with an international postage coupon.)

Notes and References

1. R.J. Stewart, *The Way of Merlin*, Unwin Hyman, 1991
2. This visualisation and others are available on stereo cassette, performed with music by R.J. Stewart. A list is available from Sulis Music BCM 3721 London WC1N 3XX. The full Sulis Music list featuring work by various authors, poets and musicians is distributed by Element Books.
3. R.J. Stewart, *Cuchulainn-A* short legendary biography, Firebird Books, 1988. Also *Cuchulainn* (cassette recording) ancient Irish epic poetry performed by Van Morrison (Sulis Music SUL 590).
4. *Robert Kirk, Walker Between Worlds.* A new edition of the *Secret Commonwealth of Elves, Fauns and Fairies* (by Robert Kirk, 1690) with a detailed commentary by R.J. Stewart, Element Books, 1990
5. R.J. Stewart, *The Underworld Initiation*, Aquarian Press, 1985/1988. Also *Journey to the Underworld* (cassette), a visualisation with music, Sulis Music EBEN 902. Also *The Underworld, Within and Beyond* (Two Volumes) forthcoming Element Books, 1991 and 1992.
6. R.J. Stewart, *The Prophetic Vision of Merlin* and *The Mystic Life of Merlin*, Penguin/Arkana, 1986, 1987. Translations and commentaries upon the medieval merlin texts of Geoffrey of Monmouth.
7. See references 1, 6 and 8.
8. R.J. Stewart, *The Merlin Tarot*, (book and deck of colour cards, illustrated Miranda Gray), Aquarian Press, 1988.

THE THERAPIST'S CHAIR AND SIEGE PERILOUS –
Totem Beasts and Therapeutic Counselling

by Ian G. Rees

INTRODUCTION
R.J. Stewart

A few years ago Ian Rees began to correspond with me on matters relating to Celtic tradition: we had exchanged several letters via my box number, and entered into some interesting levels of discussion, before I had to admit that we lived within a mile of one another. Thereafter we met frequently and exchanged various views on these traditions, which for each of us (Ian being Welsh and myself Scots with a Welsh mother) form a rich family and racial inheritance, even though we are, undeniably, modern individuals divorced forever from the old ways of life in which such traditions were embedded.

When Ian described how he had used legendary material in his therapeutic work with offenders, I invited him to present a talk on this work at the 1989 Merlin Conference. The chapter which follows was developed from that talk. I must say that until discussing the subject with Ian I had not considered the directly therapeutic aspects of the old spiritual traditions as practised by ancestral healers. I feel that there is an inherent danger in using meditation and inner techniques solely for 'therapy', and this danger is frequently abused by unscrupulous operators within contemporary fashions for spiritual therapy, channelling, and the like. It is partly the danger of becoming addicted to the healing-trip, the energy-buzz, the psychic-boost. If people choose to meditate and visualise with ulterior motives, such as personal therapy, they are perhaps missing the entire purpose and heart of meditation, which is that one becomes one's true eternal self with no motive or concept of gain, no desire for benefit. Indeed, becoming one's true self can lead to pain and misery just as easily as it leads to love and light: very few people will face up to this truth.

My own involvement with ancestral lore has been with techniques for individual inner transformation or initiation, and the cathartic methods inherent within the Mysteries and the almost lost Underworld tradition. Yet there is a vast mass of evidence from folklore and tradition of healing ceremonies, arts and families of healers. Many of the techniques used by such healers are different from those of modern spiritual healing, and different again from modern psychotherapy or alternative therapies. The emphasis in traditional healing is always upon the directly miraculous, through a line of contact from an ancestral past. This belief is amply described by Robert Kirk in his *Treatise of Spells and Charms*, incorporated in the *Secret Commonwealth* (see my edition of Kirk cited in Notes and References, p 75). Kirk's treatise is just one collection among many examples known from Celtic or Gaelic healing lore. As I have mentioned in Chapter 5, Kirk does not describe spiritual or totem animal traditions at all, but gives many other aspects of Gaelic lore as practised in the seventeenth century, particularly those connected to the second sight and fairy contacts.

Ian Rees suggests that the miraculous quality of traditional healing, often said to be vested in certain orders, castes or families, is inherent in the visionary narratives, and so may be directly used in therapy. I am not entirely certain about some of the implications of this suggestion, despite its obvious benefits as described in the chapter that follows. It tends to sidestep the core of the tradition concerning other worlds, otherworld beings, and non-human forces. We have discussed this amicably many times.

That the imaginative techniques found in legendary tales or native mythology might be directly applied in their own right in modern therapy and counselling is a considerable departure from their original roots, but not necessarily one which is alien to the development of tradition. A tradition, after all, cannot remain undeveloped, or it atrophies. The essential difference between the approach described by Ian Rees, and that of using myths and legends (such as those of classical Greece) often found in psychology, is that here the myths are not forcibly incorporated into an intellectual framework and thus removed from their true world or worldview. They are left alone, to work in their own way. This is different indeed to using myths to 'explain' problems or as examples of archetypical interactions. In this sense Ian's approach is very traditional, for explaining is not considered as significant as actual experience.

It is, however, removed from the tradition in the sense that it allows a broader scope for the imagination of the client, and this is more in keeping with the practices of modern therapy, free association, and so forth. So many people cite mythology and tradition as being rich sources for the imagination, which indeed they are, but there is also a strict level of enclosure and limitation in a magical or mythic tradition, particularly in the practical applications for changing consciousness and energy. So the modern therapist seeking to work directly with the old visualising arts, must allow, for example, for the element of modern entertainment fantasy, which is often a destructive or enervating force. Ian touches upon this in his chapter, particularly in the context of clients whose imagination and self image are severely impaired.

★   ★   ★

There is a tradition in Wales of the existence of wise men and women who functioned as healers and counsellors to their communities. They were often guardians of sacred wells, lakes, caves, mounds or the heirs to ancient ancestral knowledge. While not having a specifically religious role they had a quasi-priestly status and were often regarded as otherworldly, uncanny people whom it was unwise to offend. Their knowledge was linked to folk traditions of their localities but often looked back to the Druids and bards as their source, with particular reference to the figures of Merlin and Taliesin. The folk beliefs and legends that were the foundation of their practices may be found collected in the Mabinogion and in fairy stories that are still told to Welsh children.

While details of their practices differ there are core elements which are common to most. There is an emphasis on making connection with figures from the past who are endowed with a numinous quality. These figures may be Merlin, Taliesin, Celtic Saints or might be the family line of personal ancestors. There is a sense not of apostolic succession but of tapping into a pool of power and wisdom. They often drew inspiration and guidance from an otherwordly woman – like the physicians of Myddfai who became the court physicians of Prince Rrys Gryg and whose remedies and treatments are still preserved in manuscript. The legend says that an ancestor of the Physicians, described as the son of a widow, sees a woman sitting on the surface of Llyn y Fan Fach. He offers her bread which she rejects as too dry and then vanishes. On a second occasion, after following his mother's cattle, he sees her again and offers her bread that is rejected as too moist. On a third visit he sees cattle walking on the surface of the water followed by the maiden and this time he offers her slightly baked bread that is acceptable. She promises to be his wife but tells him that if he ever gives her three blows without cause she would leave him.

She then disappears but two women and an old giant man appear. The women are identical and the giant tells the son of the widow that he will give him his daughter in marriage if he can tell him which one she is. So identical are they that he is just on the point of saying that he cannot, when one of them thrusts her foot forwards, giving him the indication he needs. The giant agrees to their union and gives her as a dowry as many sheep, cattle, goats and horses as she can count at a breath. He is warned that if she is struck three times without cause she will return to the lake with all her stock. She counts as rapidly as she can by fives and the exact number of animals counted rise out of the lake. The young couple go to live near the village of Myddfai where they live happily for years and have three sons.

One day the couple are invited to a Christening in the neighbourhood but the wife is unwilling to go, saying it is too far to walk. The husband tells her to fetch a pony from a field while he goes into the house. On returning and finding that she has not gone, he taps her on the shoulder saying 'Go, go'. She warns him that he has given her the first causeless blow. On another occasion she cries at a wedding and again he strikes her and receives the second warning. Years later she laughs at a funeral and the third blow is given. Leaving her husband she exclaims 'Farewell, the last blow is given.' She returns to the lake, calling with her all her stock who follow her. Her husband and sons attempt to drain the lake but are prevented by a monster. She appears later to her sons and teaches them the art of healing, which makes them famous.

This story is a familial mythology and contains very ancient motifs which we find in the Mabinogion and related literature. Lake ladies possessing supernatural power who confer wealth and fertility are found right through Welsh folklore. In the Middle Ages we find them a key part of the Arthurian legends, where a lake lady confers a magical sword and scabbard that heals all wounds on Arthur. In the legend of the Physicians much stress is laid on the role of cattle, for example, a strayed cow leads the son of the widow to the lake lady at the beginning of the story, the bride principally brings cows with her from the lake and they return with her when she leaves. We may conjecture from this that the cow may have been the totem beast of the Physicians. In tradition the cow is a source of fertility, feeding and generation and an important Celtic cult animal. We see also the husband tested, having to solve a problem and enter into an agreement which he subsequently breaks through attending to conventional notions of birth, marriage and death. This deprives him of his fairy wife and her riches but these are subsequently bestowed on her sons in the form of healing gifts, becoming the fountainhead of the family tradition.

The role of the fairy wife is reminiscent of the figure of Rhiannon who is one of the major figures of the Mabinogion in that she also emerges from the Otherworld (from a mound in this version), acts as a tutor to a foolish husband and bestows wealth upon him before retiring into the background to guide and support her son.

It is difficult for us, living in a different age and society, to understand how a personal myth like the legend of the Physicians of Myddfai would be used. For us, storytelling is a trivial though enjoyable act, whereas in traditional societies, stories are the soul of the people and the telling of a story releases that soul, breathing it into the ears of the listeners and changing them forever. To get a sense of this, try for a moment to imagine that you are a son or daughter of Myddfai and about to be apprenticed to the healing art. On Candlemass night you sit waiting beside your fireside feeling excited and afraid. The older healers come for you and under the full moon lead you along an old forgotten track down to Llyn y Fan Fach to the stone at the lakeside called the Healer's Chair. You sit in perfect stillness on this stone while the eldest of the family tells you the story, describing it vividly so that you see with your mind's eye the son of the widow, the lake maiden, the aged giant, the fairy cows. You feel the pain of the three causeless blows, the loss of the maiden and the joy of her reappearance to teach the Physicians. Now the eldest recites the deeds and skills of the healers down the generations. Each of your ancestors seems to rise before you, adding his or her skills and blessing to you until finally the story comes to its continuation point in your entrance to it. The eldest tells you to look into the lake for the rising of the maiden, the first ancestor and source of the healing art. As you gaze into the water's depths, the story mysteriously becomes a part of you and you feel the Otherworldness of your lineage as the lake maiden overshadows you, beginning your interior instruction.

We cannot, of course, know that this is exactly how the Physicians of Myddfai inducted their apprentices; they are long dead and their secrets with them, but this is how the ancient story-telling tradition worked. It built up a series of images in the mind of the listener which had the effect of transporting him or her into the mind of the story, to convey a powerful emotional experience. Different healers would have different stories woven around the sites and objects in the cave. Their methods of healing were related to their own mythical tale of origin. Those who consulted them would be taken on a journey perhaps to a cave, a lake, a well and so on, they would be given an ancient object to handle such as a chalice or the skull of a distant ancestor. For example, one such object was the Nanteos Cup, a wooden cup which was reputed to be the Holy Grail. Sufferers would drink from it, having been prepared by the recitation of the legend of the cup. Latterly only a fragment of it remains and it seems that the healing method was to immerse the fragment in water and use that water, which was seen as impregnated with the blessedness of the relic, in healing.

In some cases, such as the Melchior family of Pembrokeshire, we find methods combined. Here the ill person was taken to the

Well of Saint Teilio and water drawn from the well in a skull said to be Teilio's skull.

These journeys or encounters were accompanied by ritualistic prayers, practices or the recitation of the history of the place, object or relic. This typically would form part of the family myth, concentrating the attention of the recipient on to what was perceived as the source of the healing power possessed by the family line.

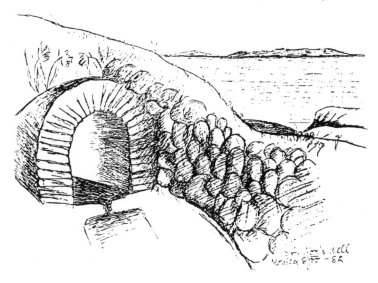

Fig 4 St Non's Well *by Monica Sjöö*

Anyone who consulted a healer in this tradition would visit the healer over a relatively brief period of time and be given a powerful evocative experience. This would connect the seeker with the core of the family tradition, which was itself based upon the more ancient Celtic bardic tradition. As well as physical healing, healers dealt considerably with problems such as depression, unhappiness and so on.

This tradition, far from being dead and buried in the medieval past, remained active right through the nineteenth century and traces of it remained within my lifetime. In the small South Wales village I grew up in was a group of men who met in the Cobblers Shop to compose bardic poetry. In popular imagination they were said to have inherited the bardic knowledge. The old stories were still well known in my childhood and local folklore beliefs were still vivid and powerful.

While the stories, imaginative material and folklore customs vary considerably, there are certain basic patterns which underlie them, such as the entrance to and experience of the Otherworld via cave, well, lake and so on, an encounter with a guardian and transformation experience conveyed through the agency of an Otherworldly woman. The experience involves the journeyer giving up something in exchange for the gift of the Otherworld. In the deepest examples of exchanges it becomes a death and rebirth experience in which one gives up one's self and is reborn as a new self. Another key element is the sense of tapping into a pool of ancestral power and experience which is applied to the problem at hand.

This tradition of healing and counselling is radically different from modern approaches. Modern psychological counselling might be said to have begun with Freud, Jung and Adler and other such depth psychologists at the beginning of the century. Here the emphasis is on prolonged periods of time spent in analysis, tracing back present day attitudes to their roots in childhood. The analysts' main methods were discussion, analysis of dreams, the use of the famous 'Freudian slip' and so forth to make conscious the presumed unconscious difficulty. Here the analyst acts as a guide and interpreter in the most detailed manner and indeed is a vital ingredient in the healing process, being a figure on whom emotions from the past are projected, thus enabling old emotional scenarios to be played out to a conclusion between patient and analyst. The Freudian approach may be said to direct itself principally to the resolution of childhood conflicts which were set up during the patient's early life and never resolved.

Jung, while accepting much of that approach, developed his system in a wider and more optimistic way by including the notion of individuation or personal psychic growth in later life as crucial to psychological health. He concentrated on the importance of religious ideas and symbols as applicable to the individuation process and out of his studies of his own mind and the study of different cultures separated by both time and space, developed the notion of the collective unconscious. This, he postulated, is a part of the psyche which is common to all humanity, containing within it mythical patterns and figures – these he called the Archetypes and considered that connection with them and their right expression was important in mental health.

In addition to the standard methods of analysis, he pioneered work in the method of 'active imagination' which was similar in technique to the bardic imaginative arts. Substantially, however, the therapy method still involves considerable periods of time whilst the various layers of the psyche are explored, much as an archaeologist explores an ancient gravemound.

Adler concentrated on the notion of power and social influence and his psychology emphasised the need for personal power. Again here the therapy methods were similar to the other analytical schools. A great host of schools and varieties of analysts arose from the work of the founding fathers. The ideas and theories of Freud, in particular, have had a wide general influence and have been incorporated into many training programmes in counselling.

Diametrically opposed to this school of counselling is that of the Behavioural Psychologists, of whom the most prominent early exponent was B. F. Skinner. Behaviourists take the stance that man is an animal whose behaviour is based on learned reflexes. They dismissed the notion of mind altogether and concentrated on teaching their patients how to modify their behaviour by a process they called Operant Conditioning. This is a form of learning whereby behaviour is broken down into small units and useful behaviour rewarded whilst maladaptive behaviour is discouraged by association with something painful or unpleasant. This is an approach that can be effective but it relies on the problem being able to be divided up and expressed in behavioural terms. For example, one can train somebody not to be nervous about getting on a bus but to transform a generally nervous person into a confident one would take a considerable period of time. Another difficulty with this approach is that while it enables the control and modification of behaviour, it is less successful with the feelings that underlie the problem. Phobics, for example, will often report that the problem is still in existence but is now manageable. Since its beginnings this school has become less extreme in its approach and more accepting of the role of cognition. It has combined with other approaches in a variety of ways and remains one of the most generally popular schools of counselling.

There are two other major approaches which remain influential in counselling. Humanistic Psychology teaches that we live in a cold and uncaring society and it is important that the client experiences strong emotional support from the therapist who is supposed to exhibit what is called, in the Rogerian variant of this approach, 'unconditional positive regard'. While there is much value in this, I have to say that personally it can be difficult to summon unconditional positive regard on a wet, cold Monday morning when waiting for a client who on our last meeting had compared me unfavourably to 'a baboon's bum'. There is a danger that this approach, if applied without sensitivity, could transform the counsellor into a smiling robot. It is clear, however, that genuine warmth and regard for the client is a vital component of counselling and the various schools of humanistic psychology have valuable work in this area, whilst also providing an active optimistic approach to life.

Finally, we see a variety of sociologically derived schools such as the group work movement, family therapy and feminist inspired schools of counselling. Group work takes as its guiding principle the idea that people in like situations are best qualified to help each other; family therapy that problems are rooted in the structure and processes of the nuclear family and can only be resolved through working with the whole family; feminist therapies address the inequalities of power and roles forced on women through society's reverence for and elevation of patriarchal values. Here again, these approaches have combined with others to produce a wide variety of methods, approaches and philosophies. There are many other approaches and schools of psychology but the foregoing have had the widest influence in the general sphere of counselling.

Modern counselling is no longer carried out by the local wise man or woman but through the National Health Service, Social Services Departments, Probation Service, Citizens Advice Bureaux and voluntary organisations such as Women's Aid, Help the Aged, Cruse and so on. Private analysis and counselling, in Britain at least, remains a minority interest of the affluent. The majority of counsellors are generically trained with levels of skill and experience that vary considerably. Most training courses tend to be eclectic, teaching many of the methods outlined above. As a result, the variety of styles and approaches are almost infinite with new books and theories proliferating by the year.

However, there is one characteristic they all share. None of the mainstream schools profess to produce radical qualitative change in the way that the older bardic traditions maintained. We see the transformation motif prominent in accounts of the old healers in the form of miraculous cures and also in its surviving literature which abounds in images of transformation. We see the bard Taliesin taking the shapes of all animals, fish and birds during his initiation at the hands of Ceridwen. We are shown also shifting landscapes, shapeshifting people, trees one side of which are green of leaf, the other red with flame. Suffusing all is the sense of a potent, protean Otherworld whose gifts may be perilous but can be life-transforming.

The majority of my time as a counsellor has been spent with the probation service and for years I have grappled with the issue of qualitative transformation within a manageable period of time.

Probation clients are generally at the bottom of society's pile. They can be poorly motivated, their lives are frequently in chaos and subject to a variety of social strictures, legal and otherwise. Most of them have experienced considerable personal damage from an early age. Moreover the client group I concentrate on are those who have already experienced counselling and found it ineffective. Approaches which need a long time before results show, or which require stable living conditions whilst internal instability is dealt with, are not likely to succeed here, as external conditions frequently change and overwhelm the internal work. Similarly, uncovering painful areas without some way of the client being able to tap into a source of inner strength can be very difficult for people whose daily life contains much pain and misery. I can vividly recall, from approximately five years ago, the response of a client whom I was encouraging to talk about his unhappy marriage, 'Don't you see! I'm just about keeping myself together. All this talking – IT JUST DRIVES IT DEEPER.'

It was this experience and others like it that turned my mind back to the traditions of my childhood. Lacking a handy well, cave or even a store of ancestral skulls, I relied on the imaginative and visionary exercises which seem to be at the heart of the tradition. I drew principally upon the Mabinogion, for here are found the major themes and motifs which are localised in the folklore traditions. Most of the texts are organised around a quest theme which begins in this world and then ventures into the Otherworld to obtain an object or perform a task before returning to this world. The quest often begins with an encounter with an animal figure who acts as a guide and helper to the questor.

I found a suitable scene for my purpose in the story of 'Owain and the Countess of the Fountain' and used its imagery as an introduction to imaginative work. I have used this with individuals and groups and its first stage is simply to get the client/s to relax using simple muscular and breathing exercises. They were then asked to imagine themselves sinking down into a warm velvety darkness until they found themselves standing in front of an old oak door with the symbol of a bear holding a ragged staff carved into it. On opening the door they then find themselves standing on the edge of the wood. A path leads into the wood towards its centre and they follow this until they come to a clearing. In the centre of the clearing is a mound and standing on the mound a man who is the guardian of the forest.

They are challenged by the guardian and must make an appropriate response; if satisfied, the guardian then beats a club on the ground and the sound resounds through the wood. In response, the clearing fills with animals; one of the animals approaches the client and leads them away. At this point the client is left to encounter the animal for a time and then retrace their steps or they may take a further journey which involves a descent into the mound accompanied by the animal.

This exercise I have found best used very early in the contact between counsellor and client. It is important to establish it as a key way of wishing to cause an alteration in the client's view of themselves and their problem. It is normally the case that when a client first consults a counsellor they will describe their problem in detail and in such terms as to suggest that it is insoluble. It is a common experience among counsellors to feel weighed down and imprisoned by the client's pain and depression at this stage. The use of the visualisation exercise at a first or second meeting frees up this feeling and focuses attention away from the unproductive aspects of the past on to the present therapeutic encounters.

The bardic traditions that are being drawn on here describe this process as entering the Otherworld; a description which at first could strike one as being primitive and superstitious. However, in practice it is an elegant example of Occam's razor, for the experience is precisely that of discovering another world or dimension, and it avoids paradoxes of terminology such as how the unconscious can become conscious. The ambiguous nature of the definition is also useful, for it directs attention on to the experience itself rather than allowing the mind to concentrate on learning a new therapeutic terminology.

One of the features of this traditional imagery system is that it functions in a cathartic way, breaking down already existing preconceptions, beliefs and attitudes, freeing people to be more creative and spontaneous than hitherto. The imagery can be disturbing and very unlike that used in relaxation exercises or manuals of popular psychology. To illustrate the difference, the following exercise may be helpful.

Close your eyes and imagine you are standing outside a cave. On your left hand is a rowan tree glowing with berries and on your right a yew tree. Together they form an archway above the cave. Above the rowan sits a black crow and above the yew a white cow. Hold this image for a moment until you get a sense of what it would be like to enter the cave. Contrast this with more popular visualisation imagery. Imagine that you are standing at the gateway to a white temple with corinthian columns, looking beyond them to an inner court where fountains play and many beautiful flowers can be seen. Once again, contemplate this image until you have a sense of what it would be like to enter this place.

The first image normally produces disturbing feelings; it may feel sinister and dangerous. The second generally produces feelings of peacefulness and serenity and while it is a useful palliative does not contain the same potential for transformation and the destruction of outworn and poisonous attitudes as the first image. Individual reactions to the material differs widely, but these are some general conclusions and patterns that can be perceived. Important experiences generally occur at the point when the totem animals have been summoned. A common experience, and one that has parallels with folklore, is for the great crowd of animals to be perceived as hostile or threatening. This sense of hostility vanishes once an animal has approached the visualiser.

I have often been asked what totem animals are and whether they are within us or external beings. To the first question I can only answer that they are guides and to the second – yes. The totems themselves will explain and reveal their natures to you as you work with them. On a first journey with a totem animal it is common for the person to undergo a powerful, emotionally intense experience – often a pleasurable one but sometimes disturbing, indicating areas that need to be worked on or specific problems that need to be solved. For example, Helen, a trainee therapist, first encountered a rabbit which played with her before turning into a mythical animal, depicted in the Genesis song 'Track of the Tail', and indicated that it would show her the way to a city of gold if she would believe in him.

This, for her, was a powerful positive experience which validated the reality of her natural imagination which her behavioural training had diminished. Peter, a creative but somewhat work-obsessed psychologist, was induced to play in a corner of a wood with a young deer. Trev, a 35 year-old man on probation for offences of violence and who had been through a bitter divorce and custody battle, encountered a dog he had had as a child and re-experienced the sense of emotional richness and fulfilment that had existed between himself and his pet. Janet, a 27 year-old depressed mother, encountered a horse who gave her a sense that within her was both power and the ability to direct that power to gain control over her life.

Of the more disturbing experiences: Maureen, a trainee therapist encountered a snake which showed her life as a stagnant swamp. Arthur, a probation client, a lonely, isolated man who had always denied his feelings and whose mother had recently died, was led by a small bear to his mother's grave, provoking a reaction in which his feelings of grief poured out. Darren, another probation client, was shown scenes in his life when he'd been dishonest and hurtful to others. Cas, an aggressive young woman, was surrounded by barking dogs and the hostile figures of her parents.

To summarise, therefore, the initial experience is almost always intense and may be positive or negative depending on the need, and the ability to sustain shock, of the person who is visualising. To date, I have not come across a single person who was not able to make some constructive use of the experience.

The exercise is then repeated on the next appointment. The totem animal now meets the visualiser at the edge of the wood and leads them through the forest to the centre or to some other location in the forest. In this and repeated experiments we see an individual inner landscape developing, forming a structure within which further imaginative work develops. The variety of such landscapes are infinite and may contain houses, castles, towers, valleys, mountains and so on. During this phase there is a curious interplay between client and counsellor in which the counsellor enters the inner world of the client and may at various points be inspired to suggest modifications to the inner landscape. The imaginative forms often dramatise episodes from the client's past and present or show aspects of their nature in symbolic form. While initially these may seem random, through repeated work they become tied together in the shape of a quest to obtain a desired goal or object or to overcome some restrictive barrier.

The messages derived from these visualisations can be described as emotionally profound but intellectually simple. They do not normally require detailed intellectual knowledge of symbolism and dreams. Frequently, riddles and cryptic images emerge but the unravelling of these requires emotional and intuitive effort rather than intellectual effort.

The role of the counsellor here is to discuss, clarify, reassure and occasionally to direct. It is the role of a helpful companion rather than an all-wise teacher, assisting the client as they explore together the path that opens out before them. Emotional honesty and trust in the value of the work is important, just as it would be if one was engaged in a journey in an unknown region in outer life. In the early stages both client and counsellor will have little notion of the way the work is developing. One must learn to trust the totem beasts and allow them to guide you.

An example of such a quest was Arthur's quest to find a box in which he had buried his heart. His mother's grave was part of his inner landscape and his path lay directly over the grave. Other quests have involved a search for a stone of stillness, the knowledge of balance represented by a pair of scales, an idealised self – one's sexual complement, for example a man seeking a goddess figure. The object of the quest arises naturally as work with the totem beast proceeds. It is important to use patience and not try to rush the process.

During this formative stage the counsellor may suggest tasks that the client can carry out on a daily basis to link the inner work with everyday life. For example, it was suggested to Arthur that he spend some time at his mother's grave; Rachael, a young woman we will hear more of later, was given a stone which she was to call her stone of tranquillity and asked to hold it once a day and simply sit quietly with it. Other tasks might involve painting a picture of a scene or figure and looking at it daily or simply thinking about some aspect of the imaginative work. The tasks also emerge naturally out of the work and are very individual. There would be little point in listing them as that would give an artificial sense of completeness to something that by its very nature must remain open ended.

As the quest develops, the role of the counsellor becomes more passive and the work acquires its own momentum. It has its own rhythm in which great leaps are followed by periods of consolidation; the leap taking the form of powerful experiences which reveal unknown parts of the client's nature or experience. There are times of great difficulty when the client will encounter obstacles which seem insurmountable, be asked to solve an impossible riddle or confront a frightening figure which bars the way. This is an important traditional device which is often shown in the stories. For example, in the tale of Owain and the Countess of the Fountain from which the visualisation comes, Owain, before he can gain the hand of the Countess, has to do battle with a knight in black armour. In the tale of Peredur[1], Son of Evrawag, the hero must fight the Black Oppressor, slay a monster called an Afanc and finally do battle with a black man on a bony horse before achieving the object of his quest. Again, in the highly elaborate and important tale of Culhwch and Olwen, which contains some very old material, Culhwch is set a wide variety of tasks by Chief Giant Ysbaddaden before he can claim Olwen as his wife.

It is a feature of the tasks that they are daunting and seem impossible at the outset. They need heroic effort if they are to be achieved and the same can be said of the tasks and problems that arise through visualisation of the totem animals. The counsellor must now encourage the client to keep working with the task. There is no trick or technique that can be used, for the person must be brought firmly face to face with the frightening object, person or situation. For example, let us say that the client finds him/herself trapped in a cleft of rock with no way of moving forwards or back. The counsellor will assist the client to experience this to the full, to work with and struggle with the obstacle, until meaning emerges in a release of emotional energy and insight. Overcoming an obstacle is normally accompanied by a release of energy and the gaining of strength which gives the confidence to go forwards.

In time, the work builds to a culmination point; the achievement of the quest. This is an unmistakeable point, for here all the threads are drawn together. Immediately prior to this, the inner work will have taken on a life of its own and the rate of progress will have accelerated. The client, through succeeding in earlier tasks and by being in tune with the totem animal, is much more in control than the counsellor, and that is exactly the right situation. It is astonishing at this stage to see the degree of growth in the client both in terms of their understanding of themselves and in the way they conduct their lives. The work builds into a final visualisation which is climatic in its effects – not necessarily in the sense of internal fireworks; it can often be a thing of stillness.

To illustrate this process let us look at the case of Robert, a trainee therapist, and Rachael, a client that he worked extensively with. Robert was part of a group of inexperienced counsellors that I worked with for approximately twelve months. He is a man who has lived a varied life having been a marine and a systems analyst working at a high level in industry. More recently, he runs a day centre for the probation service. He has powerful emotions, which over the years he had learned to suppress under what seemed a formal and controlled exterior. On his first encounter with a totem beast he found himself confronting a tiger with peaceful eyes. The tiger led him to figures of people with blank faces. The tiger encouraged him to touch the figures and as he stroked their faces so the features became visible and tangible. This was a powerful experience for him, which he interpreted as his need to express emotion and get close to people. The tiger has become an important figure for him; the combination of its ferocity and the peace in its eyes symbolised the balance he was seeking between the different sides of his nature. For him, an inner landscape developed, containing a house which was a form of sanctuary and in which he and the tiger did much work. For example, when he needed to bring himself into a state of balance he would visit the house and visualise the tiger sitting in front of him staring into his eyes. This had the effect of making him feel alert and centred, thus enabling him to release his energies in such a way that they did not overwhelm either him or other people.

Through this work he has developed his already powerful natural intuition and a great capacity to help others along the same path. He joined a small group of other counsellors who were working with images from the Grail tradition and concentrating on the notion of healing. He moved on from there to develop his own style of work, defining his quest as 'becoming a painter of mind pictures'.

One of his first clients, Rachael, was a young woman with three children who had received considerable assistance from the local Social Services Department, had no self confidence or sense of self worth and drew her sense of identity from a skinhead group. This group often abused and exploited her, using her house as their club house. She was also very dependent on boyfriends and would feel desperate and depressed if she did not have one. She was prone to violent rages and mood fluctuations and would exhibit attention-seeking behaviour such as mock suicide attempts.

Rachael initially attended a group I was running but did not make much headway with the totem animal visualisation. She could only visualise cartoon animals and her visualisations did not have the depth and power necessary to cause transformation. This is a phenomenon I have come across from time to time and is an example of the way people's imaginative powers can become encumbered and corrupted by the superficial use of images in society.

It was decided, because she had a strong and sincere desire to overcome her problems, that Robert would work with her on a weekly basis. Counselling lasted a little under twelve months. After some initial introductory work she produced a visionary landscape within which the work took place. The landscape began with a description of a womb-like room in which she found a person she called 'the Inner Rachael' who was a replica of herself but on a larger scale and possessing all the qualities she felt she lacked. The 'Inner Rachael' was to function as a stabilising, comforting figure which gave her strength and a feeling of peace. Beyond and below the womb-like chamber was a place called the Cavern of Doors. This cavern was inhabited by a horned, demonic figure that she called the Keymaster. He was so-called because he held the keys to the doors in the cavern. Behind the doors were feelings, attitudes and memories of great power and she sensed that the Keymaster opened the doors as he willed, letting out great floods of negative emotion which then exploded into her outer life. Her quest became defined as defeating the Keymaster and wresting the key from his grasp.

There then followed a series of imaginative encounters with the Keymaster that were of great power and intensity in which he, in battling with her, exposed areas of painful memory and feeling. Notable amongst these was a particular occasion when the Keymaster appeared as her father but with rotting, corpse-like features. This experience brought to light memories of having been sexually abused by her father. During this process of battling with the Keymaster, Rachael discovered a great deal about herself and was able to see that there was a path opening out for her which could be productive.

Robert's role at this time was to encourage her, to suggest imaginative scenarios and to be frank and honest with her about her progress or lack of it. The work called on him to use his own intuition and imaginative abilities to enter the world Rachael was working within. It was very important that the counsellor and client moved as one here. Robert had to resist the temptation to push Rachael more quickly than she was capable of going and he also had to handle his own feelings of fear at things being out of control when she was moving very quickly.

Following her encounters with the Keymaster she made rapid progress and increasingly took charge of the direction of counselling. The process is not unlike that of someone learning to read; initially the work is fragmentary and stumbling, but once a certain threshold is reached work proceeds by leaps and bounds. The therapy came to a conclusion with a powerful visionary experience which tied together and resolved the preceding themes and provided a basis for her new journey. This concluding experience introduced a new figure, an old wise woman who was called the Guardian of the Gate and who gave her the gift of strength with which she could overcome the Keymaster. Rachael then entered the Cavern of Doors and confronted the Keymaster, who was now diminished in size and power due to their previous encounters, seized the key from him and locked him away in a cell. She then encountered the 'Inner Rachael' and the two became one.

This experience summed up all Rachael's previous work and had the effect of freeing her from the pain of unpleasant memories but also led her to discover a source of creativity and strength which she learned to draw on. On an objective level the changes in Rachael have been profound. She broke away from the skinhead group she had been enmeshed in and established her own identity. She now takes pride in the fact that she is independent and in control of her life. Her emotional life is now much more stable and she no longer exhibits the sort of attention-seeking behaviour that formerly characterised her. It was particularly interesting to note that when her boyfriend proposed marriage to her recently, rather than accept immediately, she has chosen to wait and see how their relationship develops.

The Keymaster figure illustrates very clearly the role of the guardian and testing figures that one encounters in this imaginative work. These figures are well documented in the folklore literature and they are key components in the work of transformation. It is by struggling with the guardians and overcoming them that the questor rouses his or her inner energies and brings to light areas of conflict and difficulty.

There are three main components to this form of imaginative work.

1. *The Guide* – exemplified by the totem animal but who can emerge in human form. In this case the guide was the 'Inner Rachael'.

2. *The Guardian* – described above. Here, the Keymaster.

3. *The Transforming Power* – normally a female or goddess figure. Here the Guardian of the Gate – the old woman fulfilled this function[2].

The imaginative work is capable also of bringing people into the spiritual dimension. The word 'spiritual' is a difficult one, suggestive of pious puritanism and a dedication to a bloodless heaven populated by Rubenesque cherubs. The spirituality that emerges out of this work is unlike this and might be described as organic or natural spirituality.

It is exemplified by an episode in Geoffrey of Monmouth's Vita Merlini, in which we see the mad Merlin wandering in the wood lamenting the coming of winter. His only companion is a wolf; the wolf is dying, there is no food to be found and he is totally alone. Here his pain and problems arise out of the nature of things and he cries out against the natural order, questioning its purpose. As a result of his pain and his questioning he encounters Taliesin, who teaches him about the cycles of transformation which underlie all things. This spiritual level addresses the great questions of life and death and problems that are not to do with individual pathology but about an encounter with the hardness of life[3].

Examples of tapping into this level would be that of Larry, a trainee counsellor, who on his first encounter with a totem animal was confronted by a King Stag who faced him down and made him enter the mound. As he entered the mound he felt as though he was dying and then suddenly felt as though he and the Stag were one being and that the world outside was now contained within him. This experience gave him cause to ponder on the relationship between inner and outer worlds and became the foundation for later work on his part.

Other such experiences have involved the totem animal leading the visualiser to a figure of light sometimes seen as Christ, sometimes as a pagan figure or in an entirely non-traditional form that gave the visualiser the vision of a Force of Love working beneath all things. Still others have experienced a vision of the stars being contained within the body of the earth, giving them a sense that all things are interconnected. Others again have experienced a death and rebirth experience of being buried in the earth and emerging naked and newborn.

In some cases, deliberate choices are made to explore this deeper dimension. One small group of counsellors in the continuation of the work found that visualisation using imagery derived from the Grail legends was very effective – an appropriate symbolic focus for a group who were learning to heal others, as the Grail is said to heal all wounds. This again has parallels with the folklore traditions, particularly those that involve sacred caves. This particular line of tradition involves visits to a cave to obtain objects to solve personal problems. Within this cave sleep Arthur and his knights, representing a set of transformative archetypes of more than personal significance. The questor is warned not to wake them before their time. For the group in question the time had come.

The imagery that follows arose naturally within the group. The general plan and overview was suggested by me, but details and immediate ideas arose out of the collective imagination of the group. The work began by the visualisation of a Great Hall containing a round table with a rose carved at its centre. The quest began with the group imagining themselves seated at this table. A white hart followed by a pack of hounds ran round the Hall. The hart then vanished into the wood beyond the Hall while the dogs gathered around the table, each dog choosing a counsellor to sit with. The dogs functioned as totem beasts, guiding the counsellors through an inner landscape which included journeying to a hut where a male and female hermit provided advice and experiences concerning ideas of balancing and healing. It also contained a castle within which was a wounded king whose sickness blighted the land. The quest for the Grail was the quest to gain the power to heal and in a sense the counsellors were seeking to become the Grail – to be a vessel through which healing is achieved.

The white hart, after a certain point, took over from the dogs, guiding individuals into an experience whereby they were able to find the power to heal within them. The visionary work here, while it did bring out individual difficulties, concentrated on notions like mental health, pain and healing. Insights into the nature of counselling and images of clients were common, as were powerful experiences which seemed to increase their potency as healers.

As in the case of Rachael, the various insights, encounters and experiences formed a continuum of learning which came together in a powerful visionary experience. In this experience, the white hart conveyed each person through a process in which his or her identity as a counsellor was affirmed and made potent and, as with Rachael, this formed the foundation for future work.

Traditional imagery dealing with the spiritual level is organised into mysteries using the classical Graeco-Roman definition of that term, that is, a ritual drama whose components and images deal with the theme of death and rebirth. The Mabinogion and folk material abound in such structures. One such sequence that I have found useful is a fragment of the story of Culhwch and Olwen entitled 'The Search of Mabon, Son of Modron'. This fragment represents the myth of the search for the Blessed Son of Light and involves a journey deep into the Otherworld, in the course of which one encounters the oldest of the totem beasts: The Blackbird of Cil Gwri, the Stag of Rhedenfre, the Owl of Cwm Cawlwyd, the Eagle of Gwernabwy and the Salmon of Llyn Llwch. At each encounter the totem beast challenges the visualiser, demanding a gift and bestowing a gift in return. The underlying theme of this tale is the search for an imprisoned power of light which heals and redeems. The totems concentrate on assisting the visualiser to dispose of any obstructions within them to the power of light.

The phrase, 'Mabon, Son of Modron' means 'The son, son of the Mother' and the quest for the lost child of light is associated with the idea of a wasted and destroyed land that needs healing. The tale of Culhwch and Olwen is a very elaborate and somewhat confused account of this ancient myth, involving also the quest for the daughter of light and including a great series of tasks which require the assistance of Arthur and his entire court.

This particular tale, if worked with, combines the personal with the transpersonal and can extend the transformation process to deeper and deeper levels. The same can be said of many of the folklore myths, such as those of the Physicians of Myddfai – there is much more to them than an initial reading would suggest and images and thoughts that are taken purely personally at first can, with developing work, relate to themes of life, death and renewal.

The spiritual dimension is one that normally arises when the personal difficulties that brought one to this work have been resolved or partially resolved. It is an important dimension, for deep counselling inevitably brings you face to face with the great questions of life. It is, therefore, something that no counsellor can afford to ignore and I feel that it is important that these areas are addressed prior to doing this sort of work with clients.

Often, when discussing or teaching this subject to counsellors, I am asked what totem beasts are, whether they are parts of ourselves or objective beings and how they relate to various systems of psychology. Frankly, the best explanation is simply that they are guides. One of the weaknesses of our culture is that we are over-analytical, wanting to define, limit and explain away, rather than experience. My own experience suggests that the explanatory devices used by the ancients such as Otherworld, Guide, Guardian and so on are precise and effective ways of describing the process that is undergone.

This leads us on to a consideration of the qualities that a therapist needs and the therapeutic style that this work leads to. There are two crucial qualities that must be possessed: the ability to make a connection with the tradition and the ability to make a connection with the client. Both these qualities in large measure depend upon the clarity of attention of the therapist. It is an important part of any counsellor's training to keep attention focused in the present moment and to attend to both inner and outer senses, but it is particularly crucial in this approach where one of the key parts of the work is to keep the client focused upon his or her quest. The major cause of failure is the client giving up before the quest is achieved and thus it is important that the counsellor be in rapport with the client, providing support, encouragement and so forth. It is also vital that the counsellor has developed his or her own imaginative abilities and is able to enter into the inner world of the client, not just to assist the client through discussion but also to be a link between the client and the tradition.

We have seen in the folklore tradition that the family myth and the connection with antiquity in the shape of ancestors, or connection with an ancient sacred place, is very important. The wise man or woman is a representative and point of contact with the ancient tradition and brings to bear all its strength and wisdom to the problem at hand. This may seem like an absurd and superstitious idea but experience of working in this way gives one a sense of drawing on a pool of energy and knowledge which amplifies and extends therapeutic potency.

This connection with the tradition is best illustrated by drawing a parallel with the art of oral story telling. In telling a story to an audience you find that each time the story is subtly different – it shapes itself to the needs of the audience. The story teller is acutely aware both of the audience and their responses and of the story itself. It feels as though the story is telling itself through you and often you feel as if you are hearing it for the first time. Therapeutic work is very similar in that traditional material adapts itself through the counsellor to the needs of the client. It is in the maintenance of this linkage that the Otherworld comes into its own, for there is a sense of being linked with something purposeful which operates according to its own laws and which has a creativity beyond the two people engaged in the work.

It is necessary therefore that a counsellor who wishes to use this method explores and uses it initially on his or herself, thereby testing out notions like the Otherworld, Guide, Guardian and so on. The most accessible way into the tradition is via the stories, legends and folklore that encapsulate its essence. There is no shortage of material to work with. From the early traditions we have the collected stories from the Red Book of Hergest and the White Book of Rhydderch, now gathered into the Mabinogion, the Triads of Britain[4] – a collection of cryptic mnemonics which provide flashes of imagery any one of which might open a door, and we also have the Taliesin poems from the Book of Taliesin, The Black Book of Carmarthen.

Later in time we have the voluminous Arthurian tradition containing a great host of books. My own preference is for the works of Geoffrey of Monmouth – *The History of the Kings of Britain and the Life of Merlin* and also for Malory's *Morte d'Arthur*[5] – a beautifully written corpus of stories which summarises the Arthurian legends. There are also two poems written by an anonymous poet – 'Gawain and the Green Knight' and 'The Pearl' – which have much relevance[6]. In addition to the literary tradition described above there is the great body of folklore and fairy tales such as the legend of the Physicians of Myddfai.

All of the above mentioned texts are derived either directly or at several removes from the oral tradition and retain the same qualities of interaction with the listener or reader. It is important in reading such texts to build up the images vividly. Some of the early examples, such as the Mabinogion, spend much time in describing detail in order to aid this process. As you do so you may find that the text is becoming alive for you – images may alter, new story lines may develop or the story may seem to have significance to the other aspects of your life.

Selection of a text or story depends purely on inclination. In the old familial traditions, the themes and stories chosen would be linked to family history, but in this more general renaissance you are free to choose any that appeal to you. As the chosen text responds and shapes itself to your work, you will find that your own style develops and you will establish the basis of your own tradition.

Traditional training laid great stress upon developing powers of concentration and attention by, for example, observing the motion of the breath, concentrating on a tree or a stone, hearing the environment and observing the transformation cycle of the year in plants, animals and the earth itself. This initial training is important, for it enabled the apprentice to develop his or her senses, the ability to focus and direct the mind as well as grappling with ideas of growth, death, blossoming after winter, and so on. It also had the effect of thoroughly rooting the apprentice in the everyday world before attention is directed inwards through the use of the story, which is used as the exercise I have described to link the apprentice with the Otherworld, pursue the quest for personal healing and thereafter the deeper death and rebirth experience which conveys the capacity to heal.

Some of the features of the traditional training can be reproduced through the use of relaxation exercises and simple concentration and meditation exercises. It is important to choose objects that are natural to the environment and that suggest the ideas of natural growth and change as the foci of concentration experiments.

It is important to remember also that the key elements of the imaginative work are:

1. *Entrance into the Otherworld* – via a well, lake, cave, secret door, etc.
2. *The Guide* – normally in the shape of a totem beast.
3. *The Guardian* – testing figures which challenge and arouse your energies.
4. The generation of an *inner landscape* based on the tradition particular to you and your needs.
5. *The formulation of a quest* for healing or the resolution of a problem.
6. *The achievement of the quest*, often as part of an encounter with a female transformative power either overtly signified as a woman or goddess, or covertly such as a cave, a tomb – the body of the earth. The experience is one of giving up and being given to. The deepest example of this is the death and rebirth experience in which you give up your old self, surrender to the transformative power and are remade.
7. Return to the outer world as the *Guardian of the gift* and bearing the responsibility to use it wisely.

In the exercise which I have used as the principal introduction, an old oak door is the entrance point, the Guardian of the forest is the testing, challenging figure, the guide is the totem beast and the transformative power is the mound, although in some variations reference is made to the Old Woman of the Mound.

It seems to me that these old methods are as relevant today as they ever were in the past. They appear to be effective even for very severe problems. They do not rely on intellectual knowledge or capacity to be effective and they seem much quicker and more effective than conventional psychoanalysis and psychotherapy. It is perhaps best to conclude in the words of one of the old texts which give a feel for the entrance into the Otherworld:

And he came his way towards a river valley and the bounds of the valley were forest and on either side of the river, level meadows. And one side of the river he could see a flock of white sheep and on the other side he could see a flock of black sheep. And as one of the white sheep bleated one of the black sheep would come across, and would be white; and as one of the black sheep bleated, one of the white sheep would come across and would be black.

And he could see a tall tree on the river bank and one half of it was burning from roots to tip, and the other half with green leaves upon it. And beyond it he could see a Squire seated on top of a mound and two greyhounds white breasted, brindled, on a leash lying beside him. And he felt certain that he had never seen a squire of such princely mien as he. And in the forest fronting him he could hear staghounds raising a herd of stags. And he greeted the squire and the squire greeted Peredur. And Peredur could see three paths leading away from the mound, two paths wide and the third narrow. And Peredur asked where the three paths went.

'One of these paths goes to my court, and I advise thee one of two things, either to go on ahead to the court, to my wife who is there, or that thou wait here and thou shall see the staghounds driving the tired stags from the forest into the open. And thou shall see the best greyhounds, and the strongest stags. And when it is time for us to go to our meat, my groom will bring my horse to meet me. And thou will be made welcome there tonight.'

'God repay you but I will go my way.'

'The second path goes to the town that is nearby and therein meat and drink will be found for sale. And the path that is narrower than the others goes towards the Addanc's cave.'

'By thy leave squire, toward that place I will go.'

Notes and References

1. *The Mabinogion*; trans G. Jones and T. Jones, J.M. Dent and Sons, 1976.
2. R. J. Stewart, *The Underworld Initiation*, Aquarian Press, 1985.
3. R. J. Stewart, *The Mystic Life of Merlin*, Arkana, 1986.
4. *The Triads of Britain*, trans. R. Bromwich, University of Wales Press, 1978.
5. Malory, *The Morte D'Arthur*, ed. Prof. E. Vinaver, Oxford University Press, 1971.
6. *Pearl, Cleanness, Patience, Sir Gawain and The Green Knight*, ed. A. C. Cawley and J. J. Anderson, Everyman Classics, 1985.

Further reading

T. Gwynn Jones, *Welsh Folklore and Folk Custom*, D. S. Brewer, 1979.
A. and B. Rees *Celtic Heritage*, Thames and Hudson, 1989.
J. Rhys *Celtic Folklore, Welsh and Manx Vols. I - II*, Wildwood House, 1980.
W. F. Skene, *Arthur and the Britons*, ed. Bryce, Llanarch Publications, 1987.
R. J. Stewart, *The Prophetic Vision of Merlin*, Arkana, 1986.
W. J. Thomas, *The Welsh Fairy Book*, University of Wales Press, 1952.

AUGURIES, DREAMS AND INCUBATORY SLEEP
Among the Celts of Britain and Ireland

by John Matthews

INTRODUCTION
R. J. Stewart

In this chapter John Matthews offers extensive evidence of dream therapy in the ancient world, specifically that of the pagan Celts and Greeks. In the case of the Celts, of course, paganism and primal Christianity intermingled, and many ancient practices were retained well into the Christian historical era: some persist in Celtic culture to this day.

It seems likely, from such evidence as we find in this essay, that the therapeutic arts related to dreaming were sophisticated and widespread. That they were attached to sacro-magical systems stemming from primitive or primal roots does not in any way detract from their sophistication: the techniques outlined by John Matthews are clearly an aspect of the profound philosophy and metaphysics of the ancient world, far removed from modern folk superstition or idle popular belief such as we still find in glossy magazines – 'your dreams and yourself revealed'.

It has always seemed remarkable, and perhaps a little depressing, to me, that modern pioneers of psychology paid so little attention to the dream therapies of the ancient world. My guess is that over-specialisation and an unwillingness to be accused of pandering to outmoded superstition have caused a mass of very valuable information, techniques and methods to be passed over. But we need to be cautious in extending comparisons between the modern use of dreams in therapy and the ancient.

While modern therapy involving dreams is mainly concerned with reassessing and interpreting images, symbols and sequences of dream-events that arise and are recalled or intentionally remembered, this was not, apparently, a major emphasis of ancient dream therapies. In many

cases the dream therapy was aimed at specific information – a contact
was made with a deity who advised upon healing techniques. This is
rather different from the contemporary notion that one dreams *about* a
mythic figure or archetype, and that this dream is, or may be, potentially
therapeutic. Here we touch upon one of the most important and most
ignored differences between the classical or magical psychologies and the
materialist: the ancients took the Otherworld for granted. It was a reality,
not merely a property or expression of the imagination, or a generally
unconscious area of the psyche.

Modern people have problems with this difference: we repeatedly find
that modern psychological theorists and practitioners treat mythic figures
and locations as imaginative or archetypical, using what suits modern
theory from within ancient myth and religion, while denying the central
thesis of all religion, which is that there is more than one world.

John Matthews also deals with the range of initiatory and augury or
predictive sleep techniques that we know of from the Celtic and Classical
worlds. In the pagan world concepts of augury, therapy and initiation are
not separated as we tend to expect them to be today. While dream therapy
is quite acceptable now, dream augury is generally regarded as superstition,
or rationalised into various techniques involving the response of the
unconscious to problems and questions. Dream initiation or profound
transformation is often looked upon with some suspicion, though it
does have parallels in modern transpersonal psychological techniques.
The difference always rests upon the Otherworld and its inhabitants, and
our acceptance or lack of acceptance of their reality.

One other important theme is touched upon by the evidence that John
Matthews has assembled, and that is the connections between the Celts and
the Greeks. There are many similarities between the earliest strata of Greek
myth religion and magic and those of Celtic cultures. Setting aside (in such
a limited space) the lengthy racial and anthropological theories concerning
the Indo-Europeans, it seems likely that at one time they shared a common
foundation, certainly in the form of the Great Mother Goddess who was
widely worshipped in early Western societies.

But we can be more specific, for this connection between the Celts and
Greeks is highlighted, curiously, by the figure of Merlin, known primarily
from medieval sources, but dating to a much earlier period. He is originally
a type of Divine Child, prophetic, light bringing, but deriving his power
from the Underworld. This divine child, appearing as Mabon in Welsh
legend, is very close indeed to the earliest descriptive images of Apollo
among the Greeks. The attributes of therapy, prophecy, music and totem
animals are all held in common. Furthermore the ancient Greeks believed
that Apollo was a god originally hailing from Hyperborea in the north, and
classical writers have tended to identify this with land of the Celtae, just as
modern interpreters have felt it to be Britain.

The location for this reference is Diodorus Siculus, quoting from a much
earlier text, the lost *Circuit of the Earth* by Hecateus (circa 500 BC). Apollo, son
of Leto, was worshipped in Hyperborea with music of the harp and dancing,
and he returned there every nineteen years, to a circular temple of stone.

While comparing the classical and Celtic dream therapies, John Matthews examines in some detail the famous Temple of Nodons at Lydney upon Severn, and compares it to those therapeutic Temples of Asklepios in ancient Greece. In this context it is worth remembering that another temple, not far from Lydney, but on the opposite side of the Severn, is sometimes considered by archaeologists to be part of the same Romano-Celtic cultural region in the South West of England. This is, of course, that of the goddess Sulis-Minerva, at Bath, sited over the hot springs.

But this temple site was not solely dedicated to the goddess, for on a separate hot spring within the temple area, was a small worship site associated with Apollo and Asklepios. Carved stones bearing the symbols of Tree and Serpent can be seen today in the museum at Bath, while the carving of Apollo playing a harp, from the great altar that originally stood outdoors before the Temple of the Goddess, has been built into a medieval church buttress at nearby Compton Dando. Presumably this carving was carted thither by industrious medieval monks who raised it from among the extensive masonry of Roman period ruins found underground in the region of the hot springs in Bath. Thus the ancient god of therapy and music, British and Greek, still upholds, to this day, a Christian worship site.

★   ★   ★

When the body is awake the soul is its servant, and is never her own mistress . . . But when the body is at rest, the soul, being set in motion and awake . . . has cognisance of all things – sees what is visible, hears what is audible, walks, touches feels pain, ponders.

                                                        Hippocrates: Dreams

AUGURIES

The search for omens and their meaningful interpretation is one that has long been recognised as a major concern of human beings. Ellen Ettlinger, in an article on the subject of 'Omens and Celtic Warfare', sums this up precisely:

The life of primitive man depended upon his unceasingly vigilant attitude towards the phenomena of nature. Among these were uncanny incidents, strange coincidences or vivid dream-impressions which took hold of his imagination. By pure intuition, and without any analogy, man interpreted a stirring natural happening as a warning of trouble ahead. Similar or recurrent experiences caused the attribution of . . . foreboding to a particular event. The newly won knowledge was passed on to the medicine-man who handed the facts and the meaning of the 'omen' down to his successor. As time went on the functions of the medicine-man gradually separated more and more from each other and developed along their own lines. Magicians, diviners, leeches, judges and poets emerged and were initiated into the omen-language in order to satisfy the requirements of their respective activities.[1]

The first principle of which we become aware when the subject of precognition among the Celts is studied is the importance of dreams in which the subjects learn something of considerable import to their circumstances. A typical example of this is to be found in the Irish text of the *First Battle of Moytura* in which the arrival of the Tuatha de Danaan is preceived by King Eochaid in the following manner:

> 'I saw a great flock of black birds,' said the king, 'coming from the depths of Ocean. They settled over all of us, and fought with the people of Ireland. They brought confusion on us, and destroyed us.' And he said to his Druid, Cesard: 'Employ your skill and knowledge, and tell us the meaning of the vision.' Cesard did so, and by means of ritual and the use of his science the meaning of the king's vision was revealed to him; and he said: 'I have tidings for you: warriors are coming across the sea, a thousand heroes covering the ocean; speckled ships will press in upon us; all kinds of death they announce, a people skilled in every art, a magic spell; an evil spirit will come upon you, signs to lead you astray . . . they will be victorious in every stress.'[2]

Two factors become immediately apparent from this: 1. that the king recognises his dream as important, implying that precognitive dreaming was a normal matter, and 2. that he required an interpreter for the meaning of the dream – in this case, the druid Cesard. A third factor, that the symbolism of the dream involved creatures (specifically birds), and water (the sea), will be seen to possess an importance of their own.

Prognostication from the actions of animals or birds are well attested in Celtic literature, and were a part of the substantial shamanic tradition once prevalent in Britain and Ireland.[3] Two treatises preserved in a Middle Irish manuscript in the Library of Trinity College Dublin (codex H.3.17), refer specifically to the interpretation of the flight patterns and songs of the Raven and the Wren – birds long recognised as sacred in Celtic myth. Of the Raven, it is said that if it calls

> from above an enclosed bed in the midst of the house, it is a distinguished grey-haired guest or clerics that are coming to see thee, but there is a difference between them: if it be a lay cleric the raven says *bacach*; if it be a man in orders it calls *gradh gradh*, and twice in the day it calls. If it be warrior guests or satirists that are coming it is *gracc gracc* it calls,

or *grob grob*, and it calls in the quarter behind thee, and it is thence that the guests are coming. If it calls *gracc gracc* the warriors are oppressed to whom it calls.[4]

Of the Wren we are told:

If it be between thee and the sun, it is the slaying of a man that is dear to thee . . . If it be at thy left ear, union with a young man from afar, or sleeping with a young woman. If it call from behind thee, importuning of thy wife by another man in despite of thee. If it be on the ground behind thee, thy wife will be taken from thee by force. If the wren call from the east, poets are coming towards thee, or tidings from them.[4]

The observations here are of a very general kind and are perhaps not to be taken too literally; however, they do indicate the divinatory importance of birds and suggest that at one time the practice was both more sophisticated and more precise.

Aside from this there were a number of specific kinds of omen which occurred frequently, notably before a battle: weapons that shrieked or cried aloud, the appearance of the Washer-at-the-Ford (see below), or the behaviour of animals – notably horses or dogs. Among the death omens which surrounded the last days of the great Irish hero Cuchulainn, is that in which he is offered a vat from which to drink before departing for battle. Hitherto this had always been a sign of certain victory for him, but on this occasion he finds the vat filled with blood.

DREAMS

By far the most significant documentation of augury concerns precognitive dreams, not only of the kind discussed above, which are primarily spontaneous, but also self-induced visions, which may be brought on in a number of ways, including the position of the sleeper, bodily contact with other men or women, and with the skin of an animal on which the sleeper lay to have his or her dream.[5]

Several texts mention the positioning of the sleeper between two pillar-stones, as in the case of the Irish hero Cuchulainn, who could not sleep inside a house until a special bed was built for him at the behest of the king. First two tall stones were erected, then the bed was placed between them. Cuchulainn is then able to sleep – though when he hears 'the groans of the Ulstermen', his comrades, in a battle, he stretches forth and breaks both the stones. Another text mentions Condla Coel Corrbacc resting on an island 'leaning his head against a pillar-stone in the western part of the island and the feet against a pillar-stone in its eastern part'.[6]

Neither character is described as having any vision or dream in this instance, but it seems likely that the depiction of this unusual method of sleeping with its orientation east/west, once held a great significance as the position assumed by the seeker after dreams of predictive visions. Elsewhere we read that when the druids wished to make an important prognostication, and had tried all other methods available to them, they made 'round hurdles of rowan, and spread over them the hides of sacrificed bulls with the fleshly side uppermost'.[7] Whence it was said, remarks the historian Keeting, that 'anyone who had done his utmost to obtain information . . . that he had gone onto his hurdles of knowledge'.[8]

The importance of sleeping on the skin of a particular beast is well attested throughout Celtic literature. The best known example is in the story of *The Dream of Rhonabwy* from the *Mabinogion*, in which the hero is in pursuit of an actual historical figure, known to have lived in the Middle Ages in Wales. Seeking shelter one night in the dank and evil-smelling hut belonging to a hag, Rhonabwy sleeps on a yellow bull's hide and dreams a long and astonishingly complex dream of the hero Arthur and his men, who are all depicted as larger than life and much saddened by the fact that Wales has come to be occupied by such little men![9]

Apart from the obvious shamanic nature of this idea, it is clearly a reminder of the *tarbh feis*, or 'Bull-Sleep', practised by the Irish druids. In this, after having sacrificed a (usually white) bull and made a broth from its flesh, the druid wrapped himself in the freshly flayed skin and slept a profound sleep, in which he would dream the answer to a great question – usually the secession of a king or something of equal importance.

The eating of the sacrificed creature's flesh suggests a further connection with methods of prognostication described in *Cormac's Glossary*,[10] a medieval compilation of lore which discusses such methods at length. Among the techniques mentioned is *Imbass Forosnai*, generally translated as 'Knowledge that Enlightens'. This was achieved by the subject chewing 'a piece of (the) flesh of a red pig, or of a dog or cat', after which he 'pronounces incantations on his two palms, and he lays his two palms on his two cheeks and (in this manner) falls asleep'.[10]

I have discussed the manner in which this relates to world wide shamanic practice elsewhere;[11] but it is worth noticing that among the Okinawa, as among the Esquimaux, the Wintu and Shasta tribes

Fig 5   Dream Incubation *by Monica Sjöö*

of North America, and the African Zulus, shamans frequently receive their 'call' in the form of dream or vision, and that often animals or bird are involved as in the examples of raven and wren lore quoted above.[12]

The practice of sleeping on a hide was attested as late as the eighteenth century, by Martin Martin, in his *Description of the Western Isles of Scotland* of 1795, where he describes the rite known as *Taghairm* as follows:

> A party of men, who first retired to solitary places, remote from any house . . . singled out one of their number, and wrapp'd him in a big cow's hide, which they folded about him, his whole body was covered with it except his head, and so left in this posture all night until . . . (he gave) the proper answer to the question in hand.[13]

This wrapping of the dreamer in a hide recalls the descriptions of patients at the Asklepion, who were wrapped in tight bandages, from which they were symbolically cut free after their incubatory period as a sign of their healed state. The objectives here are different, but the method of obtaining the vision once again curiously similar. We do not know whether this was practised as a mimesis of the swaddling clothes of babies, whose fontanelles would still be open to allow the ingress of spirits and visions, but this is a factor to be considered.

Finally, we must mention the idea of physical contact as a further means of enhancing the visionary state. We do not know if the priests of the Asklepion were present or watched over the patient during their incubatory sleep; it would seem, on the whole, unlikely. However, in most of the accounts from Celtic literature, the sleeper is described as being watched over by his friends, or by the druids who initiated his state of being. In some cases they are described as chanting 'a spell of truth' over the sleeper;[14] in others as being near at hand and shaking him awake after his period in a darkened room. Often there are four guardians mentioned, as in the description of the Bull-Feast mentioned above. Elsewhere, in the text known as *The Voyage of Bran*,[15] one of the characters is described as ascending every day to the top of the royal rath with his three chief druids in order 'to view all four points of the heavens that the *sid* (faery) men should not rest upon Ireland unperceived by him'.[16] We may guess from this that a watch was to be maintained at all times over the sleeper to ensure that his sleeping, or wandering, spirit was not carried off into the Otherworld, as might happen all too easily at that time.

Whether or not the guardians were actually touching the sleeper is not stated, but in several other texts such a contact is specifically noted. In the *Mabinog of Math, Son of Mathonwy*, for instance, we learn that Math spent most of his time with his feet in the lap of the royal foot-holder;[17] while in a later story a child who is experiencing difficulty in remembering the Psalms has only to sleep with his head resting on the knees of the Irish Saint Aengus in order to awake with the entire canon of the scripture secure in his memory![18]

This seems to point to the idea of the passing on of knowledge by direct contact with the master. It is no large step from here to the idea of knowledge gained from the dead, who were frequently consulted on matters of import, and who could be contacted by either visiting their graves or summoning them in necromantic fashion. The Roman author Tertullian states (*De Anima* 27) that the Celts were given to sleeping on the tombs of their ancestors in order to receive knowledge and inspiration; the same idea was current among the Norse; places where the dead rested were regarded as sanctuaries, and the act of sleeping upon them seen as likely to result in a revelatory experience.[19]

INCUBATION

The method of obtaining information from inner sources (primarily the Otherworld) most often attested to, not only among the Celts but in a much wider sphere, is that of the incubatory sleep. This is especially true of ancient Greece, where the temples dedicated to Asklepios concerned themselves specifically with the healing of ailments through this method. Here the sufferer, after being suitably prepared, slept in a special cell in a part of the temple called an *abaton*, and there dreamed a dream in which he or she either received a visitation from the god himself, whose touch brought healing; or else was instructed in a method of self-cure – sometimes cryptically and in a form requiring interpretation; though this does not ever seem to have been done by the priests of the temple.[20]

To early man, who saw sickness as a reflection of spiritual health, if a person suffered from a physical ailment (excluding loss of limbs or wounds acquired in war) there must be something wrong with his soul. For this reason Asklepios, who became the god of physicians, was seen not only as a healer, but also as a 'saviour' god, whose actions were intended to counteract those of other deities whom the patient might have offended, or whose observance he or she might in some way have neglected. Incubatory sleep was the god's principle method of working his cures – much as in modern psychoanalytical treatment, where the patient is encouraged to discover the disaffection in his or her soul through the study or interpretation of his dreams.

Unlike the modern practice, however, the dreams were seen as specifically emanating from the god, and the whole process took place within a specific *temenos*, the sacred precinct of the god. (The word *incubare* is translated as 'sleeping in the sanctuary'.) The resultant dreams (and few seem not to have experienced something) either effected an immediate cure or gave a method by which this might be achieved.

Preparation for the ritual of dreaming was also carefully controlled. After undergoing rites of purification, involving a lustral bath and preliminary sacrifices (usually of a cockerel) to the god, the patient went to sleep in the place 'not to be entered by the unbidden'.[21] It appears that he or she underwent some period of waiting, until 'called' by the priests, or even by the god himself, to enter the *abaton*. The importance of preparedness is stressed in every account of the Asklepiae; if the patients were not in a proper state of mind they were likely either not to experience a dream or to have one which was unsatisfactory. Those who did so were likely to be sent away, perhaps to try again later on, after a further period of preparation.

It is also clear that the period of incubatory sleep took place at night, an important point for our argument in the light of the stress laid upon absence of light on the part of the Celtic poets and prophets, who frequently gave forth their precognitive visions after being enclosed in a dark place, watched over by friends or priests, and afterwards brought forth into bright light. It is apparent in the case of patients at the Asklepion who failed (perhaps from excitement or pain) to sleep at all, that they received some kind of direct vision of the god. In this they were instructed as to how they might achieve healing, in the same way as if they had experienced a dream.

Asklepios himself appears to have begun life as a mortal physician who, taught by the centaur Cherion, was struck down by Zeus after he had successfully raised the dead. A still earlier strata suggests a more shamanic personality, in which his name is *Aischabios* and he is represented by totemic animals – the dog and the snake. The latter continued to be Asklepios' theriomorphic form, so that whenever a new Asklepion was founded, one of the sacred snakes kept in the temple was taken to be installed with due ceremony in the new one.[22]

The Asklepiae were generally founded near a grove of trees or a spring, indicating their connection with both the elements and the Underworld. As Dr Chadwick has noted in her study of dreams in ancient Europe:

> The most striking features which these dreams share in common . . . are 1. that they generally relate to the underworld . . . and 2. that they are for the most part shared with the rest of the community.[23]

This in itself indicates the chthonic nature of the Asklepiae, and of the god himself, and it of course also recalls the accounts of sleeping on the graves of dead heroes or druids in order to obtain dreams in which their wisdom could be plumbed. That this was a very central aspect in the design of temple precincts where incubatory sleep took place is demonstrated by the account of the Greek historian and geographer Pausanias. He personally experienced initiation into the mysteries of Trophonios, an early Greek hero who became deified and took on many of the aspects of Asklepios. Initially he was shown to have lived in a cave at Lebadeia in Boetia, again an indication of chthonic aspects. Pausanias' account makes this even more apparent:

'When a man decides to go down to Trophonios, he first lives a certain number of days in a building which is consecrated to Good Fortune (Fortuna) and the Good Spirit (Agathadaimon). Living there he purifies himself and uses no hot water; his bath is the river Herkyna'.[24] The initiate is then bathed in the river Herkyna and anointed by pubescent boys, called the *Hermai*. 'From here he is taken by the priests, not straight to the oracle, but to the water-springs, which are very close together. Here he must drink the water of Forgetfulness, to forget everything in his mind until then, and then the water of Memory, by which he remembers the sights he sees in his descent.' (ibid) After a period of worship here, he is taken to the mountainside above a sacred wood, which is surrounded by circular platform of white stone, about one and a half metres high. On this are bronze posts which are linked by bronze chains. Passing through the doors down into a chasm, the initiate descends through the kiln-shaped orifice of the earth, descending six metres by means of a ladder. On floor level here is a small passage – thirty centimetres high and sixty centimetres wide to admit the initiate. The man going down lies on the ground with honey cakes in his hands and pushes his feet into the opening and then tries to get his knees in. The rest of his body immediately gets dragged after his knees, as if some extraordinary deep, fast river was catching a man in a current and sucking him down. From here on, inside the second place, people are not always taught the future in one and the same way: one man hears, another sees as well. Those who go down return feet first through the same mouth. 'When a man comes up from Trophonios the priests take him over again, and sit him on the throne of memory, which is not far from the holy place, to ask him what he saw and discovered.' (ibid) Pausanius' account says that only one person had ever been killed here. He himself had passed these dangers and wrote from personal experience. All who have consulted the oracle had to write down their story on a wooden tablet and dedicate it to the shrine. Such a collection of testimonies would be most interesting to read.

That mysteries such as these, and of Asklepios, were once current among the Celts, is evident from accounts in widely scattered sources. As these are pieced together we begin to see a pattern emerging.

Clearly water was seen as a conductor of healing or information from beneath the ground. Numerous instances could be quoted from Celtic literature in which omens or precognitive dreams are vouchsafed beside river or springs. In the poetry of the Welsh poet Taliesin (a probable contemporary of Merlin) there are more references to water than to any other element, and this can be seen to reflect the complex matter of visionary insight as it connects with both darkness and light, as in the story of Nechtan's Well, which those who looked into it unprepared were at once blinded by light from within, but whose waters also gave inspiration to those who had undergone the necessity preparation (as in the case of the visitors to the Asklepiae).[25]

Examples of omens received at or by rivers include the following from the story of 'The Siege of Howth'.[26] In this the king (Mes-Gegra) and his charioteer have paused behind the main body of the army to rest awhile. The charioteer sleeps first and while Mes-Gegra is watching he sees a large nut floating down river. Seizing it the king cuts it in half and eats it. As he looks he sees the charioteer 'lifted up in his sleep from the ground'. When the man wakes the king asks how he is. 'I have seen an evil vision,' replies the charioteer and asks about the nut. A quarrel then breaks out and the king is severely wounded and the charioteer killed. Though the connection between the dream and the nut is not made clear, we should remember that nuts are almost invariably connected with visionary insight, and of course once again we have the themes of precognition and water.

Badbh, the Irish War-Goddess, announced the approaching death of eminent heroes by taking the form of the Washer-at-the-Ford, who was to be seen washing out bloody clothes or bloodstained armour in the river near the site of a forthcoming battle – a possible memory of a time when priestesses, trained in the arts of prophecy, kept watch at fords or springs, and were called upon to give prognostications before battle was joined.

There is no clear evidence for the existence of incubation temples of the kind discussed above in Britain or Ireland; however, one site has caused more than one commentator to suggest that it may have been put to just such a use – the inference being that if one such temple were operative in this country, others of which we have no current knowledge may well have existed also.

The site in question is at Lydney in Gloucestershire. It is of Romano-British provenance and was built between AD 364 to 367. It was excavated by Sir Mortimer Wheeler in the 1940s and found to possess a building consisting of several small cubicles. It was then noticed that the ground plan of the temple complex bore a marked resemblance to the layout of the Asklepion at Epidavros: including a bath-house and dormitories. Casts representing a disfigured hand and a heavily pregnant woman were also discovered at the site, suggesting that these may have been representations of the ailments suffered by those who attended the temple. At Epidavros, similar effigies were found in profusion, having been hung up in the temple as thankful offerings by patients who had been cured.

All of this led Wheeler to suggest that:

> Here, then, we seem to have a recurrent feature of some of the principle classical shrines of healing, and we may provisionally regard the Lydney building as a member of this series. On this line of thought it may be that the Long Building was indeed an 'abaton', used to supplement the 'chapels' in the temple itself for the purpose of that temple-sleep through which the healing-god and his priesthood were wont to work.[27]

If we accept this suggestion, the question arises as to whether the Lydney temple was the province of a native god, or was a copy of the classic foundations.

The dedication of Lydney was undoubtedly to the Celtic god Nodens, of whom little is, unfortunately, known. The presence of a priestly diadem at the site in Gloucestershire has lead some commentators to the belief that he was a solar deity, a belief substantiated by the great Celtecist Sir John Rhys,[28] who also pointed out the probable links between Nodens, the Irish Nuada Argetlam (Nuada of the Silver Hand) and the Welsh Llud Llaw Eraint (a title applied to Nodens in the hero list from 'Culhwch and Olwen' in the *Mabinogion*); both of whom derive from an earlier Brythonic version, Ludons Lamargentios.

Nuada was the possessor of an artificial hand, made for him by the Smith god Creidne with the help of the leech-god Dian Cecht. Llud can be identified with Llyr Lledyeith (Half-Speech). These are interesting as they are both suffer from physical defects, and are connected with a god who may have been responsible for a healing temple.

However, the diadem mentioned above, which depicts the god in a chariot drawn by horses and surrounded by neriads and spirits of the winds, suggests not so much a solar deity as a god of the sea. William Bathurst, who first drew attention to the Lydney site in 1831, translated the name Nodens as 'God of the Abyss' or 'of the Depths',[29] an evocative appellation since it suggests connections both with the sea and with the chthonic depths of which, as we have seen, Asklepios was identified. Interestingly, like Asklepios, Nuada was eventually struck down by a bolt of lightning at the battle of Mag Tuired.[30] Llyr was also connected with the sea, and together these watery references recall the provenance of so many Celtic dream visions beside streams or rivers – though this analogy should not be pressed too far.

It is possible, then, that we have in the figure of Nodens a native equivalent of Asklepios, and on the site at Lydney a British, Romano-Celtic temple where incubatory sleep was practised. We have seen from the evidence presented above that the idea of sleep as a means of discovering information or precognitive vision was common among the Celts. That a tradition of shamanism was also current at least as late as the sixth century A D is also certain. The combination of these two strains of thinking and belief make it more than likely that the idea of incubatory sleep for healing purposes would have been readily acceptable; though whether it was imported from the Classical world or already existed in the native islands is less certain. However, one final piece of evidence does remain, which suggests that it may well have been current at least in Ireland.

We are used to hearing accounts of Sweat-Lodges in the Americas, which are frequently associated with both healing and vision-seeking activities. What is not commonly known is that such practices were also current in ancient Ireland. 'Sweating-Houses' (*Tigh 'n Alluis*) were known in the nineteenth century and seem to have been in use for much longer than that. A number of such houses have been discovered, notably on the island of Inishmurray. They are usually about two metres long inside, and entered through a low, narrow door. A turf fire was usually kindled within and then the door closed up until the interior became like an inferno; then the ashes were swept out and those who wished went in and were enclosed until they were bathed profusely in sweat.[31]

The similarity between these structures and the ancient howes or burial chambers of Britain and Ireland is marked. Martin Brennan first drew attention to this in his book *The Boyne Valley Vision*, in which he noted that at sites such as New Grange, Knowth and Dowth, huge stone basins had been discovered in some of the side chambers. The use of these had passed unnoticed until Brennan realised that also present in the tombs were round stone balls which displayed signs of having been heated many times. He suggestion was that:

> The enigma of these objects may easily be explained by filling the vessels and stone basins with water and by heating the stones and placing them in the basins. Water and heated stones produce steam and the chambers in the mounds contain steam, thus easily and efficiently creating a steam bath.[32]

Brennan goes on to note that this was an ancient and well attested method of inducing an altered state among the shamans of many parts of the world. The combination of this idea with that of incubatory sleep and the Celtic love of augury, suggests a very strong argument in favour of these being such practices in these islands, perhaps from a very early date.

To end on a personal note. A few years ago, while suffering from a bout of 'flu, I received a visit in dream-state from an inner guide who communicated to me a specific method of helping myself to recover quickly. I had virtually forgotten about this until a few weeks ago, when I was again laid low with a virus. Lying in bed, suffering alternate bouts of hot and cold, I began to dream 'lucidly'. I recalled the previous instruction clearly: I must seek and find a pattern of negative promises: for example, I promise to feel very much *more* ill in a moment; I promise to bite my thumb very hard when I wake up. When I had successfully established this pattern I would awake refreshed. It proved extremely difficult to do. The tendency was to think: I will feel *better* when I awake; I will *not* bite my thumb hard on waking and so on. But eventually I was able to discover the right pattern, helped by a specific symbol which remained in my mind until I had finished. I then woke up feeling a great deal better.

The symbol is depicted in Fig 6 on the opposite page.

Subsequent meditation on this has revealed more of the image: that of a temple portico, with seven pillars and a wide entrance standing open before me. It does not require too great a stretching of credulity to believe that this is an image of the healing temple – whether the mother foundation of Asklepios or the native one at Lydney. Either way, it suggests to me very powerfully the

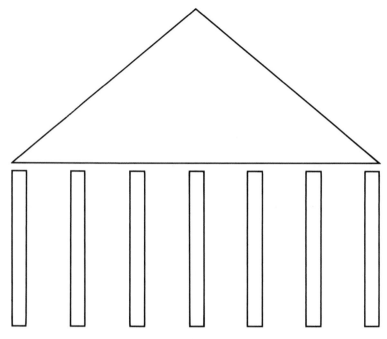

Fig 6   Healing Temple

continuing efficacy of incubatory sleep, as it was, I believe, once practised in these islands.[33]

To end I should like to append an 'Incubatory Invocation', to be recited by the priest/priestess of the shrine over the sleeper. It was written by my wife, Caitlin Matthews, after a discussion of the material presented above:

> Learn to the gifted with the night,
> With the words of wisdom.
> From the depths of darkness' dazzling
> The story will rise
> As a circling snake.
> May the sacred curve
> of Her arm enfold you!
> May the stars of Her
> dark veil cover you!
> May your sleep be founded
> in the deep night of Her own lap!

116   *Psychology and the Spiritual Traditions*

Notes and References

. 1. E. Ettlinger, 'Omens and Celtic Warfare' *Man* XLIII (1943), No 4.
  2. J. Fraser, 'The First Battle of Moytura' *Eriu* VIII (1915) pp. 1–63. See p. 19.
  3. J. Matthews, *Taliesin: Shamanism and the Bardic Mysteries in Britain and Ireland*, Unwin Hyman, 1990.
  4. R.I. Best, 'Prognostications from the Raven and the Wren' *Eriu* VIII (1916) pp. 120–126.
  5. E. Ettlinger, 'Precognitive Dreams in Celtic Legend' *Folk-Lore* LIX (1948), pp. 97–117.
  6. ibid.
  7. C. Plummer, in *Vitae Sanctorum Hiberniae* (I (1910), No 5.)
  8. G. Keating, *History of Ireland*, (II (1908), pp 348–50.)
  9. *Mabinogion* ed and trans J. Gantz, Penguin Books, 1965.
 10. *Cormac's Glossary* ed and trans J. Odonovan. Irish Archaeological & Celtic Society, 1868.
 11. See note 3 above, especially Chapter 7.
 12. S. Krippner, 'Dreams and Shamanism' in *Shamanism* ed S. Nicholson, The Theosophical Publishing House, 1987.
 13. M. Martin, *A Description of the Western Islands* 1703.
 14. See note 5 above, p 104.
 15. K. Meyer, *The Voyage of Bran*, D. Nutt, 1895.
 16. See note 5 above.
 17. See note 9 above.
 18. See note 5 above.
 19. See especially *The Underworld Initiation* by R. J. Stewart, Aquarian Press, 1985 where this topic is dealt with in some detail.
 20. C. A. Meier, 'Ancient Incubation and Modern Psychotherapy' in *Betwixt and Between*, ed by L.C. Mahdi, S. Foster and M. Little, Open Court, 1987.)
'21. See note 20 above.
 22. C. Kerenyi, *Asklepios* trans R. Manheim, Pantheon Books, 1959)
 23. N. K. Chadwick. 'Dreams in Early European Literature' in *Celtic Studies*. ed J. Carney and D. Greene, Routledge and Kegan Paul, 1968.
 24. Pausanias, in *Guide to Greece*, Penguin Books (1971), pp 393–395.
 25. P. K. Ford, 'The Well of Nechtan and "La Gloire Luminesse"' in *Myth in Indo-European Antiquity* ed G.J. Larson, University of California Press, 1974, pp. 67–74. See also J. Matthews, *Taliesin*
 26. W. Stokes, 'The Siege of Howth' *Revue Celtique* VIII (1887) pp. 47–64.
 27. R. E. M. Wheeler, *Report on the Excavations of the Prehistoric, Roman and Post-Roman Site in Lydney Park, Gloucestershire*, Society of Antiquaries, 1932, pp. 51–52.
 28. J. Rhys, *Celtic Folk-Lore, Welsh and Manx*, Wildwood House, 1980.
 29. W. Bathhurst, *Roman Antiquities at Lydney Park, Gloucestershire*, Spottis-

woode and Co, 1897.
30. J. Hersh, 'Ancient Celtic Incubation' *Sundance Community Dream Journal* III (Winter, 1979), pp. 81–90.
31. P. W. Joyce, *A Social History of Ancient Ireland* I, Longmans Green & Co, 1903, pp. 626–7.
32. M. Brennan, *The Boyne Valley Vision*, The Dolmen Press, 1980.
33. Several people are working with the idea of incubation at the present time. They include James Hersh of Salva Regina College, Newport Rhode Island; and Eugene Monick, who is a Jungian analyst practicing in New York City and Scranton, Pennsylvania. The Dragon Project Trust, under the guidance of Paul Devereux, have recently begun a new programme of experiments into incubatory sleep at ancient sites which have been found to possess unusual geophysical properties. For further information write to: The Dragon Project, P.O. Box 92, Penzance, TR18 2XL, Cornwall, UK. (I am grateful to Paul Devereux for putting me in touch with some of the material used in this essay, and for providing a copy of the article by James Hersh.

ANIMAL TRANSFORMATIONS IN ALCHEMY

by Adam McLean

INTRODUCTION

R. J. Stewart

In this chapter, Adam McLean discuss a wide range of animal symbolism in alchemy. The relationship between alchemy and modern psychology, deriving from the work of C.G. Jung, has been an interesting and unusual one. The historical fact that a major founder of modern psychology fastened upon alchemy as a symbolic system connected to processes of individuation or transformation of the psyche has had a twofold effect. Firstly it has tended to obscure the essentially physical aspects of alchemy, and Adam leaves us in no doubt whatsoever that these physical aspects are a major part of alchemy in operation, and that it should never be limited to visual symbolism alone.

The second effect of psychology upon our understanding of alchemy has been more positive, for there can be no doubt that new generations have discovered alchemy through its publicity in psychological works. Thus fresh attitudes to alchemy have arisen in addition to the purely psychological or symbolic non-practical approach. Today we have a new generation of alchemists, actual practitioners of the physical and spiritual art.

Adam McLean lists the major animals and birds in alchemy, and their traditional interpretations, showing how they have their counterparts in physical manifestations and transformations generated by the alchemists' experiments. It is this lore of animals and birds that alchemy partly absorbed or shared from within the older traditions of spiritual creatures and otherworld journeys. In alchemy the mineral, vegetable, animal, human and spiritual worlds are harmonised by physical processes, showing that they all partake of and derive from one universal source of Being.

*   *   *

As far as I am aware there are few direct links between the alchemical tradition and the Grail and Merlin legends. One of the few borrowings from the Celtic myths is the important alchemical story the *Allegory of Merlin*. However, in this case, it seems most likely that the 'Merlin' name was associated with this allegory only during the Elizabethan period when there was some revival of interest in the Merlin figure. The *Merlin* allegory was written a century or so earlier and in its original version lacked the name 'Merlin' in its title. Needless to say there are no internal references in its text to anything remotely connected with Merlin mythology. There are a couple of other such short alchemical works which draw on Celtic myths, 'The Transmutations of King Arthur' being one of the more obvious. However, like the Merlin Allegory there is nothing of substance for the student of Celtic and Grail mythology in these texts either. There are a few other borrowings from the Celtic/Grail mythos, but these are peripheral to the core of alchemical ideas.

Despite this rather negative conclusion about the textual parallels between alchemy and the Celtic/Grail mythos in the extensive body of literature which has survived, I believe if we look deep at the symbolism itself we will find more inner esoteric links than can be grasped by a mere scholarly analysis of the texts. Although the flowering of Alchemy occurred in mid-sixteenth through the seventeenth centuries, when printer/publishers developed a market for the enigmatic symbolic copperplate engravings, and the strange oblique convolutions of alchemical language. Many great and influential writers emerged during this period; Henry Khunrath, Robert Fludd, Michael Maier, Daniel Mylius being among the best known; as well as a wealth of anonymous texts – the Rosarium, Splendor Solis, the Parabola of Reusner, the Basil Valentine material and so on.

As brilliant as these writers were, they were drawing upon a tradition which went back centuries earlier, rather than devising the mass of symbolic material entirely out of their own imaginations. Their works borrow quite extensively from an earlier stratum of alchemical material dating from the ninth through to the thirteenth century – the writings of such as Ramon Lull, Arnold of Villa Nova, and various alchemists of Arabic origin, Geber, Rhases, Khalid and so on. The fundamental set of alchemical ideas in the Western tradition was formed during this time, influenced during its early period by texts and ideas emanating primarily from the Arabic world which were transmitted to Western Europe during the Moslem conquest of Spain where, in the eleventh to twelfth centuries, Northern European scholars travelled to learn and translate seminal works on mathematics, astronomy, astrology and alchemy.

The Grail cycle seems to have emerged in a similar way from an encounter of European scholars with an earlier layer of esoteric ideas carried within the stream of Celtic mythology. The main formative period for the sets of ideas at the basis of both the Alchemical and Grail traditions is the eleventh and twelfth centuries. So it should not be at all surprising to us that inner links are found between these two separate traditions, in the shape and texture of their fundamental set of ideas. For they arose out of the same interior struggle in the soul of Northern European humanity which was taking place at this time, and reflect the energy and the dynamics of these inner soul experiences.

The most obvious parallel, and the one I want to explore today, is that of the use of animal symbolism to echo or act as a picture for interior experiences. I will here deal only with the ramifications of animal symbolism in the alchemical tradition – others can follow up the appearance of these symbols in the cycle of Celtic and Grail legends, and examine the parallels further.

Alchemy, as I perceive it, is a spiritual tradition, a means for exploring our inner space and the layers which clothe the previous essence of our innermost soul. It is a path, a way, a practical method for investigating the substance of our being, by meditating upon chemical processes. The alchemists worked with their retorts, heating, calcining, subliming, distilling substances, watching all the while the transformations within their experiments. They used events in their experiments as seed images for meditations, forming visual mantras from chemical changes. The alchemists reflected and mirrored these outward events into their interior world. They saw the processes in their flasks as an interaction and linking of the spiritual and the material. The spirit rose up, separating from the substance at the bottom of their flasks and descended again to spiritualise the material into an essence or tincture. As the alchemists reworked these experiments over in their souls, they further drew parallels with the greater laboratory of Nature. They saw the work within their flasks as a kind of microcosm of macrocosmic Nature. The living energies and beings in Nature were metaphorically drawn into their retorts, as they began to picture the living alchemical processes through animal symbols. For example, a black toad was a good image for the seething black mass of substance digesting in the flask, while a white eagle was a beautiful way of describing the white steam or fumes which rose up into the neck of the flask from the substance being heated below.

I would just like us to consider some of the more important of these animal symbols. Alchemists were, of course, individualists who worked alone, rather than being members of sodalities or secret orders, yet despite their writings being a result of their own experiences, the animal metaphors rapidly developed into a universal language. In the centuries before the invention of printing, key alchemical manuscripts, often with beautiful illuminated illustrations, circulated quite widely. Works such as the Aurora Consurgens (attributed to Thomas Aquinas), the Buch der Heilig, the works of Ramon Lull, Roger Bacon, Arnold of Villa Nova, exist in many manuscript collections from this period, and with this exchange of ideas a quite coherent set of metaphors emerged in the European Alchemical tradition. It was the coherence and universality of this set of alchemical symbols that led Carl Jung to the concept of the collective unconscious. The alchemists, though pursuing their inner work independently as individuals, nevertheless found in their interior descent a coherent language of symbols.

At the core of this was a vision of an alchemical process occurring through a cycle of colour changes, from an initial blackness to the perfection of the quintessence.

The alchemist envisaged each stage of the process being heralded by a colour change and a meeting with certain animals.

Blackening – Black Crow, Raven, Toad, Massa Confusa.
Whitening – White Swan, White Eagle, skeleton.
Greening – Green Lion.
Rapid cycling through iridescent colours – Peacock's Tail.
White Stone – Unicorn.
Reddening – Pelican feeding young with its own blood, cockerel.
Final transmutation – Phoenix reborn from the fire.

The phase of Blackening, which usually marked the beginning of the work, was brought about either by heating the prima materia in the process of Calcination (the 'dry way' of the alchemists), or by the process of Putrefaction, a slow rotting or digestion over a period of weeks or months (the so-called 'wet way'). The Black Crow or Raven was often associated with this Calcination, for on vigorous heating the calcined material would usually carbonise and layers would flake off and move like a crow's wings in the flask. The Toad was a better symbol of the Putrefaction, the decaying mass slowly pulsating and shifting as gases were given off, while the substance rotted down to a black mass. Another symbol of this stage was the dragon, a familiar inhabitant of the alchemists' flasks. The dragon is however a more complex symbol and is also used when winged as a symbol for the spiritualising of the earthly substance.

Thus to the alchemists the dragon appeared at the beginning and at the end of the work.

The alchemists paralleled these experiences in their souls as a withdrawal into the darkness of their interior space, a darkness pregnant with possibility. We have to a great extent lost the sense that still lived in the medieval and renaissance alchemists, that this darkness contained all potentialities. Like children we fear the dark, and for twentieth-century humanity darkness often holds only an existential dread – philosophers of science have in the last decade brought us this terrible image of the 'Black Hole' which swallows up and annihilates everything that comes into its orbit. Perhaps we do not gaze enough at the blackness of the heavens. For if we look deep into the blackness of space on a clear night, we will sense more stars hidden between the known visible stars, especially in the vast star fields of the Milky Way. Cosmic space is pregnant with the possibility of other worlds as yet unseen. It is this image of blackness we must try to recover if we are to become alchemists. An echo of this perhaps remains in the often-used phrase 'a profound darkness'. In alchemy, to meet with the black crow is a good omen. Thus in the Chymical Wedding of Christian Rosenkreutz, as our hero sets out on his journey of transformation, he meets with a Crow which by a turn of fate decides which among the various paths open to him is the one that will lead him to the Castle of the King.

The temporary phase of whitening which followed on the black stage was symbolised by the white eagle or white swan. As the black mass of the calcination was reacted with other substances and heated, it took on a white crust or dusty layer which sometimes puffed up and flew in a cloud in the flask, as heat exploded bubbles of gas out of the black substance below. This was the White Eagle of the dry way. In the wet way, the dark putrefying matter sometimes began to form white patches, often fungal growths floating on the surface, or white crystals growing out of the mass. This could be pictured as the White Swan, which was at home upon the surface of the water yet fed from the dark mud at the bottom of the stream or lake. Its whiteness contrasting with the mud on which it is observed to feed, made it a fine symbol of how spiritual purity could be gained from the unpromising primal material.

The whitening is a phase when we sense or have a prevision of the end of the work. It is a polar swing from out of the blackening – the appearance of seeds of the future development of the work. It is that stage of catharsis after some intense experience of being consumed in the crucible, when we glimpse the appearance, however fragmentary, of a new possibility – a flickering light in our souls which draws us towards its promise of change. We all experience these alchemical phases in our inner life, though nowadays, immersed as we are in twentieth century images which often lack a spiritual core, we usually fail to recognise these to be of any value. If we are able, however, to use the alchemical view of inner transformation, which we might need to mould and shape to suit our present consciousness, we can gain much inner perception and growth. For our blackness becomes a pregnant space, and a mere fleeting show of the whiteness is a significant step towards our goal of integration of the spiritual and the material in our beings.

Thus in alchemy these two phases, so fundamentally linked, were sometimes seen as the chaining of a toad and an eagle. The eagle of the spirit is held down by the earthly weight of the toad, while the earthly part of our being (the toad symbol) is lifted up towards the spirit. The hermetic philosopher Michael Maier incorporated this symbol into his coat of arms. The image of the earthly dragon bearing wings was sometimes used to express this same idea. If we can sense within our souls the need to link the spirit and the material, the spiritualising of the material and the materialising of the spirit, then we truly have made progress through the blackening to the stage of the whitening.

At this point the alchemists would often encounter the Peacock's Tail, a sudden appearance of a rush of colours, an iridescence on the surface of the material in the flask, which made some think they had achieved their goal. This could arise through the formation of a layer of oil on the surface of the watery mass (in the wet way) or some oxidation–reduction reactions, say on the surface of liquid metal (in the dry way). It was a fleeting show of colour changes that pointed to the fact that one was on the right path, and this reabsorbed the energies released in initial emergence of the polarities. It was a midway point of the process, which could be seen as a false conclusion. Many people who have this experience in their inner life often falsely assume they have reached the end of the work, and attained inner transformation and enlightenment. The inner vision of the Peacock's Tail, beautiful though it may be, is merely a digestion of the polarities of the black and white stage. These must be transformed further into spiritual tinctures, if we hope to have any permanent transformation within the soul.

Not all alchemists used the symbolism of the Peacock's Tail, and another stage often met at this point in the cycle was the meeting with the Green Lion. Physically the Green Lion was usually a name for vitriol, or the sulphuric acid created by distilling the green crystals of iron sulphate in a flask. Iron sulphate was formed when iron ores rich in sulphides were left to oxidise in the air; it was readily available to medieval alchemists. The sharp, penetrating sulphuric acid could create major chemical changes in many materials, even to the extent of dissolving metals like iron and copper. The Green Lion could also be the nitric acid formed from heating saltpeter or nitre and iron sulphate. Nitric acid, when mixed with the acid derived from common salt, hydrochloric acid, produced aqua regia, a greenish-tinged liquid that could dissolve even the noble metal gold. The Green Lion devouring the sun is a famous image in alchemy; it is depicted in many manuscripts and engravings, and can be thought of as aqua regia dissolving the solar gold and forming a solution which could readily tinge metals with gold.

To other alchemists, who worked primarily with vegetable matter and processes, rather than the mineral work, the Green Lion was an image of the green raw energy of nature, 'the green fuse which drives the flower' as Dylan Thomas elegantly expressed it in one of his poems. Here the Green Lion which devours the sun is the green pigment chlorophyll. The green leaves of the plant are formed out of the energy of sunlight. Alchemists often attempted to create living processes in their flasks and looked especially for precipitates or crystallisations which resembled leaves or plant forms. The Green Lion here could be a plant sap extract which was often the prima materia for their alchemical work. The Gryphon, half-eagle and half-lion, was sometimes associated with the end of this stage. The eagle nature of the Gryphon gave this hybrid being an ability to ascend in the flask, so it marked, in a sense, the spiritualisation of the Green Lion.

In the work with minerals, the metal antimony was referred to as the Grey Wolf, because when molten it greedily swallowed up many other metals, such as copper, tin and lead, by forming alloys. In this sense it behaved like metallic mercury which also readily amalgamated with metals. The Grey Wolf of antimony became especially important in early seventeenth century alchemy – its curative properties were popularised through the writings published under the name of Basil Valentine. To an extent, with its work with minerals it became an analogue for the Green Lion and the work with plant substance.

After the Peacock's Tail or the greening of the Lion, alchemists looked for the appearance of a stage of whitening then a reddening in their flasks, marking an new integration of the polarities which had emerged in the initial blackening and whitening and then been digested.

The white stage was the formation of the white tincture or stone, and was derived from, though not to be confused with, the earlier whitening, which followed the calcination or putrefaction, for to have proceeded to this stage meant one was on a higher level of spiritual attainment. This was often pictured as the appearance of a queen dressed in shining white robes in the flask. The white tincture marked a process of inner charge when the alchemist was able to experience and bring into an integrated harmony the feminine component of the soul. Often this sexual element is stressed in alchemy. The Rosarium Philosophorum, a key work of the mid-sixteenth/century, shows the coupling of the male and female as a central facet of the process. Regrettably, some twentieth century commentators have sought to link this symbolism with the practice of so-called 'sex-magic', in which people seek to use the sexual act as a basis for magical working. The alchemical manuscripts and books do not seem to support such an interpretation at all. The male and female copulating in the flask were for the alchemists symbols for aspects of our inner being uniting together. They saw metals, plants and minerals as being masculine in some degree and projected the transformations of these in their retreats into their inner space, in order to explore their own masculine and feminine natures. Acids, for example, which could penetrate and dissolve metal ores, were seen as masculine. Substances exhibited a femininity when they were connected with the forces of growth and nourishment of processes in the flask and the melding of substances together into a new unity. Metallic Mercury was seen as hermaphrodite as it both dissolved and brought together other metals into an amalgam.

The White Stone was sometimes symbolised by the Unicorn, partly because of its white horn, but also because the Unicorn could only by tamed by the touch of a pure woman. Thus the White Tincture can only be experienced by purifying the feminine forces within our beings.

The reddening or formation of the Red Stone was pictured through the symbol of the Pelican. The white pelican bird with its long bill reaching down over its breast, was in medieval times mistakenly observed piercing its breast with its bill and feeding its young on its own blood. What actually happens is that the bird regurgitates food it has caught earlier to feed its young. Bits of fish fall on to the breast of the pelican and it appears as if its breast is bleeding. This myth of the sacrificial act of the Pelican, in feeding its young on its own blood, was more powerful than the prosaic reality and during medieval times the Pelican became a symbol for Christ's sacrifice of his blood. Alchemists also took this symbol aboard and readily incorporated it into their symbolic menagerie.

The reddening marked the formation of the Red Tincture, which transformed the masculine forces of the soul, ennobled them, and brought them into a new harmony. This was often symbolised by the appearance of a Red King in the flask. In our inner work, we begin to possess the red tincture when we have entered on the task of transforming the raw energies of the masculine component of our souls, sometimes pictured by the alchemists as a knight brandishing a sword, into a more creative force.

The tinctures in alchemy relate also to the substances of the Mass, the red wine – the blood; and the white wafer – the body of Christ. Administration of the Sacraments was seen as spiritualising the souls of the partakers. In alchemical terms these white and red stones or tinctures served much the same purpose, though the alchemists achieved this, not through the intermediacy of a priest but by their own inner work of transmutation. Here alchemy links directly with the Grail stories which use similar parallels between the Grail and the Sacraments. The red tincture was occasionally symbolised by a stag bearing antlers – the stag was seen as a noble, masculine animal. This links in with the Unicorn as a symbol of the white or feminine tincture. In some alchemical illustrations, such as that of the late sixteenth century Book of Lambspring, the Stag and Unicorn meet in the forest of the soul as part of the process of inner transformation.

The final stage of the work was often symbolised by the Phoenix rising from the flames. This goes back to the Greek myth of the Phoenix bird which renewed itself every 500 years by immolating itself on a pyre. This is a kind of resurrection and was paralleled by the symbol of Christ rising from the tomb. In interior terms it marks the rebirth of the personality from out of the crucible of transformation. The alchemists, in meditating on processes in their flasks, threw themselves into a sea of strange experiences, and as they worked these within their meditations and sought to grasp the inner parallels and significance of each of the stages of the process they had embarked upon, they experienced in a sense an inner death and rebirth in attaining the Philosophers' Stone. This stone was actually experienced as the formation of a solid ground within the shifting sea of their inner world. Once this solid ground in the soul was found, the alchemists were able to take hold of their lives in a creative way; they could root their personality on a solid foundation or ground of inner experience.

One symbol of the stone was that of the Ouroboros, the snake holding its tail. As we begin the work, we are all rather unformed (the 'Massa Confusa' or confused mass is a good image) and often victims at the mercy of the sway of polarities in the soul, psychic energies that constantly shift from one pole to another, from joy to despair, from overbearing positivity to deep melancholy and negativity, from light to dark, energy to inertia. Our consciousness naturally follows the cycle of wakefulness and sleep, reflecting the cycle of day and night and the Seasons in Nature. This duality becomes reflected in many of our inner experiences. The snake was often used as a symbol for duality – its long, drawn-out body separating the polarities of head and tail. Sometimes the figure of a winged dragon was used here in place of the snake, in order to close the circle with the dragon at the beginning of the work. When the snake or dragon seized its tail it united the polarities into a circle, a symbol to the alchemists for achieving solidity amongst the dualistic energies of the soul forces. The creation of the Philosophers' Stone was the formation of solid inner ground upon which the alchemical philosophers could build their personalities, and experience the full potentiality of being human.

Thus alchemists could pursue their cycle of inner transformation as embarking on a journey in which they met with archetypal animal figures. The steps on their journey were paralleled in their experiments in their flasks, and the detailed images of processes of change were worked together with the animal archetypes of that stage into a mandala-like picture which they used as the basis for their meditations. In some ways this is similar to the journeys of the various characters in search for the Grail, and it is obvious that these stories were arranged so that the experiences the knights met on their quest, which often involved animal symbolism, led them through a cycle of inner transformation.

It is in this inner esoteric sense that the Grail Cycle and Alchemy have elements in common, though, having presented the alchemical picture, I must now leave it to others to follow up the links in detail.

PATTERNS OF WESTERN MAGIC

by W.G. Gray

INTRODUCTION

R. J. Stewart

This chapter from William G. Gray, one of the senior figures in twentieth century magical arts and the exposition of the Western Magical Traditions, is reproduced from *Transpersonal Psychologies*, ed. C. Tart, published by Harper & Row in which it originally appeared in 1975. It contains a wealth of insight, information, and potential material for the developing student. In the fifteen years or more that have passed since this chapter was first published, there has been a great expansion of interest in the Western Tradition, and a veritable flood of books upon various aspects of it. This is, however, a classic essay on the Western Tradition couched in the author's inimitable, highly individual style.

★   ★   ★

First, it is extremely important to recognise the fundamental difference between those Eastern and Western systems of spiritual development which might be classified as Magical. This is essentially one of Individuation aims and techniques. Briefly, the main Eastern aim is absorption of the Individuality into whatever Ultimate Nil lies behind all Life and Existence. The Western aim is actual achievement of Eternal Identity as a responsible integer living in the Unifying Principle of entire Existence. Thus, Occidentals would identify their beings with the 'Energy of Existence' expressed as Eternal Entity, whereas Orientals evidently prefer identifying with the Inertia principle providing passivity for such a Primal Power to operate Itself from. Perhaps one might broadly say that the East favours a 'feminine-passive' Life-angle, while the West prefers a 'masculine-active' approach to problems of the psyche.

It should also be realised that neither Eastern nor Western systems actually oppose each other, both being complementary extensions of a central spiritual consciousness that will ultimately lead individuated members of Mankind towards the 'Light of Truth' explaining the Eternal Enigma we all seek to solve. East and West simply approach the same solutions of spiritual living from alternative angles or 'Paths'. Nevertheless, it is a fact of Inner Life that those who belong fundamentally to any specific spiritual Path should develop themselves along its particular lines rather than attempt inherently alien Life attitudes. Since there is a definite 'Way of the West', it is surely the responsibility of advancing Westerners to find and follow their own Inner Tradition. This means evolving within their natural Ethos.

The Importance of Ethos

Inner Traditions consist of inherited patterns of progress towards an instinctive Ultimate. Such patterns amount to our 'spiritual genes' or 'family Life-faith'. Just as we are born with specific ancestral traits and characteristics which condition our living consciousness, so do we have definite spiritual inherencies stemming from our people's past links with Life. The 'Soul of a People', or Ethos, is shared proportionately by every member of that ethnic association. We establish either favourable or unfavourable working associations with these vital 'trace elements' of our metaphysical makeup. This means it is best for all to acknowledge their inbuilt ethnical 'psychosomes' and live along lines these indicate as aims for future Inner expansions of Identity. Conflicts of consciousness between surface interests and our deepest-seated basic beliefs implanted at Identity levels cause serious psychological damage. So it is just as wise to recognise our ethnic elements as to know our physical blood groupings.

Denying our deepest derivations results in a type of spiritual schizophrenia. Carl Jung had a great deal to say about this in his preface to Wilhelm's *Secret of the Golden Flower* (Wilhelm, 1962). The sum of his remarks comes to a conclusion that each ethnic grouping should support and follow its own Inner Tradition while reaching through this towards a sort of central Collective

Consciousness. He put it quite bluntly that we of the West must make our own Inner way, rather than be beguiled by intricacies of Orientalism which have become alien to our present lines of advancement. Jung says finally: 'It is sad indeed when the European departs from his own nature and imitates the East or "affects" it in any way. The possibilities open to him would be so much greater if he would remain true to himself.'

The broad spiritual spectrum of the Western Inner Tradition fines down to a number of parallel Paths, linked together on deep levels, yet offering opportunities for every different category of developing consciousness. Since the particular Path we shall consider here is so often called 'Magic', we had best define this blanket term to fit present purposes.

Definition of 'Magic'

There is much misunderstanding about defining the term 'Magic'. It means something different for most of its practitioners, and many people still think of it in childish terms like some sort of superior stage conjuring. The roots of this misused word stem from *maj*, meaning great, royal, and similar superlative states of being. Magic is properly 'magistery', or *mastery* in the sense of mastering one's own self-state before contemplating control of anything else. Therefore the word 'Magic' should stand for the means of attaining the greatest spiritual state of Selfhood reachable by initiated Individuants. As an art, it is consequently both sacred and secret, however much it has been misrepresented through the centuries. Re-establishment of its pristine meaning should be a major concern of Initiates in our modern era.

Psychological Background of Western Magic

The historical origins and developments of Western Magic have a highly interesting social and psychological background. Because of its essentially individualistic nature, it largely became a secret or semisecret counterculture in which practitioners sought spiritual independence from imposed patterns projected by Temple, Church, State and other organised establishments of human society in general.

There is a fascinating possibility that motivations behind Magic go back to our most primitive times when sharp distinctions appeared between the two main classes of Mankind dividing into

Hunters and Herders. Man first *hunted* for food and essentials. In this practice, Hunters developed intensely individual skills, making great personal progress in all arts of sharpening senses and coordinating consciousness. Hunters became the chief providers for, and saviours of, their close family and tribal associates. A Hunter was virtually the 'King centre' of his own Magic Circle.

Later on, as the practice of herding arose, the old Hunter-King became increasingly deposed. Working collectively rather than individually, Herders became able to supply the foods and raw materials their contemporary civilisation needed. They were probably the first supermarketeers in history. So the role of the Hunter slowly downgraded to that of soldier. His place became that of protector for the Herding Establishment's property against predators. The Hunter naturally resented this usurpation of his place and significance in human society. His individualism had been swamped by collectivism, and he felt frustrated and rejected. In fact he carries this sense of injury subconsciously to this very day.

Intelligent and Initiated human Hunters learned how to translate all their self-skills into Inner fields of action where the Quest became that of their own spiritual attainments, and the Quarry was Individuation into Eternal Entity. By and large, Hunters tended to become Western Magicians, while Herders remained Eastern ones. Looking at the general outlines of our world today, we should see this pattern fairly plainly.

There is a very interesting sidelight on this point in the present popularity of our 'Saint Christopher' image. Early representations of this Figure are those of the Hunter, with animal-skin cloak and club-staff like Heracles, whose name could stem from roots meaning 'Earth-Keys'. Christopher (Christ-bearer) gained his name by carrying the 'new' religion, but he himself is the old Hunter-God-Sacred-King Figure of the oldest faith known to Man on this earth. He typifies the fundamental Life-faith of humans for all time, and as such is instinctively revered today. Whenever humans feel their real spiritual roots threatened, they reach for these with every protective device they can find. The roots of our deepest beliefs lie with Magic in its real sense, and not all the intellectual influence in the world will alter our adherence to that ancient Inner anchor.

The modern resurgence of 'Christopher' as a symbolic patron of those seeking their ways along Paths seems to be a cry for help from a humanity feeling the very foundations of its Life-faith shaking intolerably. This is a direct appeal not to the Christ-Image now associated with that Church-State establishment which has betrayed so many beliefs, but to the Old Avatar of the Hunter-King who might carry us through the dangers of our crazy civilisation with some degree of spiritual safety. Today, Man needs Magic more than ever.

Modern Value of Western Magic

The function of Magic in our times lies largely with fulfilment of an almost desperate need for advancing individuals to maintain a sense of spiritual Identity in the swelling seas of Collectivism threatening to swallow all our souls. If entities are ever to evolve efficiently, they need to become exactly what they ought to be in and *as* the Selves they fundamentally are: not anything they are told to be by others, compelled to seem by circumstances, or otherwise altered to suit anyone else's ideas of Selfhood, except their own *as conceived by the Consciousness of Cosmos working through them.*

Such a spiritual need may be felt as urgently as drowning people need air or starving folks crave food. It is actually our deepest Life-drive, transcending all others associated with purely physical functioning. In Mass-mankind, it is usually dormant like the senses of a fetal child, but once awakened (which was called the 'second birth'), this drive becomes more and more dominant and directive of every individualising instinct and activity.

Some Magical systems claim to awaken this spiritual Self-sense by processes often involving stress techniques and ritual psychodramatics. Be that as it may, the field of genuine Magic in the West does afford unique scope for souls struggling to Individuate in a modern world.

The Real Inner Tradition is Independent of Earthly Organisations

It will probably be most difficult for many to appreciate that the real Inner Way of Western Magic is something quite apart from all Earth-based organisations claiming connections with it. One hears of many different 'schools' and systems such as Rosicrucian, Druidic, Hermetic, Templar, Martinist, and all the rest purporting Western ways of Initiation. At best, these are only *agencies* for the Tradition and are neither better nor worse than those operating them. The Tradition itself exists independently of them all, and can be contacted by whosoever has the needed links or 'Keys' within himself.

The real home ground of the Western Inner Way is not in this world of material manifestation at all. It is in another level of spiritual consciousness which has to be reached from ordinary 'Earthstates' by specific symbolisms or 'consciousness converters' available to initiated intelligences at each end of the linkage. Different systems use different types of symbology and agreed arrangements of action to suit definite categories of human awareness seeking solutions to our Eternal Enigma: 'What am I and It to each other?' Such variants, however, belong to the same Tradition, so they relate with each other at appropriate angles.

Once we can see our Tradition as something apart from its purely human makers, we must admit that other orders of Life than those are concerned in its construction also. Whatever we choose to call such orders is largely a matter of common convenience. They, however, deal with the spiritual structure of the Tradition on its own Inner ground, so to speak, whereas we in this world are concerned with it in the midst of material Time-Space-Event affairs demanding focal attention on much lower Life-levels. We are therefore likely to get somewhat distorted views of Inner actualities which would appear quite clear when seen from higher spiritual angles.

Providing we remember that whatever organisations we meet with in this world claiming contact with the Western Way can interpret it only along their particular lines, these may serve useful purposes. Yet it is the realisation that the Tradition exists in its own right apart from incarnate individuals or combines which makes real spiritual sense of everything.

Elusiveness of Western Inner Way

Partly for these last-mentioned reasons, a remarkable characteristic of our Western Magical Tradition is its amazing elusiveness. In the East one finds gurus and expounders of spiritual systems everywhere, and evidence of Inner Traditions all over the place. In the West, things are quite the opposite. The harder one seeks an Inner Magical Tradition the more rapidly it recedes into near-inaccessibility. It is like following someone always disappearing around a corner ahead. What may not be so obvious is that such a withdrawal causes suitably sincere seekers to follow much further Inwardly than they might have done otherwise.

Actually the Western Way is far more mysterious, mystical, and truly Magical than its Eastern equivalent. It has to be sought out with considerable devotion, and its contacts are discovered only after some difficulty. Only those who locate the links leading through all the obstacles deployed before the 'Doors of the Western Mysteries' are likely to penetrate those Inner portals. In other words, there is a sort of spiritual aptitude test for selecting worthwhile entrants.

This is why the overall picture of the Tradition is so puzzling until its structure is understood. Externally it presents a scattered and seemingly stupid medley of myth and muddle. Traces of fragmented old faiths, almost forgotten folk customs, and a welter of apparently isolated incidentals make everything look rather a silly and superstitious mess. This is just how it is meant to appear from a world's-eye view. It really offers a complicated yet spiritually soluble IQ problem, which only those who naturally belong inside the Tradition are likely to suspect, let alone solve. For IQ, read Inner Quest.

Lines of Western Initiation

In earlier times, initiation into the Western Secret Tradition tended to be hereditary, more or less restricted to definite family frameworks which later widened into associative clans and classes of limited social structure. The 'Passing of the Blood' from kingly levels to peasant ones was once enjoined as the sacred duty of a monarch or noble for the sake of his people's spiritual future. By implanting the 'sacred seed' in selected virgins, it was believed that blood lines would go on incarnating which could eventually prove the people's ultimate salvation. That is to say, the psychogenetic patterns of human perfection and Individuation would become set up and consolidated by processes of biological breeding.

Later on, this custom was honoured as a psychological rather than a physical actuality, although *droit de seigneur* continued for many centuries into its modern attenuated versions. The spiritual side of the Tradition was disseminated by secret or confidential communications handed through families from one generation to another. This always had to be from father to daughter and mother to son, or older generations of one sex to younger people of the other – a sex-polarized transmission of Tradition. Where this proved practical it worked out very well, but human nature being what it is, errors of teaching and other inaccuracies became far from few over the centuries.

With the rise of Church-State control of society, the older Western Tradition associations either had to go underground or else assume Christian disguise. This resulted in a wide division within the Tradition's framework. On one hand, the wealth-accumulating aristocracy commanded the best facilities and commodities, and on the other a poor peasantry possessed but the most elementary wherewithals, but held an inherited and instinctive faith in Nature and the Spirit it stood for. Between these two extreme Pillars of the Western Tradition developed the mysterious 'Middle Way' which has become, as it were, a backbone of belief supporting so many seekers right into our present times, even though we may not yet be a completely classless society. We have to remember now how very sharply distinctions and divisions of human society were marked in olden days. It was almost inevitable that magical methodology had its corresponding divisions then.

Among the privileged circles of the Western Way, elaborate and expensive procedures were possible. There were writers, poets, artists, designers and experts of all kinds to employ in this 'spiritual secret service'. Musicians arranged sonics, apothecaries compounded drugs and aromatics, while artificers made beautiful symbols and ceremonial accessories. Everything became expensively exclusive and eclectic. In some ways a good deal of progress was made, but in others a lot of touch was lost with Nature, the common Mother of Mankind.

Down at the other end of the Tradition, an illiterate and impoverished peasantry kept up what they could remember of 'old times' with a kind of instinct that if they persisted long enough, things would come right for them in the end. As best they could, they contrived symbols and simples of their own from the commonest materials freely available from the countryside. Every flower and leaf had its Inner meaning for them, and they read the book of Nature for themselves in its oldest language that needs no speech for communication.

Against all Church-State ordinances, these simple folk still kept touch with their 'Old Ones', now nameless verbally but always identifiable Inwardly. Here and there they met on hilltops or old-time sacred sites, unless the warmth of barns tempted them closer to civilisation. It was almost inevitable that their customs coarsened and crudened until accusations of demonism and worse were hurled at them by members of Church-State society. Even so, such rustic rowdyism was true only among some circles of surviving pagan practice. Others went quietly along their own Inner lines, skilfully avoiding open conflict with authority, yet remaining loyal to the Tradition they honestly believed would always be best for them.

Those humble and faithful followers of the 'Secret Faith' would have been horrified to hear themselves described as any kind of 'witch'. In those days, witches were just what the word 'meant: 'workers of wickedness'. It is only recent mistranslations and reiterations of error that have given the word 'witch' its present ambivalent sense. An Anglo-Saxon dictionary will clear this point entirely. Adherents of the Old Religion had no special name for their religion among themselves, and they believed in nothing like the Christian devil at all. If anything, their beliefs were not unlike those of the American Indians. They certainly never bothered much about what Church people said of God, since they could seek this Spirit for themselves in all Nature around them. Such was their simple code of conscious Individuation.

The Two Streams of Western Magic

So along such main lines, Western Magic went two ways. It is tempting to call these the Magics of the Poet and Peasant. One was sophisticated, intellectual, artistic and polished, the other home grown and instinctual. One might say Urban and Rural Magic, perhaps, or that of the Lodge and Land.

It is important to recognise this division of Western Magic into distinct streams, because that explains so much of the whole Tradition. Neither stream was the 'one true, etc', inheritor of the Tradition, and both distorted it in different directions.

There is one point for investigators to bear in mind. The Urbanites were usually literate, whereas Rustics were seldom so. What has been written of Rustic or 'folk magic' was not put down by the people who practised it, but often by 'non-Magical' Urbans who wrote what the Rustics told them. This was often deliberately twisted or exaggerated, or else just muddled and misremembered. What country folk told 'foreigners' with nice smiles, bright coins, and busy pencils was often very different from what they said to children and grandchildren in ways familiar to the family.

Therefore, whoever looks nowadays for traces of the Western Tradition in literary lines of approach needs great gifts of deduction, appreciation of inferences, not to mention quite real contacts with Inner sources of spiritual awareness, in order to make much of what is available in written shape. Most of what was written got cast into very involved allegories and complicated codes of consciousness. In those days of Church-State dominance, genuine Traditionalists no more dared express their deepest spiritual realisations in writing than a modern Moscovite would dare scrawl 'Marx is a Bum' on the walls of the Kremlin. Points like that have to be borne in mind by moderns looking for Magic in old Western literature.

Possibly the best way to treat written relics of Magic from the past is to transcend their literality altogether and use them like 'launching pads' for making excursions into Inner Space in search of the Tradition they link with so tortuously. There is more chance of reaching real truth that way than by trying to reconstruct it from mutilated mosaics of meaning scattered sparingly over such a wide field.

Examples of the Two-Stream Tradition

Here are four examples, two good and two bad, from the Urban and Rustic streams of the Western Tradition. We will take the Urban Poetic stream first. The good example is the Grail Mythos. Under a light disguise of Christian symbology, the best aspects of the old Sacred-King sacrificial beliefs were perpetuated. All the elements of initiated circles, disciplined ideals, pure purposes, 'in-group' phraseology and the rest of those old Questings revolving around the Magical meaning of the Mass-Rite are to be found by anyone knowing what to look for. The 'Last Supper Cup', for example, was an euphemism well known to initiated members of the Mystery. The 'Grail' was not so much of a 'what' as a 'who'. Whoso 'gained the Grail' was the one chosen to die Sacred-King fashion for the sake of salvation among the remainder: a noble death by a noble individual on behalf of his beloved people – a life-giving death, they all believed. Later, this extended to a 'life-until-death' offering of a lifetime dedicated to spiritual service in the common cause of God and Man together. As such, this ideal is with us yet.

The bad example of the same stream was Satanism, or anti-God and anti-Man ideas and activities devoted to sheerly malicious destruction of ordered living so as to gratify the worst propensities of human people. It was sometimes called Black Magic. Here again, the system centred on the Mass–Rite perverted to its most horrible potentials. It is easy nowadays to suppose that the Evil Entity concept connected here might be some old Fertility Figure gone wrong, or perhaps vilified by Christian commentators. That could be most misleading. The intention behind Satanism under any name was and still is sheer Evil, and old Fertility Figures were never intended to be evil in any way. Therefore the personification of Evil conceived by Satanists was a product of their own relations with Evil as a Principle, and resemblances to previous God-Images of earlier generations was probably due to subconscious desires for denigrating those ancient deities, in addition to insulting the Christ-concept associated with the Church-State enemy.

At the opposite end of the Tradition, one good example of its 'Peasant' part emerged as a 'Fairy-faith'. This was a hand-down from old animistic sources. Nature-spirits were believed to be involved everywhere with events influencing human affairs. In other words, learning how to make good spiritual relationships with the ordinary things and events of Life would lead more deeply Inward toward Individuation on higher levels right out of this world. The Fairies were the 'Little People' or lesser beings of 'Spiritland' who pointed out paths to the 'Great Ones' behind them who were never to be mentioned except by inference or allusion. There was much more to the Fairy-faith than ever appeared in print, and there are still fascinating blanks to be filled in by whoever interprets the clues correctly.

The bad example of the Peasant end can be classed as witchcraft in the real sense of the word, 'the skill of working wickedness'. It was deliberate encouragement of Evil through applied spiritual and natural agencies. This included the use of herbal poisons and abortifacients, calling down curses, and what we would now call 'psychological warfare' on other humans, such as preying on their fears and weaknesses. In fact the word 'witch' stems back to 'weak', and there is an implication that witchcraft involves working on people's weaknesses. Rustic witchcraft means an instinctive, inherited, or instructed ability for using the finer forces of Nature against one's fellow creatures for reasons of malice or personal profit. This type of spitefully directed subtle energy always works best within the relatively closed circles of association such as were commonly found among country communities. The wider the area the less effective it becomes as a rule, unless correspondingly larger groups of ill-wishers are involved.

So called 'Witches' Sabbats' of medieval times were seldom more than orgiastic assemblies of an oppressed peasantry with undertones of pagan memories. That happens among humans without any witchcraft at all, being simply the worst elements of any community behaving badly, as they always do through all the centuries we have been trying to civilise ourselves.

The Middle Magical Way of the West

Very quietly and steadily, a main stream of 'Middle Magic' grew up among the 'Men of the West' who were far-sighted enough to consolidate workable ways of consciousness calculated to lift spiritual levels of living towards highest possible human aims. A central theme developed among the various branches of the Tradition in terms comprehensible to initiates from each separate system.

Perhaps the most significant item of this centralising trend was the formation of what became generally known as Cabalistic philosophy and practice. This is often assumed to be purely of Hebrew origin because that language was largely used in its literary formulas. It actually derives from many spiritual sources, all Westernising in nature. Its uniqueness lay in compressing the metaphysics of Western Magic into mathematically acceptable spiritual symbology serving as a central Codex from which advances of Inner awareness could be developed during successive generations. It was spiritually what the famous Einstein formula meant physically in later times, though of course it attracted far less publicity.

The word 'Cabala' literally means 'mouth to ear', or signifies the Secret Tradition which could only be whispered by Initiates directly into the ears of worthy recipients. It also implies transmission of the Tradition through 'Inner ears' attuned to purely spiritual sources of instruction – that is to say, a kind of 'Master method' or summation of Western Magic into a Key-symbology giving access to the truth behind the Tradition by making direct links with what could only be called Divine Consciousness. While so-called vulgar or mere gold-grasping Alchemists sought chemical formulas for discovering the principles of health (Universal Elixir) and wealth (Philosophers' Stone), initiated inheritors of the Sacred Science sought means of transmuting the earthiest parts of plain human nature into the finest states of being achievable. This was symbolically described sometimes as 'making demons subject to God by means of angelic agencies'. Unluckily a great deal of misunderstanding arose through wrong interpretation of such metaphors.

Magic Misunderstood

It was the printing press which brought private Magic into public possession for the sake of profit regardless of authenticity or anything whatever except making money. There can scarcely be a bigger metaphysical muck-heap than most medieval books about Magic. Their badness lies mainly in their motivations, based on the meanest and nastiest aspects of human nature. Cast into contemporary commercial cant, their sales blurbs might have read something like: 'Defy Demons and Find Fortunes! Eliminate Your Enemies and Fool Your Friends!' or maybe: 'Millions by Magic. Wealth through Wickedness', or perhaps: 'Fun with Fiends. Satanic Supersex, Masturbate by Magic!!' or just: 'Glorious Grovels and Demonic Delights.' One could go on inventing idiotic titles like those for a long time, but that was more or less the literary level of those books. Unhappily, they still sell, and many moderns get their inaccurate ideas of Magic from such stupidity.

Into print for profit went all the ridiculous rubbish and torrid trash that authors and booksellers could compile from available sources, especially including their inventive imaginations. Peppered among this, of course, were quite genuine items of folk faith and odd fragments of interesting information. Possibly the greatest sales promotor of this stuff was its illegality in the eyes of the Church-State enemy hated by more and more of mankind. This seemed like a chance of hitting back at resented authority, and books on Magic sold for big prices as status symbols of defiant daring. Their reputed wickedness made owners feel wonderful. Few feelings stimulate compulsive conventionalists so much as a luxurious sense of sin.

Sad to say, much of that same story applies today. The so-called occult explosion has probably pushed more mental junk into a buyers' market than most of the dangerous drugs causing chemical damage to physical brains. Moreover, if drugs destroy addicts in a few short years, whereas books produce mental effects lasting for centuries, one is tempted to wonder which evil is worse in the long run. Now that almost no publisher will handle material that does not promise computor-calculated sales well above a high profit mark, works of genuine scholarship are bound to be few in relation to the hackwork easily marketable among so much of Mankind.

This is a problem which has to be faced by all who seriously seek evidence of the Western Magical Tradition. Books are becoming very chancy means of making any true contacts with it through literary links. Besides, even if every book on the subject of Magic were read right through, these would only supply *information*, which is not the same as *initiation* into the actual Tradition at all. Everything depends on what will trigger the right reflexes in any entity to initiate a search for its own True Identity. The combines of consciousness needed for this most Magical of operations might arise from many suggestions over a wide reading area. On the other hand, some single symbol could initiate a chain reaction of consciousness leading in exactly the right direction. Sometimes it may take years of muddling around with Magical literary material before even a dull Inner Dawn begins to break. Magical Dawns are much more often leaden than Golden.

Basic Beliefs

Because of its essentially individualised character, there are no dogmatic beliefs imposed by any obvious authority in Western Magic. Nevertheless, owing to similar spiritual findings reached by independent Initiates, a convenient body of belief and practice has indeed grown up through the Tradition as a whole. It could, perhaps, be covered in very general terms something like this.

First, a belief in whatever amounts to the Ultimate of Unbeing, Zoic Zero, or Infinity of Inexistence, which has 'No Name but NIL' behind all Being. This supreme act of Magic is regarded as emergence of Eternal Entitised Energy from a preprimal state of Perfect Peace Profound. Something out of Nothing always symbolises Magic to some degree, even with stage symbolism of a rabbit (a lovable living creature and fertility emblem) out of a hat (Emptiness – Ultimate Unconsciousness). Note the *white* creature from the *black* circular 'creation-crater' – Birth of Being and so on.

After the Supreme Spirit of Life is accepted as the One Self in Which or Whom all other selves live, each individual self is considered as an idea conceived by Cosmic Consciousness. This could be simplified in childish terms by saying that we should be as God intended us to be originally. So why are we obviously not? Here, the 'Fall' is postulated. The basics of this belief are briefly that Man was not meant to be a biologically bred entity on this Earth at all. This Earth was set up for animal ecology only, and Man, in spiritual shape, was supposed to lead those lesser beings up the Ladder of Life as they evolved into higher states of entity. Once the first 'Adamic' specimens of Man had made the fatal mistake of 'falling' into materialisation and begun breeding as the prototypes of humanity on Earth, the damage was done. More and more members of Mankind were dragged into incarnation through the gates of sexual intercourse, and humans became an almost alien species of being, having a spiritual entity attached to an animal body. Only a long series of evolving incarnations may breed out animal traits and breed in those more suited for essentially spiritual entities.

Thus, the 'Great Work' or Life-aim of Magic is seen to be that of making the right relationships with Divinity and Humanity which will 'redeem' our spiritual situation and result in attainment of original Intended Identity so that Cosmos can complete its Plan of Perfection through itself. This implies a belief in the principles of reincarnation, equation of energy, cooperation of and with other orders of intelligent Life in Inner dimensions of Existence, and individual responsibility for self-salvation in the entire scheme of Corporate Cosmos. That not only means 'Know thyself,' but also '*Be* thy self'.

Many attempts have been made to formulate a 'Golden Rule' of Magical living. One such is phrased:

These words our Ancient Rule fulfil,
An thou harm none, DO WHAT THOU WILL.

The true meaning of this is the signification of the word 'Thou', which is taken to be the Divine Will working in the individual, far above levels of personal wants or desires. However the formula may be expressed, it means the same thing – Individuate. The methodology by which this becomes possible is the only Magic recognised as such by Initiates of the Western Mysteries. Now let us see how the psychology of all this might work out under various suggested headings so that we can get a reasonable picture of the whole subject.

The Function of Man in the Universe

From a Magical viewpoint, Man is a Microcosmos living in a Macrocosmos, and is himself a Macrocosmos relative to the lesser lives comprising his corpus: a sort of 'atom in the Body of God, and God of an atomic body'. One lovely old Magical legend says that when Archetypal Man fell to Earth, he broke up into millions of pieces which all became tiny men and women running around after each other. One day, they will discover the secret of coming together as One again, and then all will be happy forever in Heaven.

Magically, Man is seen as a sort of spiritual anomaly. Our proper place was supposed to be a kind of Life-link between physical animals and nonincarnating orders of Life much higher up the spiritual spectrum. Since we 'fell down on the job', our immediate function is perfection of our species until we evolve enough to Individuate away from Earth altogether. Sooner or later we have to learn living independently of incarnate bodies, and realisation of this necessity is part of Magical practice.

Meanwhile, we have to act as agencies on these Life-levels for that Power which intends Perfection everywhere – in a sense, to become 'Deputy-Divinities'. Our finest function is becoming focal points for that single spiritual Universal Intention.

The Nature of Human Consciousness

Strictly speaking, there is only One Consciousness, that of Creative Cosmos Itself, the Life-Spirit as the Energy of Infinite Awareness. The reflective reaction of this Energy through every category of

Creation can be considered as the consciousness of whatever class of created entity it may be. This again subclassifies until individual awareness is indicated in each and every entity.

Thus, human consciousness, per se, covers a fairly broad frequency band. If we accept the Consciousness of Cosmos to extend over the entire spiritual spectrum of what can only be called Divine Omniscience, we must also admit that humans are capable of consciousness through a segment of that spectrum however small in relative terms.

Our consciousness is therefore a limited waveband of the Inner spectrum which links with many Life-categories. We are rather like radios with transmission and reception covering a limited set of frequencies. Few humans bother to explore anything like their available range, let alone attempt to increase or improve it.

Because of our imperfect and unsatisfactory states of being, we are highly unstable and potentially dangerous creatures as 'connectors of consciousness' in Cosmos. Conversely, on account of our unique positions in the Life-scheme, we may yet prove invaluable innovations for furthering its fulfilment.

Central control and correctly aligned arrangements of consciousness are considered a very major job of practical Magic. This is one 'first on the list' exercise on all authentic training programmes, and consciousness is treated as the natural 'raw material', out of which a Magical artificer has to make everything he needs – especially his own entity.

Consciousness is undoubtedly the most important energy that humans have to handle. Since so much may go wrong with it or be deliberately misused for malicious reasons, we might say that our entire future as entities depends on our 'Cosmic commodity of Consciousness'. Genuine Magi respect their art as a means of controlling and directing this most elemental Energy of Existence for the sake of our spiritual safety and prospects of perfection.

Personality (or Pseudoself)

Personality is regarded as a fractional and frequently faulty presentation of energies from different Life-levels concentrated into incarnate organisms. It is virtually a buildup of bits obtained from many sources fitted into a fundamental framework integral to the presenting entity. Ideally the personality should disintegrate like a defunct physical body after its useful purpose has been served, and a finer fresh one be built up for future incarnations if these are unavoidable. This is why Western Initiates are so strongly discouraged from trying to remember past lives, or attempting to 'bring back the dead' as they were known in personal guise.

Persistence of past personalities is normally a serious spiritual disadvantage to be dealt with very carefully. Personality is an *effect* of Identity, and not the Individuality at all. That is the reason why real Magic and so-called Spiritualism are incompatible. The Magical view is that recall of past personalities after physical death may interfere with the Individuals who should be in process of liberating themselves from these outworn encumbrances. Besides this, a disintegrating personality is a poor proposition to deal with. Much of the unreliable rubbish obtained via so many dubious 'spirit-guides' comes from these low levels. Communication with discarnate entities is not denied as a possibility, but it is strongly discouraged as a practice confined to personality levels alone. The experience of centuries is that communication with disintegrating personalities is a waste of time and energy.

Persistence of personality from one incarnation to another eventually builds up a kind of artificial ego or Pseudoself which can cause very serious spiritual trouble if it tries to 'set up in business for itself', regardless of best Individuating interests. This is something on the principle of a theatrical role specially created by an actor persisting after the play has ended and making difficulties for its designer. Just as such temporary constructions of consciousness have to be equated out of existence for the sake of mental health, so do our incarnationary personalities have to be dealt with likewise if spiritual health is to be safeguarded. Practical Magic offers many formulas for coping with this problem.

For reference purposes, it is generally taken that we derive our personalised presentations by combination of consciousness from Brain (our animal component), Mind (its metaphysical counterpart), Soul (feelings and emotions), and Spirit (our remotest Inner reality and True Identity). It should not be forgotten also that we have connections with the vegetable and animal kingdoms in us, and may present the best or worst of those Life-levels through our own living. In fact we are 'compendiums of consciousness' coming from natural spheres as well as spiritual ones. Constructing worthwhile personalities amenable to Cosmos-control is a valuable project in the Western Magical programme for the perfection of people.

Emotion

Emotion (literally, 'outmovement') classes as 'Soul' or ability of empathy with Existence in general and specific spiritual qualities in particular. This pushes people between the Life-pillars of Pain and particular. This pushes people between the Life-pillars of Pain and Pleasure up towards the 'beatific balance' of Perfect Peace Profound which equates these exactly.

Emotion is the correct complement of Intellect, and those two faculties should always be kept in harness with each other if a straight course is intended along the Path of Life. This is very highly important. Employment of either Intellect or Emotion unilaterally always leads to spiritual trouble, and correct balance of both is regarded as a most vital Magical operation. Treated as a team, the qualities are invaluable and indispensable, but allowed to run wild they can be disastrous.

Unguarded emotions in Magical practice are a very real hazard, and a large proportion of early training is usually devoted to emotion employment and equation, balancing emotions so they can be kept hold of. Theoretically, emotions are used to contact many Inner sources of direct energy supply, and Intellect is applied to direct and dispose the power provided. Magic utilised irresponsibly is a potent producer of emotions, particularly in young people. Unless correct channelling is also available, far more harm than good is likely. Emotion, however, remains a principal provider of those 'raw' energies needed especially during early stages of Magical practice. Hence the construction of an adequate 'emotion apparatus' is a valuable procedure of primal Magical training.

Motivation

All motivation goes back to a primarary 'need to BE', and this diversifies through all Life-levels until there are so many varied needs and drives that they conflict with one another if improperly related in common areas. Our bodies alone have motivations coming from mineral, vegetable, and animal levels which all have to be mutually equated until we can begin living with them to any degree of success at all. Above animal levels, our metaphysical motivations come from every Self-state of spiritual being insisting on survival.

Magically, the only sensible thing to do is make all these motivations subservient to our 'One NEED' of Individuation into spiritual Selfhood. Otherwise the constant conflicts going on within our 'invisible empires' will exhaust us by attrition if nothing else. Unless a clear line of consciousness connects our manifold motivations and 'centres them in', so to speak, relative to a pivotal purpose-point, Life is liable to get very difficult for

Memory

Strictly speaking, 'memory' is intentional conscious contact with 'stored' life experiences or information either in one's own brain cells or any other available supply. Theoretically we inherit all 'memories' of every ancestor with our genes. Theoretically also one should be able to project these forward along Inner levels. The issue at stake is how from our 'here–now' we might influence the course of such deep consciousness to our ultimate spiritual advantage. Through our genes, we should be able to remember all our ancestry and contact the Inner epitomisation of their Life-experiences. By spiritual equivalents, we may 'link in' with pre-and post-incarnationary processes not as pictorial representations, but as pure awareness translatable in symbolic or other terms.

One of the chief reasons why old-time Initiates attached so much importance to genealogical tables with all the 'begats' was because when ritually recited these had an effect of extending an Identity-sense past personality levels into more spiritual spheres. So did poetic identifications with imagery such as: 'I was a hart in the forest and the tree in which its horns were caught. I was a cloud in the lonely sky, and the shadow it cast on the cornfield beneath.' Magical memory has to work in much wider fields than mere brain memories.

Equally important to memory is the faculty of clearing consciousness so as to remove from any Selfstore whatever might have harmful effects on future progress.

Manipulations of memory in order to improve Individuation are part of Magical practice. A great aim also in Magic is to transcend purely personal memories altogether and gain access to Cosmic memory banks. Mild examples of this may be found with what was once called 'psychometry', or an ability for reading metaphysical 'memory impressions' associated with inanimate objects, especially stones. The use of ESP can allow one person to read the memories of another. Once memories limited to a single physical brain are exceeded by Magical means, a very wide field of discovery awaits awakeners in Inner dimensions of living.

Learning

Learning is regarded as an ability of life-appreciation at all levels. To be useful in any degree it has to be backed by memory and spearheaded by interest. It is for more than feeding information into computer banks of consciousness and recalling this to order. True learning involves a faculty of some identification with what is learned. This means absorption of subject into Self, analogically to Self-absorption into an Ultimate Awareness. It is a vital part of the perfection process.

Magic postulates that humans increase learning by Inner contacts with superior sources of intelligence on higher Life-levels, not necessarily by specific conscious instruction, but mainly through opening out areas of awareness in line with human intentions of advancement. In other words, the knowledge already exists in different dimensions of living, and we simply catch up with it in ours – if we can.

Learning is the Inner equivalent of eating and drinking. Our bodies must feed or die, and our Selves must learn or cease living. Magic treats learning as 'Inner alimentation', necessitating correct choice and diet. It is considered very important that learning should call for equal and more care than physical feeding. Just as food metabolises in our bodies and builds them into whatever they are, so does what we learn metabolise in our minds and souls, making us Inwardly into the Self-states we assume. The related functions are very parallel indeed, and Magic makes much of this both symbolically and practically.

Magic especially recognise the extreme importance of continuing with learning all through Life. Refusal to learn amounts to spiritual starvation, and mental malnutrition can be a severe complaint indeed. Most of all, Magic specialises in learning not so much from externals of any kind, but by looking inside one's own Self. Many Magical formulas are designed for that very purpose. They all amount to much the same message, which could perhaps be translated as something like: 'You don't have to depend on somebody telling you or seeing it in a book. Go inside yourself and dig out what you need from there. That will also lead you to whatever externals are related which you may need.'

Mind-Body Relationship

Here, the Magical view is that Body with its brain constitutes an animal in its own right, deserving the care and attention as a creature for which its attached Individuant is responsible to a common Creative Consciousness. The ideal should be to establish a relationship of friendly confidence between each end of the partnership. Mutual recognition of each other's faculties, functions and potentialities is essential for a good working agreement between Mind and Body. Magic aims to inculcate such an awareness and develop it with advantages for both ends of entity.

In Magic, it is very necessary to realise that bodies are temporary focal accommodators of Mind in these material dimensions of Life. As a creature, the body has an instinctive awareness of its own. At physical death this either breaks up altogether and reverts to origins, or it may be absorbed into and integrate with surviving spiritual principles which it served faithfully during incarnation. This is how immortality works: the awareness of an entity withdrawing its focal projections from one Life-level into the wider field behind it. That in turn is focal in relation to levels behind it again, and so on until Ultimation.

Man has to learn how to live apart from embodiment, yet in close friendship with physical associations. That is one great value of fellowship with other animal dependents. This should teach us how to appreciate our bodies and what they mean for us. It ought also to remind us that the body can be a dangerous animal if ill-treated or not properly dealt with. Once good relationships can be established between the body and mind of an Individuant, Life becomes better for both, and many Magical methods are concerned with creating such a happy condition.

Death

With regard to this event of universal concern, the broad teachings of the Path of Magic are possibly the simplest of all. Fundamentally we are entities of pure energy temporarily inhabiting animal-type bodies in the biological range of existence which have very limited lives. Those bodies die, decompose, and are elementally recycled through natural channels. Assuming our entities have not evolved to a point of living entirely apart from physical projection, then we generally reincarnate to continue the course of our spiritual development. In ancient times, Celts believed this so strongly that instances were noted of some who actually lent money to friends for repayment in some future incarnation as cash or favours – possibly a graceful way of covering what was intended as a pure gift, but in any case indicative of faith extending beyond bodily bounds.

Ultimate immortality, however, is not considered automatic, but depends entirely on individual intentions and actions spread over a wide spiritual spectrum. In every being exists the 'Original Intention' of the Supreme Life Spirit indicating the cosmic condition of such a being if it ever became 'Perfect'. That is to say that there is a Divine Intention of Ultimate Perfection behind all 'Being' as a 'Whole', and each individual item of that Whole has its own degree thereof integral to itself, what used to be called 'the Will of God within oneself'. That, and that alone, leads us through Life towards true Immortality by a process of Individuation.

As mortal humans in our present imperfect life state we have two mainstream options. We may follow the 'Perfection-pattern' imprinted in our spiritual genetics and individuate towards our own Ultimate state of spiritual Entity in 'PERFECT PEACE PROFOUND'. Conversely, we may try breaking away from this pattern and setting up apparently on our own in a state of 'pseudoself', which steadily separates from 'Universal Life' until its eventual extinction as entity and reabsorption into the Life-cycle as raw energy. Put in crude old-fashioned metaphor, we either 'Live with God or die with the Devil'. Both processes take a very long time indeed in human terms, but they go on continually in the Cosmos. We are normally instinctively rather than consciously aware of this, but as we evolve we become more and more conscious of it, and increasingly able to influence its course volitionally. In fact a major aim of initiation on this Path is to train and develop this faculty advantageously.

During earthlife we build up a sort of artificial, personal pseudo-self which should die a natural death subsequently to our bodies. Theoretically, our imperfect self states should become 'absorbed back' into successively higher levels of Life until Ultimate Entity is reached. Failure to perfect this in practice leads to reincarnation or reprojection into higher than human biological conditions of consciousness. We simply become as and what we make of our own beings. To that extent, both 'Heavens' and 'Hells' as states of awareness have indeed reality for all sharing experiences of consciousness to any degree of those conditions. Both are purely self states, and no one gets us into or out of either except ourselves, however long it may take us to realise this and live accordingly.

Therefore the word 'death' on this particular Path is purely a relative one signifying cessation of function along any specific line of living and redeployment of energy otherwise. Everything depends for us on our sense of identification. The more we 'identify' purely with our physical bodies, then the more spiritually traumatic their deaths will be to us, unless a merciful unconsciousness supervenes, and 'Inner reawakening' becomes a very gradual process. The more we learn to identify with our spiritual structure, the less losing our bodies will bother us. It should be noted that neither 'Heavens' nor 'Hells' are regarded as any kind of ultimate condition for advancing Individuants, but purely as 'temporary accommodations', so to speak, for souls in such states of relation with the Spirit of Life.

'Death' in any sense of ultimate finality can be considered only as an eventual total loss of individual identity, which is normally determined by the entity concerned of its own accord. The pros and cons of this are quite beyond discussion within limits imposed here. The main issue is that the death of a physical body should be regarded as one incident in a very long chain of conscious life, whereas the death of an individual soul is to be deplored as a loss of Life as a Whole which cannot be replaced by any means so readily. A truly dead individual is a contradiction in terms, for the genuinely dead are altogether nonexistent. An individual apart from a physical body is *alive*, whatever state of being that entity may exist in. It is very important to realise this distinction between Life and death in relation to ourselves as principles of being and nonbeing.

It can scarcely be overstressed that this concept of Life-continuity through all levels of Cosmic Creation is virtually central to this Tradition. Unless our lives are realised to reach very far beyond the limits and death of one biological body, nothing else of the Tradition has the slightest meaning whatsoever. Furthermore, no amount of external teaching, offered opinions, or even spectacular demonstrations can really bring about such a realisation for anyone. That is something we all have to reach for ourselves within ourselves entirely, by means of the relations we make with Life itself. All that this or any other Tradition can do to help is to provide integrals for people to build their own beliefs and experiences with. The Tradition does indeed appear to fulfil exactly that function for its mortal followers who have made themselves vital to its spiritual structure.

Psychopathology

Magically, psychopathology can be seen only as faulty relationships among the Body-Mind-Soul-Spirit combination comprising a human entity. Causes and remedies are quite beyond this basic introduction. States of Inner unbalance cannot be fairly described as 'abnormal' in the sense that mass-average humans must necessarily be the norm. The only 'Norm' (so far as this exists) recognised by Magical Initiates is the most direct degree of relationship between the centre lines of Body-Mind-Soul-Spirit stages of both individual and collective Mankind.

Since this varies so greatly, it could be possible for a mass of 'abnormals' to consider a few 'normals' among them as quite crazy. Magic has no interest in enforcing a rubber-stamp artificial 'abnormal-normality' upon anyone. Its chief concern is with establishing conditions of balanced relationships among integers of individuals and their collective Cosmic circles.

Perception

As an animal body and brain perceives by its sensory organs, so does our spiritual sensorium make relationships with environing and internal energies by equivalent Inner sensors. Again, as with physical sense organs which we must train to function well in our external world, these Inner 'estimators' take a good deal of training and practice for accurate working and coordination. Many exercises are devoted to that purpose.

This is one reason why Magic makes use of symbology so very widely. It is about the most reliable 'converter of consciousness' into terms relevant at all Life-levels. Moreover, it enables perception to be directed and controlled. Literally, perception means 'by taking in', and signifies an admission of anything to at least 'outer courts' of consciousness for examination. That would be the Magical definition of perception: a sort of pre-entry consideration of anything prior to acceptance or rejection of its significance.

In old Magical workings, this was symbolised by an external circle traced around the inner area into which 'spirits' could be called for examination as to suitability for whatever purpose motivated the whole operation – a sort of preliminary interview as it were. If wanted, these 'spirits' could be directed accordingly, and if not, dismissed forthwith. Making up an actual Inner 'perception perimeter' around Individuants is part of Magical psychological practice.

Social Relationships

Magical Initiates are seldom noted as great seekers of human society for its own sake. Nor are they antisocial by nature. The general pattern is that of Individuation out of Mass-Mankind, and pioneering Paths for others to follow in their own ways if they will.

As a rule, Magical practice often begins with Lodges, Temples, Groups and so forth, but eventually Initiates must progress on their own Inner Paths as these open up within themselves. Therefore very few really close contacts on ordinary levels are normally made. Initiates are not advised to intrude themselves into incompatible company, or court any kind of publicity whatever in connection with their Inner activities. In fact any television, radio, or press appearance by people claiming some special spiritual status or authority should be very highly suspect at once by those knowing what appertains to authenticity in these affairs. True Initiates do not advertise themselves as such in any way whatever, or even imply by hints or other means that they are at all different from other humans. It is strictly forbidden to do anything like this under commonly accepted ethical codes of conduct.

There is no actual injunction against Initiates making any social relationships they please with other people, *providing* these do not interfere with processes of Individuation. Most Initiates follow personal patterns of involvement with others up to a point, then withdraw quietly from social contacts periodically and switch over to spiritual ones for a while, something on the lines of a 'retreat'. Some organise this rather rigidly by daily, weekly, monthly, quarterly and annual schedules, while others just 'take a breather' at need. All would acknowledge that it is only their Inner periods of spiritual contacts which enable them to live and work in this world with sanity and stability.

Sooner or later, Initiates of every spiritual system are forced to face the fact that they cannot possibly fulfil all their needs from or with other humans only. Human associations will take them so far and no further. To pass that point, they have to seek companionship from other Life-levels, and nothing else will answer their spiritual purposes and problems.

Cognitive Processes

A major Magical method here is Inner imagery with creative consciousness controlled by intention – that is to say, treating consciousness as the basic material of an art, and making what is willed with it. Symbols have been described as the tools or implements of this 'trade'.

That is why Masonry, for instance, relates with symbolic tools of the building trade. The significance is to work with consciousness comparable to that of any skilled craftsman dealing with whatever materials and processes are appropriate for specific purposes. There is also an implication that if as much training, application, discipline and other essentials were put into Magical practice as there must be for normal employments, Magic would become a much more practical proposition.

New Faculties

Properly speaking, humans do not so much gain any new faculties as develop inherent Inner potentials. We have only one real faculty, that of being. All whats, whys and hows are extensions of this. As individuals progress along their Paths, cognition centres tend to rise, as it were, from physical to spiritual status. So our sense of values alters accordingly. As insight increases, knowledge is acquired by 'whole understanding' rather than through serialised efforts.

Altered States of Consciousness

There are only two ways of altering states of consciousness: from Within by intention and ability, or from without by intrusions and impositions. A main aim of Magic is to so cultivate the first method that it controls or equates effects of the second. This allows the 'Central Consciousness' coming from True-Self level of Spirit to function more fully in such an altered area. That in turn should result in fractional changes of human awareness towards more perfect states of Life.

Therefore, in the higher echelons of the Western Magical Tradition, employment of chemical hallucinogens, hypnosis and the like is strictly prohibited for altering states of consciousness. It is considered essential that the individual always be in command of the consciousness involved with any spiritual situation. That is why all exercises, customs, practices and so forth are deliberately geared towards training Individuants to alter consciousness for themselves. Artificial aids are regarded as secondary and subservient to the will-work concerned with such changes.

The Path Itself

The authentic Western Way of Magic usually follows a general pattern. Applicants or candidates with interests awakened deeply enough to reach real Inner sources of guidance are normally dealt with something like this: from some established circle of consciousness operative in the Tradition, individuals are supplied with basic symbologies of spiritual significance, informed of disciplines and procedures for combining these into relevant structures, put into contact with Inner agencies of intelligence, then allowed to grow their own ways within that force-framework.

All this is not necessarily carried out in any physical Lodge, Temple or anything of that nature. That is actually somewhat rare. A noticeable difference between Eastern and Western Traditions is an apparent absence of 'Teachers', gurus, or whatever in the latter. This is especially so nowadays, when all initial information is lying around awaiting *discriminating* attention from interested Individuants. Formerly the various 'primal points' could be imparted only orally in carefully closed circles of incarnate Initiates, or else learned instinctively from Inner sources. That often took a whole incarnation to absorb. Now, the symbology and instructions can be put into plain print or other very ordinary ways – except, of course, for private and confidential matters applying only within circles entitled to regard these as purely 'family affairs'. It must be fully realised that the onus is squarely placed on the spiritual shoulders of would-be Western Traditionalists to pick up its threads for themselves from the available keys placed before them, and follow these inside themselves until they encounter the experiences they seek on Inner Life-levels.

Starting Point

There is no starting point except one's own emergence into Existence as an entity. On ordinary levels of Life here on Earth, however, there does come a point of reaching realisation right into incarnate awareness that one truly belongs to the Western Magical Tradition. This might be regarded as the starting point of each incarnation, where anyone picks up links which lead back to a sense of *belonging* – as, for example, one feels states of age, sex, nationality or other distinctive status. Usually this happens via some symbolic impact which makes contact between ordinary consciousness and deep-down recognition of spiritual realities. A word, a place, an object perhaps, almost any symbol is likely to act as a key. Once this occurs, there will come a positive Inner certainty that an affinity exists with the Western Magical Tradition. There will be an unmistakable sense of 'This is ME.' The rest will follow quite naturally.

This may or may not be encouraged or enhanced by efficient ritual psychodramatics, assuming that competent practitioners of this art can be found. Nevertheless such is not entirely necessary for initiating anyone associating with the Western Way. It is an odd fact that so many inexperienced people who are at the stage of being 'attracted to the Occult' have an almost pathetic belief or expectation that if only some marvellous Master or 'Teacher-Figure' would consent to put them through an impressive form of ceremony, they would forthwith become altered and amazing persons, full of wisdom and other remarkable qualities. So much nonsense is supposed of initiation ceremonies by those knowing nothing of them that they have only themselves to blame for anything going wrong. Perhaps it may be as well to deal with this issue here.

Any real initiation ceremony is exactly what the phrase means, a ceremonious beginning of something, in this case, the commencement of specific spiritual courses of conduct. Such affairs can have a marked psychological effect upon subjects, *providing* adequate preparation has already created a condition of readiness for effects to take place. Not otherwise. All that any ceremony does is to act as a symbol linking very deep spiritual Self-states with ordinary conscious levels, so that the candidate may realise his own Inner potentials and is therefore likely to live accordingly. Unless such a prestate is already operative, no ritual initiation will be of the slightest use whatever. In any case, it is perfectly possible to arrive at an Inner awakening quite naturally of one's own accord. One mildly witty description of the difference between this and a ceremonial initiation is that the latter is like a friend waking one up with a cup of tea, and the former is like waking up by oneself and putting a kettle on. Either way, one still wakes up.

So whoever bewails his misfortune in never meeting great Masters and mighty Secret Orders willing to initiate him into Mysteries of Magic merely reveals total ignorance of actualities. In point of fact, putting unprepared and inadequate people through inaccurate and badly presented initiation ceremonies has probably done more harm in occult circles than many less serious follies. A whole thesis could well be written on that one point alone.

Intellectual Appreciation of Path

This is mainly a matter of reading available material, making contacts with the oral Tradition where possible, and forming opinions out of collected items of consciousness. A very great deal of time, money and effort can be spent on this pastime quite pointlessly apart from intellectual entertainment. Many people spend lifetimes at it and little else. They 'shop around' from one system to another exploring something of each and gaining personal proficiency in none. It is always best to adopt some single system in particular and work with that until one is able to transcend it into auto-operative Inner areas.

The major system emerging as most suitable for present Western spiritual development in the Magical Tradition seems definitely that which is based on the Tree of Life and Circle-Cross symbology. From these fundamantals, any branch of the Western Inner Way may be entered and its Magic operated. The Tree of Life has mainly intellectual appeal, and the Circle-Cross has emotional attractions.

A combination of both is thus ideal for a framework of Western Magical workings.

Emotional Appreciation of Path

The Western Magical Way is superlative in ritual and psycho-dramatic operations involving the deepest emotional levels of Life. Ritual is probably the most perfect tool which the Tradition has forged to suit all spiritual needs. Whether the simplest or most sumptuous type of rite, the West has brought ritualism to a high point of perfection.

Ritual is an activity and participatory practice in which all concerned can combine for a common cause. It might be described as a concert of consciousness through symbolic instrumentation. As an organ of occult energy operative between human and associated entities, ritual is Man's oldest and maybe most trustworthy Magical ally. Ideally, each ritualist should be capable of constructing individual rites from basic principles. Great spiritual satisfaction is possible, however, by working existent rites of reliable form, where these are obtainable.[1]

Successful management of ritual procedures is a highly skilled art demanding considerable practice and patient training. To suppose anyone could merely say some words, make vague gestures, and Magic happens would be utterly absurd, to put it very mildly. Unless external symbology can be used to raise and release actual associated Inner energies, no ritual will prove any more effective than amateur theatrical exercises.

Dangers of the Path

There are many dangers on all Paths of Life, and the Western Magical Way is no exception. The worst danger is definitely *imbalance* in every imaginable direction. For this reason, most of the early advised exercises are concerned with poise, stability and rapid recovery of Inner equilibrium. Then, exaggerations of character deficiencies are to be expected. It is a fact that frequently after initiation ceremonies there are sudden 'flare-ups' of outrageous behaviour in the subject, analogous to inoculation reactions. Also symptoms of paranoia may develop. All these possibilities arise from spiritual structural weaknesses existing already in the people concerned. What Magic does is apply Inner stresses which will naturally show up flaws lying dormant in the individuals themselves. In fairness it must also be said that Magic may also be used to remedy those very failings.

Overenthusiasm and overconfidence are very common dangers. Again and again, adherence to a 'Middle Path' has to be emphasised and practised until this becomes second nature. A chief hazard especially of the Magical Path is breakdown of mental and physical health if safeguards are ignored. Diseases are nonetheless real because of psychosomatic origins. Most of these troubles arise through misuse of Magic applied to mind or body, and are traceable to wrong intentions, disregard of calculable risks, carelessness, or just lack of common sense. Genuine accidents can occur as with everything else, but the majority of ills through Magic are invited ones. For example, those who poison themselves with chemical drug compounds and exhaust their physical energies while contorting their consciousness into painfully unnatural knots can scarcely complain when the account for all this has to be paid. Their mistreatment of Magic deserves small sympathy. Magic makes its own retribution on misusers.

It is also true with Magic that there are dangers arising from misinterpretation of intelligence gained from Inner sources, or acceptance of influences from antihuman entities. These latter were once called 'temptations of the devil'. By whatever name they are termed, they amount to pressures and persuasions contrary to our best spiritual interests. These affect humans in general, of course, but more especially those who have awakened Inner susceptibilities by Magic or similar means, yet have neglected to take even commonsense precautions against ill usage. This leaves them extremely vulnerable in sensitive Inner areas without adequate protection.

The upshot of this results very often in troubles coming from sheer gullibility, deceived Inner senses, and plain credulity due to inaccurate Self-estimates. Human beings enjoy flattery and Pseudo-Self aggrandisement. They like supposing they have been singled out for special spiritual messages, and are delighted to discover an awakened ability to make contact with other than human types of consciousness. This makes them liable to any kind of confidence trick or subtle manipulation they may meet with from immediate Inner quarters which are not necessarily in favour of human progress. In other words, they become common or garden-variety suckers – unless and until they learn better by sad experience. It is almost amazing how those who are too clever to be cheated by fellow mortals fall for the same hoary take-ins when these are slid over the edges of Inner dimensions in their directions.

Most of the 'awful warnings' about dangers of Magic are uttered by non-Magical observers unable to distinguish between carts and horses. It is not so much that Magic is of great spiritual danger, but that spiritually dangerous people are so liable to suppose that Magic might be a wonderful weapon for their worst intentions. So many stupid, wicked, irresponsible, and other inadequate people are attracted to Magic for the wrong reasons that it is scarcely surprising that their mismanagement of it is apt to make a very bad impression upon un-Magically minded people. Nevertheless it should definitely be seen that such misfits are fundamentally bad to begin with, and Magic is simply their means of making themselves worse. They could have done as much by other means such as religion, politics, or anything else. Another thing we must remember is that the worst examples of Magic gone wrong get all the publicity, while spiritual successes normally remain secret in this world. There are no dangers in Magic that do not already exist in its practitioners.

The most sensible safeguard against misuse of Magic is adoption of and abidance by some clear spiritual standard of values against which all may be measured while decisions on energy applications are being made. Setting up and making real relationships with such a standard is a 'first and foremost' in authentic circles of Western Magic. Probably the best-recognised and most practical of these standards is that of the Tree of Life.

Techniques of Path

Most of these are described in every book of mental and spiritual exercises. The essential elements are: understanding of requirements, dedicated discipline and regularity of practice. Rituals combining physical, mental, and spiritual activities are normally in general usage. There should be no 'dead letters' in Western ritualism, but only living experiences within a controlled framework of consciousness. Every system within the Tradition has whole collections of such practices and performances which they usually reveal to followers as they seem ready to benefit by them. The vast majority of such 'secrets' are accessible in any public library nowadays. What makes them special is knowing just what will be right for any individual at particular points of his progress. It is the planning and layout of apparently quite simple factors which differentiates between an initiated expert and a dilettante. One knows how to do this, and the other does not.

Techniques of early training among responsible circles in the Western Way seem disappointingly simple or inadequate. They are specially designed along two main lines: to act as 'character revealers', and to awaken the applicant's Inner attention, which is then directed into responsive spiritual areas already 'staffed' by nonincarnates capable of dealing with exactly such types of contact – not by any spectacular or obvious objective means, but by arranging a return force-flow calculated to stimulate whatever point in the applicant seems likely to make a right Self-response. Whether or not this works depends on the inquirer's ability to answer the Inner impetus correctly.

Let us take an actual example of this. Students or candidates are told to do several quite simple things every day which differ only slightly, though significantly, from their ordinary living routines. The idea is to link spiritual progress with human activities, while initiating a gradual direction of attention away from merely mundane matters toward Inner areas of Magical importance. In addition to these acts, applicants are given a basic philosophy to follow, and a standard (often the Tree of Life) to set up for themselves.

The simple activities are frequently these: first, five minutes' meditation in the morning as soon after waking as possible. At commencement, these meditations are free choice, later going on to graduated subjects and symbols. Very brief tabulated notes are made afterwards on crucial points, such as clarity of concentration, drift of attention, unusual impressions received, and so forth. At noon, a very brief but intense 'Inner Call' is sent out. This is simply a momentary focus of all available Inner energy directed towards Divinity for aid and assistance through the Powers of the Path. Some verbal formula such as: 'Lighten Thou my Way' may accompany this. It is meant only to be a 'flash contact' for one precise instant. In the evening not more than ten lines on the 'subject of the day' have to be written into what is called a 'Magical Diary'. This has to be confined strictly to subject, and be compressed into the smallest symbolic consciousness possible, though not in shorthand. To get this compression, a good method is taking a whole page of written material, condensing that to a paragraph, the paragraph to a sentence, and then to a word, finally finishing in a wordless awareness of meaning. By reversing this process, ideas may be obtained out of Nil which will gradually expand and unfold until maximum perception is reached.

Last thing at night just before going to sleep comes the 'rapid reverse review'. This consists of running *backwards* mentally and quickly through remembered events of the day, if possible going to sleep while doing so. The purpose of this is to push serialised consciousness out of its mundane groove, and also there is an aim of 'event equation' which has an effect of balancing out long-term likelihoods, otherwise known as 'converting karma'. Dealing with events of the day this way tends to balance one instead of letting long-term, unfinished business accumulate.

All this sounds very simple and undemanding. To persist with it day after day as routine procedure for a year and more may not sound very profitable. Yet it works for Westerners who have to earn livings in this world while trying to earn rights of living away from it. There are other methods, of course, but all depend on the same principles of fidelity, devotion, and genuine spiritual humility which has nothing to do with masochism at all. It is simply a quiet confidence that the Emptiness in one's own entity will become filled with whatever is most fitting for the sake of true Selfhood in Perfect Peace Profound. In the words of an old initiation ritual:

Q. In what do you place your trust?
A. I trust in Truth alone.
Q. What is Truth?
A. [keeps silent]

Technique Temptations

In most Traditions, but particularly in the West, people are tempted to play around with practices regardless of abilities for working them properly. Mostly they only make a mess, or get themselves grubby like children who interfere with materials of adult art. Physically grownup humans seldom see their Inner conditions of spiritual childhood, and they behave with infantile abilities as they did during early days on Earth. It takes more than one human lifetime to reach spiritual maturity, and in this world we are a very much mixed-up assortment of Inner age groups.

Because desire to dress up and act like adults is a normal part of childhood, ritual Magic has an automatic appeal for those unable to handle it on higher levels. Playing with Magic is very different from working with it. Luckily, most muddlers with Magic seldom come to much harm unless they insist on releasing real evil from inside themselves or willingly act as agents for ill-intentioned entities capable of using their Magical efforts for malicious purposes. The real danger of things going wrong occurs in groups of virile energetic youngsters who get together and, as they believe, 'make Magic'. Their sex energies are an entirely natural supply of 'wild' force which can be tapped fairly easily from Inside while they are throwing Magic around so freely.

This is actually where a good deal of harm comes through misused Magic. By itself, there would be relatively few results beyond an ebullience of energy something like a geyser or other natural phenomena exploding happily. The evil lies entirely in the deliberate exploitation of the energy by 'baddies' who are able to divert and apply it for their own vicious purposes otherwise. There is nothing especially new about this, but it could be particularly nasty in modern times because of our recent relationships with Energy to such extremely dangerous degrees. This topic indeed deserves very careful study by competent investigators.

Much muddle in Western Magic comes from people trying to work its 'big bits' before gaining proficiency with small ones. Overestimation of personal importance is a fairly common temptation leading in that direction. When would-be Magi learn to look for real powers in the least evident factors of Life, they might find something they snatched at and lost so often in sizes too big for them to handle. Maybe too many of them lose altogether, or never gain at all, one most precious power of very mighty Magical import: a genuine sense of humour and fun!

How to Contact the Living Tradition

There is only one real way to contact the living Tradition of Western Magic: live it oneself and become part of it. This may not sound a very encouraging answer, but it is the truth. Let us face the issue squarely.

If anyone seriously expects to meet up with incredible 'Secret Brotherhoods of Magic' or the like outside the pages of occult fiction, he may as well forget the fantasy unless it amuses him to maintain it. Small secret and semisecret Lodges and Societies do indeed exist by the dozen, and fade out again. Some may, or may not, operate contact points within the Tradition, but none has exclusive entry rights or the power to prevent a single entitled entrant from 'belonging' to what amounts to a spiritual birthright. Whether to spend time, money, and effort on membership with esoteric 'culture clubs' must remain the decision of individual seekers. The thing to remember is that these may indeed be part of the Western Tradition, but it is much bigger than all of them by itself.

It is possible to encounter bits of the living Tradition almost everywhere: in books, conversations, pictures, buildings, designs, music – all over the place. One can make a fascinating Treasure Hunt or Grail Quest, following the Tradition around from point to point and trying to connect up a complete picture. This might take a whole lifetime, yet only provide interest. It would not make inquirers part of the Tradition themselves.

To discover the Tradition along living lines, one factor is essential: selective working with its fundamental frequencies *only*. This means strict spiritual discipline in working exclusively with Western symbology and terminology as well as employing its methods and customs. For instance, that calls for closing down all immediate channels leading directly to Oriental or other Traditions. These would still be contacted through common Inner meeting points, but because they are not appropriate to the Western Inner Way, they have to be cleared from the Paths of whoever would follow the Western Inner Way faithfully. A Tradition is a Tradition, and must be kept true to itself, or it dies out in the end.

As an example, it would be impossible to work true Western Magic while still employing Tibetan prayer wheels, African masks, Chinese drums, Egyptian jewellery, Asian costume, and a muddled medley of symbology regardless of derivation or Inner association. Then again, rituals fudged up from Tantric terms, invocations of Egyptian deities, bits of medieval misprints, and assorted junk from similar sources are not, and never will be, part of the true Western Way. To take items properly belonging elsewhere and force them into uneasy association with each other is simply incongruous and silly. Yet so many make that very mistake.

Any reputable or reliable group of initiated individuals trying to represent the Western Tradition in its best light has to insist that applicants sacrifice all such 'un-Western' associations before admission – not from any kind of prejudice or aversion, but simply for the sake of keeping clear contacts along specific spiritual lines of development. A really strict set of Initiates who knew what they were doing would have to refuse admission to anyone in a state of 'mixed Magic'. It would be just as foolish to include such incompatibles among their company as it would be to mix unsuitable chemicals together.

So if anyone is seriously seeking contact with the living Western Tradition of Magic, let this be approached for itself, by itself, and as itself alone. Otherwise it will just elude all pursuit in a very maddening fashion, leaving an impression that it does not exist at all. There is only about one really sound piece of advice to offer anyone genuinely looking for the Inner Way of the West. It is this: go down inside yourself as deeply as you can, and try to reach *your own* Western spiritual roots. No one else's. Yours alone. Never mind what other people do in different parts of the world, or even next door. You are not they, but only yourself. So dig down into your very depths and find whatever you can of a fundamental Life-faith. If this looks shaky or uncertain, then remember you weren't much to look at a few moments after conception, so do not worry if your beliefs seem crude or tenuous. If you believe you have found nothing, then hold on to that Nothing as hard as you can. Something will have to emerge from it in the end, because Everything comes out of Nothing.

Realise you came into this world through a long chain of Westernising people. Their bodies may be dead and gone long since, but their spiritual legacy is still very much alive in you genetically. You can accept this and live happily with it, or you can try to deny it and live in a perpetual quarrel with your own Inmost nature. That last course makes trouble for anyone.

Believe in yourself and your inherent ability to reach a spiritual Tradition already existing in you, however much this may be obscured by accretions and importations from everywhere else. It is your own rightful heritage, so if you want it enough, then bend down to your roots and pick it up.

Do not be afraid to ask inside yourself for spiritual help from others whose consciousness connects with yours deep down. Call clearly, call confidently, and you will be heard. Just don't demand an instant reply in English or hard cash. That would cut off communication forthwith. If you use verbal symbology yourself, keep this very sincere and simple, such as: 'Let me live as I belong.' Keep sending this out repetitively like a radio call sign. Then keep quiet and very still. Try to follow the silence Inside until it speaks in its own way. Keep anything that comes to you secret. Remember the Four Maxims of Western Magic: Know, Dare, Will, Keep Silent. Those are all meant to be observed as One.

The 'Be-it-yourself' Tradition

In bygone times, little or none of any Tradition came from books or written records. Only parts of it were transmitted orally. So where did the rest come from? Directly from within Initiates themselves by contact with higher levels of Inner consciousness. Furthermore, this is where all truly spiritual teaching *should* come from. We rely far too much nowadays on writings, records, mass media, and mechanistic means of bulk-storing information and computerised systems of collating it. This is having an effect of making us rely too little on our own powers of Inner perception, which means a loss of spiritual linkage with Life.

It was for that reason that Initiates of former days insisted on solitary Self-searches in quest of Inner Identity and a sound Life-faith. The sojourn of Jesus in the desert and the meditation of Siddhartha Buddha beneath his bo tree are examples. One way or another, all Initiates expected to undergo such an experience not only as a psychophysical actuality, but as a principle applied to living consistently. In the West particularly, the Druid system forbade learning from books past a certain point, and insisted on oral and meditational communication with other people and Nature. Most spiritual systems had formal bans of some kind on writing details of their Tradition down. No great Teachers wrote messages for posterity. Certainly Jesus left no written inspirations, and judging from his followers' behaviour over the centuries, it may have been a mistake to have written what survives of his reputed speaking.

None of this arose from prejudice against literature or unnecessary 'secrecy-mongering'. It was entirely to emphasise and ensure the importance of sustaining spiritual Traditions through individual relationships with the Infinite, rather than by ready-made recitations from previous people's findings. Eventually the utility of recording routine run-of-the-mill information was accepted, but the real 'live' spiritual side of any system continues to be communicated through purely Inner channels of consciousness. Learning what others have said or done is very valuable *providing* this stimulates or encourages souls to make their own ways from there along the Path of Inner Life. *That* is the only way the Western Tradition may be truly entered. Concentrating on the Key-Symbols will always be the best plan of asking admission. In the Western Magical Mysteries, those are the Rod, Sword, Cup, Shield and Cord. 'Five are the Symbols at your Door', as the old and most Magical song says. Those Symbols relate with both the Circle-Cross and the Tree of Life, so should be seen in that kind of Light.

Symbol Working

The fundamentals of Western magical ritualism are concerned with practical symbology specifically applied in and to the spiritual areas of activity. This basically means that the operating magician must learn how to make himself and his consciousness alter intentionally in character according to the symbol being used. That is entirely a matter of practice in what is essentially the acquired art of magic.

Thus the only real value of magical symbols is for 'calling up' or 'raising' *in the magician himself*, and consequently in his whole field of influence, whatever particular qualities or abilities those symbols demonstrate by themselves. Such a value is actually beyond all ordinary calculations and should on no account whatever be underestimated or treated casually. Symbols are virtually the literal

Keys to an Inner Kingdom which Man makes for himself by means of Magic.

For example, to use a consecrated Cup and actually become in and as oneself a living vessel of Love embracing Entity at every level of Life from Divine to human and all lesser beings. To take up a Sword and focus every available quality of keenness, flexibility and pointed purpose. To raise a Rod, and firmly uphold whatever spiritual standards are accepted as an authority in all life activities. To shelter with the Shield of a living faith in oneself and one's True Identity, from all adversities and oppositions we encounter on Earth. Those are Magical practicalities of the highest possible order.

Then there is the symbology of working in a Magic Circle. One way or another we all have to live and work in circles of some kind, but a Magic Circle is one constructed of careful and systematically arranged patterns of consciousness relating the magician and his environs of Inner energies with a maximum of meaning according to intention. In olden times this was often done by writing various names of God functions or antievil signs in a circle around the operator. Those, of course, were worth neither more nor less than the faith of an operator in their efficacy. The chalk marks did nothing of themselves unless they inspired someone to create their meanings around himself as an actual construction of consciousness and intentional arrangement of his own nature. That was the real Magic Circle.

A modern initiate of Magic would make a 'power perimeter' around himself consisting of specific spiritual qualities categorised consciously in relation to himself and all other living entities. This could be diagrammed or symbolically traced in what might nowadays be considered a 'circuit layout'. There are many possible designs for such a 'Cosmic Compass', but a good reliable one is constructible from the Circle-Cross formula of: 'In the Name of the Wisdom, the Love, the Justice, and the Infinite Mercy of the One Eternal Spirit, AMEN.' These are the four Principles or qualities directly relating Humanity and Divinity. So the Circle is made with one Principle (or some sign thereof) at each quarter, the One Eternal Spirit (or acceptable signification thereof) around the outer edge, and the AMEN at the centre.

To make such a Circle effective, the magician in the middle must raise in himself and project intentionally the four basic qualities of its quarters, which have to harmonise as a single surrounding constant of consciousness. This not only amounts to a polarised power perimeter which relates the individual rightly with Life at all angles, but also becomes the 'spirit' in which that individual

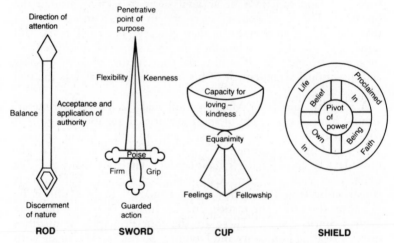

A MODERN MAGICAL CIRCLE

The

Wisdom

Spirit | Mercy | A N ● M E | Justice | One

Love

Eternal

SOME POINTS OF THE MAGICAL INSTRUMENTS

Direction of attention

Penetrative point of purpose

Flexibility | Keenness

Balance

Acceptance and application of authority

Capacity for loving – kindness

Life | Proclaimed | Belief | In | Pivot of power | Own | Being | In | Faith

Equanimity

Poise

Firm | Grip

Feelings | Fellowship

Discernment of nature

Guarded action

ROD   **SWORD**   **CUP**   **SHIELD**

Fig 7   A Modern Magical Circle and Some Points of the
Magical Instruments

actually lives. We might otherwise say that by making such a Magical Circle, the operator had achieved the right sort of spirit to live with. Few Magical operations can come much higher than that.

As a point of interest here, the central AMEN from which the operator works is capable of many interpretations. It is firstly the Name of Deity itself: AUM-En, 'I Am the Mother (Creator) of all.' The letters may be rearranged to give:

NAME: The Name of whoso works the rite.

MEAN: Median or balance of Life.

MANE: 'Soul.'

Plus of course the significance of 'May this be so.'

It is indeed worth noting that so many magical practices which became subsequently debased to superstitional depths were in fact founded on the soundest possible spiritual and psychological principles. Retrieval and restoration of these in terms of modern and future realisation is assuredly a major task for serious students of our Western Inner Way.

Looking for Light in the West

To remain in constant light, we should have to keep flying *Westward* in order to follow the sun. This is an interesting thought for those who like drawing symbolic analogies from nature. It is in the nature of the West also that its Inner Tradition may be encountered at closest quarters. Magic grows wild in the countryside, and may be met with on its home ground by those who learn the silent language of Life itself speaking through 'stems and stones'. This is meant quite literally.

Those sincerely seeking the spiritual Way of the West would be well advised to communicate directly with it through the natural features of its earthly environs. There are also many 'sacred spots' where such communion seems clearer than at other places. These are not difficult to find by anyone with an inch of imagination. One condition is essential: a right relationship. There is no use at all, for instance, in visiting places with noisy parties of restless companions. It is always best to be alone, or with only another very trusted person. Silence and secrecy are keys that open many hidden Western Inner doorways. This may be difficult to observe in overcrowded areas, but with ingenuity it is still possible to contrive opportunities. It is tempting to wonder, however, if Jesus would have learned much in the desert had a major airway been overhead, or if Buddha could have coped with his consciousness if that bo tree had been beside a superhighway.

In these days of aerial and terrestrial motormania, it can be very difficult if not virtually impossible to isolate oneself in any Western countryside for a month in search of spiritual enlightenment. Nevertheless, it is possible with practice to make every moment rewarding that is spent in close contact with the 'soul of the soil', of the Western Inner Tradition interlinking with the natural physical foci of its earthly embodiment. Learning the art of extracting this Inner content of consciousness from nonhuman sources is a fascinating facet of Western Magic by itself. It is possible only by real empathy, or one might as well say genuine *love* for the spirit hiding behind such ordinary and humble externals.

The action is simple enough. Make contact with the externals of whatever Western 'pickup point' is chosen. This could be anything from a sacred site to a natural feature or a symbol. Realise that there is a special sort of 'spirit' associated with whatever it is. Seek Inner relationship with that spirit in a friendly, welcoming and loving manner. Let such feelings arise and be directed toward its Inner objective just as if a real person were present. Try to feel a return flow from Inside. An important point here is that *no deliberate attempt should be made to translate any such receptions into visual or verbal terms at that instant.* Simply experience the Inner contact and nothing else. Interpretations make themselves later on through subconscious symbology. During the 'moment of mediation', words and pictures have to be transcended. When there is a sense of completion in this transaction, contact is best closed quietly and carefully before switching to more usual channels.

If this has been done with any degree of success, there will be a definite feeling of something 'extra' entering the sphere of personal extensions. It is difficult to describe, but unmistakable when undergone. There is something of a spiritually satisfying sensation, as if something good had been ingested – which indeed it has along Inner lines of assimilation. Again it is important not to try analysing, dissecting, criticising, or otherwise interfering with the natural processes of 'digestion' which should now be in progress. That should be left to take its normal course through the subconsciousness until effects show up by themselves on focal levels. Those vary greatly with different individuals. Some have definite dreams of significant character. Others might obtain realisations 'out of the blue', and others again feel impelled to take some line of action which will lead to clarified consciousness on this or that issue. One way or another, the original act of empathy will enter the deep psyche of participators, eventually surfacing through the subconsciousness as some favourable evidence of progress. So works Western Magic.

And So

Perhaps this has all been very disappointing and disheartening for any who expected detailed descriptions of Magical rites and methods guaranteed to induce Godlike intelligence in plain human people. In one sense, these do exist as processes extending over very long periods of wide Life-experience. What most people suppose to be Magical rites that only take moments to work are actually symbolisations of spiritual dramas played out on much more significant stages of Life than Lodge or Temple floors. These do have their uses, for those capable of construing them correctly, yet Life itself will always be the Great Initiator of all systems, Eastern, Western, or otherwise.

The aim throughout this study has been to indicate that the Magic of the West is no less than whatever special spiritual disciplines and symbology may be needed to make each individual Initiate of the Western Way achieve Self-status as a true 'Companion of Cosmos', responsible to Divinity on behalf of Humanity. This is not a matter of dogma, precept, rigid regulations or so-called scientific techniques. It is essentially an affair of constant adaptions, right relationships and empathic experience of Existence. This was once put: 'Love God and fellow creatures as your True Self.' That is the mightiest Magic of all, so why accept inferior imitations?

Real Western Magic is not in the least a curriculum of reading many mysterious tomes, concocting strange compounds, chanting weird words, wearing impressive robes, revelling in secret rites, and taking such incredible trouble for the sake of getting gods and demons alike eating out of one's hand, so to speak. Those are symbols of no value unless converted into currencies of consciousness exchangeable on much higher levels of living. They are means, not ends, and not even exclusive means. Western Magic is far wider and deeper than that. It is the root behaviour of our reality in relation to Life.

Undoubtedly it is very clever to delve into past forms of belief and make speculations about primitive practices and previous Magical methods – quite fascinating in fact. It is undeniable, however, that we should be much more concerned with making the Magic of our own times good enough for leading us faithfully toward Enlightenment in the future. Magic is always modern for those capable of translating it into contemporary idiom while yet understanding its strange 'secret speech' which is ageless and wordless. The Magic of today should matter most to us. Like the Living Tree symbolising its spiritual structure, Western Magic should constantly be growing this year's branches for bearing next season's fruit.

Towards Further and Finer Magic

Just as, a few centuries back, a modernising centre stream of Magic produced a philosophy and practice which aimed the human psyche of the West in our present directions, so now should we 'centre up' the Magical methods and metaphysics which will carry us along the Line of Life ahead. This is actually being done in many ways that moderns might not term 'Magic' at all, yet these have already become incorporated into the Western Tradition stemming from old systems of Initiation. Magic, far from being dead today, exists around us to such a great extent that we fail to see what we are standing in the middle of – the greatest Magic Circle of all, a worldwide circuit of common consciousness. What Man the Magician invokes therein will determine the fate of everyone on Earth. That is the way to look at Magic now. Once we recognise what it really is and what can be done with it, our Ancient Art will be identified with our most Advanced Arcana.

Surely few people would deny that civilisation advances from the West? In that case it is our Magic which leads the world ahead to its ultimate destiny. If the least idea of how important this implication is awakens some awareness of spiritual 'Westernism' in anyone seeking an Inner Way which is *already seeking that individual* then the mission of this little 'work within a Work' will come just that much closer to completion. For the rest, may everyone find his or her own Ways of Faith towards the same Self shared by all of us alike in

PERFECT PEACE PROFOUND.

Note

1. Given the large amount of readily available material on Magic, the aspirant must develop a great deal of discrimination. Ideally, ritual formulas evolve out of people themselves by their own efforts, and it is the basic principles of this which are important. Rites which work for some will not work for others. Some of the basics are given in my published works (Gray, 1968; 1969; 1970a; 1970b; 1971; 1972; 1973a; 1973b; 1974), but there is a vast amount of research and condensation to do in this area. As a rule, reputable occult groupings tend to adopt generalised basic rites and encourage initiates to develop their own workings out of these which, as one might expect, again tend to produce parallel patterns. The operative requirement here is realising what to select and what to reject.

Suggested reading list

The Apocryphal New Testament, trans M. James. The Clarendon Press, 1953.
The Apocrypha of the Old Testament, ed B. Metzger, Oxford University Press, 1965.
The Holy Bible, King James Version, AMS Press, 1967.
The New English Bible, Oxford University Press, 1961, 1970 (1961 edition includes O.T., N.T. and Apocrypha).
L. Apuleius, 'Madaurensis.' *The Golden Ass*, trans R. Graves, Pocket Books, 1954.
W. Butler, *The Magician, His Training and His Work*, Aquarian Press, 1959.
A. Constant, *The History of Magic*, by E. Levi (pseud.), trans A. Waite. Rider and Co, 1957; Samuel Weiser, 1969 (paperback).
A. Constant, *Transcendental Magic*, by E. Levi (pseud.), trans A. Waite. Rider and Co., 1958; Samuel Weiser, 1970.
D. Fortune, (pseud. of V. Firth), *The Esoteric Orders and Their Work*, Rider and Co., 1928; Llewellyn Publications, 1971.
D. Fortune, *The Mystical Qabalah*, Williams and & Norgate, 1935; Samuel Weiser.
D. Fortune, *The Training and Work of an Initiate*, Aquarian Press, 1955.
D. Fortune, *The Cosmic Doctrine*, Aquarian Press, 1957; Wehman Brothers, 1966.
D. Fortune, *Sane Occultism*, Aquarian Press, 1967.
D. Fortune *Practical Occultism in Daily Life*, Aquarian Press, 1969; Samuel Weiser.
J. Frazer, *The Golden Bough*, MacMillan and Co., 1935; Limited Editions Club, 1970.
R. Graves, *The White Goddess*, Faber and Faber, 1952.
R. Graves, *The Greek Myths*, George Braziller, 1957; Cassell, 1965.
R. Graves, *Mammon and the Black Goddess*, Cassell, 1965.
R. Graves, and R. Patai, *Hebrew Myths: The Book of Genesis*, Doubleday and Co., 1964.
W. Gray, *The Ladder of Lights or Qabalah Renovata*, Toddington, England. Helois Book Service, 1968.
W. Gray, *Magical Ritual Methods*, Helios Book Service, 1969.
W. Gray, *Inner Traditions of Magic*, Aquarian Publishing Co, 1971; Samuel Weiser.
W. McNeill, *The Rise of the West*, University of Chicago Press, 1963.
T. Malory, *Le Morte d'Arthur*, Medici Society, 1930; Crofts, 1940.
I. Regardie, *Roll Away the Stone*, St. Paul, Minn.: Llewellyn Publications, 1968.
I. Regardie, *The Tree of Life*, Samuel Weiser, 1969.
I. Regardie, *A Garden of Pomegranates*, Llewellyn Publications, 1970.
I. Regardie, *The Golden Dawn*, Hazel Hills Corp, 1970 (distributed by Llewellyn Publications).
L. Spence, *The Magic Arts in Celtic Britain*, Rider and Co, 1945.
L. Spence, *British Fairy Origins*, C. A. Watts and Co., 1946.

L. Spence, *The Minor Traditions of British Mythology*, Rider and Co, 1948.
L. Spence, *The History and Origins of Druidism*, Rider and Co., 1949.
L. Spence, *An Encyclopedia of Occultism*, University Books, 1960.
A. Waite, *The Occult Sciences*, Dutton and Co., 1923.
A. Waite, *History of the Rosicrucians*, Rudolf Steiner Publications.
A. Waite, *The Book of Ceremonial Magic*, University Books, 1965.
A. Waite, *Alchemists through the Ages*, Rudolf Steiner Publications, 1970.
W. Wentz, *The Fairy Faith in Celtic Countries*, University Books, 1966.

AFTERWORD

R.J. Stewart

This collection of essays has ranged widely between various schools of psychology, shamanism, Tibetan Tantric Buddhism, therapy in the ancient world, Magical techniques and traditions, and an assortment of discussions around the concept of the New Age. It could, of course, have been twice, three, or four times its present size, without losing impetus. Perhaps the publishers will, in time, decide upon a second volume.

There are no firm conclusions in a book of this sort, despite its wealth of information, rambling branches of theory, and suggestions for further work. Conclusions, after all, are valueless upon a page: the relationship between psychology and the ancient traditions must be a matter of experience. Enough has been put forward in this collection to show a number of ways towards such experience. Many more ways can and surely will be found as new generations of psychologists move away from a rigid or elitist self-image, and explore the pre-materialist psychologies of the spiritual and magical disciplines and arts.

There are always dangers in such moves . . . there are a number of books, still in print written by psychologists and psychiatrists who have expressed supernatural or esoteric interests that are little better than the most childish and superficial aspects of spiritualism. But these tend to belong to an earlier generation, working out the problems of their time and place within Western society, possibly rebelling against scientific discipline and its severely limited world-view.

Contemporary therapists and theorists seem to be drawn towards the primal magical and spiritual disciplines . . . those of the natural magician, the shaman, the seer, the Underworld. These are powerful traditions indeed, and have much to offer for our changing times. As has been said in a number of places in this book, there is always the danger that the old traditions will become diluted, even emasculated, by an increasing popularity and commercialism, particularly in the context of therapy. Conversely, there is the danger that psychologists will lose that scientific rigour which has given them a firm yet expanding discipline for the last hundred years. There is a very subtle difference between the conservatism of an organic or perennial tradition, and the conservatism of a professional body or discipline. The first both transcends and underpins many centuries, while the second is always specific to its cultural context, and must eventually be broken down and remoulded, often against bitter opposition from vested interests. We can see this today in the current interaction between alternative and orthodox medicine in the West.

There can be no doubt that we need to move away from elitism and unnecessary exclusivity in both psychology and spiritual traditions. The coming together of the ancient and modern studies and techniques of the human psyche should, for example, help with the removal of so-called 'occultism', and the public fantasies and wishful thinking concerning 'the occult'. While Freud despised such occultism (and small wonder when we consider the occultism of his century), and Jung intentionally removed the symbols and images of esoteric traditions to place them into a modern therapeutic context, we need a further synthesis between the old and the new.

This synthesis cannot be any type of 'occultism', nor can it be psychology. Both are already, did they but know it, outdated. Nor should it be the work of one single explorer, theoretician or practitioner: it must be a larger and more practical effort involving numbers of men and women. Furthermore, if it has a name, a movement, a label or a membership, it is retrogressive. We have suggested, in this book that the current fashion for New Age developments, therapies, and techniques, is far from adequate for the needs of the present and future. There are, in fact, many pernicious old monsters hidden within the New Age movement, somehow flourishing when we had assumed that they were defunct.

If we reduce the discussion to very simple terms, we are experiencing a revival of magic – that is to say, magic in its true sense, as a disciplined art of the imagination. This fundamental art and discipline of the imagination encompasses both the materialist and the esoteric or spiritual techniques of consciousness and energy. Any future developments should be built upon the simple basis of the human imagination and associated energies . . . to do this we may draw upon both ancient and modern techniques. We should always be aware, however, that theory must emerge as practice, and that the proof of any psychology (be it materialist or magical or spiritual) rests ultimately upon its effect upon human beings. Can we truly grow, transform, and mature, and thereby approach deeper levels of consciousness and higher levels and cycles of energy through the techniques that we are restating, developing and exploring? The answers will be found in people rather than in books, but at least a book of this sort helps us to formulate some of the questions.

Written over the portal of certain ancient temples was the famous dictum *Human Know Thyself*. If we are to be truthful, we must admit that most of the inner territory, that which is within ourselves which we should seek to know, is still a mystery. The ancient spiritual and magical traditions provided maps of the regions of consciousness which men and women sought to enter and understand within themselves. A map is not, of course, the territory, any more than modern psychology is the human psyche. If we are to know ourselves we need to seek out the limits of the familiar maps, ancient or modern, and extend them by direct exploration.

Every conceptual or psychological tradition filters its discoveries through a framework of reference; this framework colours and even distorts results. But this colouration is, in itself, a magical property of human consciousness . . . whatever we seek to be, in whatever form we choose to define the unknown, so will it manifest. Sometimes the manifestation is so suspiciously true to form that we must challenge it . . . and find that the illusion vanishes to be replaced by a new seed of reference. This in turn may become a convoluted growth to be disposed of, and so we continue travelling onwards in the quest for self-knowledge.

The greatest danger is the assumption that we know what is within the human psyche, or that the map is the actual territory, inflexible, unchanging. The old magical and spiritual maps, (many of which are still used in living tradition today and are by no means outdated), were open-ended. Rigidity only came in late literary presentations, such as those of the nineteenth century. But modern psychology is generally ignorant of such maps, or chooses to ignore them. It is into the zones suggested by spiritual tradition, but so far refused by psychology, that the future of imaginative arts and techniques of altering consciousness should be extended.

INDEX